Sometimes on Christmas mornin bigger and heavier than the rest, and you just knew that there was something special and substantive inside. That is what we find in this work by my friend and coworker Ross Rohde. In this treatise you will find breakthrough ideas that carry the weight of real-life stories.

—NEIL COLE
FOUNDER AND EXECUTIVE DIRECTOR OF
CHURCH MULTIPLICATION ASSOCIATES
AUTHOR OF *ORGANIC CHURCH*, *ORGANIC LEADERSHIP*, *CHURCH 3.0*,
*JOURNEYS TO SIGNIFICANCE*, AND *ORDINARY HERO*

In the earliest days of its history, Christianity was an explosive, dynamic, vibrant kingdom lifestyle that turned the then-known world upside down. Ross's own life is a living demonstration of this. Whenever we meet him, he always has an exciting new story to tell of Jesus transforming the lives of people he has encountered. In this highly readable book, *Viral Jesus*, Ross examines the principles behind the viral spread of the gospel in the early church and how a refocus on Jesus produces the deep spirituality and power that is leading to similar results today.

—FELICITY DALE
HOUSE2HOUSE MINISTRIES
AUTHOR OF *AN ARMY OF ORDINARY PEOPLE*
AND COAUTHOR OF *SMALL IS BIG*

This book is dangerous! *Viral Jesus* makes living out the Christian faith simple, powerful, and adventurous. Filled with stories that vary in degrees of success, the reader learns just how simple it can be to follow the lead of Jesus. *Viral Jesus* is a contagion that teaches every believer dependence on God and how He can use them naturally and powerfully everywhere they go. Anyone can do this!

—ED WAKEN
EVANGELIST, CHURCH MULTIPLICATION ASSOCIATES

*Viral Jesus* is an animated plea for a living faith that is unencumbered by extracurricular church forms and structures that both impede the progress of our faith and diffuse its integrity. It is global in perspective, intensely practical, and full of winsome real-life stories.

—LINDA BERGQUIST
CHURCH–PLANTING STRATEGIST
COAUTHOR OF *CHURCH TURNED INSIDE OUT*

# VIRAL JESUS

## RECOVERING THE CONTAGIOUS POWER OF THE GOSPEL

# ROSS ROHDE

## PASSIO

Most CHARISMA HOUSE BOOK GROUP products are available at special quantity discounts for bulk purchase for sales promotions, premiums, fund-raising, and educational needs. For details, write Charisma House Book Group, 600 Rinehart Road, Lake Mary, Florida 32746, or telephone (407) 333-0600.

VIRAL JESUS by Ross Rohde
Published by Passio
Charisma Media/Charisma House Book Group
600 Rinehart Road
Lake Mary, Florida 32746
www.charismahouse.com

Unless otherwise noted, all Scripture quotations are from the Holy Bible, New International Version. Copyright © 1973, 1978, 1984, International Bible Society. Used by permission.

Scripture quotations marked NAS are from the New American Standard Bible. Copyright © 1960, 1962, 1963, 1968, 1971, 1972, 1973, 1975, 1977 by the Lockman Foundation. Used by permission. (www.Lockman.org)

Cover design by Isaiah Hwang

Visit the author's website at http://viraljesusbook.com/.

Library of Congress Cataloging-in-Publication Data:
Rohde, Ross.
Viral Jesus / Ross Rohde. -- 1st ed.
    p. cm.
Includes bibliographical references (p. ) and index.
ISBN 978-1-61638-485-2 (trade paper) -- ISBN 978-1-61638-636-8 (e-book)1.
Evangelistic work.I. Title.

BV3770.R65 2012
269--dc23
                                        2011044556
First Edition

12 13 14 15 16 — 9 8 7 6 5 4 3 2 1
Printed in the United States of America

*This work is dedicated to the five most important women in my life: my wonderful wife, Margi, and my three equally wonderful daughters, Jess, Jenn, and Jo. They traveled the world with me on the journey God called us to. All of them paid a difficult price for that journey. Yet all of them are stronger and wiser for it. And to my mom, who lived the better part of twenty years with little access to her son, daughter-in-law, and granddaughters; it was a heavy price to pay for my calling.*

# ⌒ CONTENTS ⌒

## ⌖ ACKNOWLEDGMENTS ⌖

*I* WANT TO EXPRESS my profound gratitude to the pioneers in the West of that new and very old movement of God currently called organic church, simple church, or house church. No matter what it is called, it is a movement of God, birthed in the heart of the Father under Jesus the Lord and carried out in the power of the Spirit. These pioneers have graciously helped me with their writing, training, administration, and/or friendship and in so doing allowed me to learn to follow Jesus into the harvest. I am deeply grateful to my friends and mentors at Church Multiplication Associates: Neil Cole, Desi Baker, Ed Waken, Phil Helfer, Paul Kaak, Mike Jentes, and Heather Cole. Some I have met and befriended; others have just helped me just through their training and hard work. I am also deeply grateful to other pioneers in the movement whom I have gotten to know, Tony and Felicity Dale, Erik and Jen Fish, Wolfgang Simson, Chris Daza, and Frank Viola. All these people in one capacity or another used their gifting to lead the way in breaking the sod so that the first seeds of a viral movement of the gospel can begin here in the West.

I want to acknowledge my friends here in the Bay Area of California who have taken the risk of entering into organic church-planting ministry among those who did not yet know Jesus. Some are still here toiling away, fighting the good fight. Others have been called by their Lord to other places away from the Bay, some even to other countries. Still others were fruit from the harvest. So, thank you, Lyle and Kristy; Bill and Babs; Gooch and Angela; Dave and Heidi; Bum and YJ; Walt and Marci;

Humberto and Gaddy; Margi; Ryan and Marian; Shawn and Loren; Daniel and Celeste; Marcus; Mike and Leslie; Danny and Edie; John and Robin; Mike T; Dave; A and R; Jason and Marcia; Erik and Linda; Travis and Ashley; Dave and Brook; Jennifer; John and Nhi; Chinh and Rachel; Hai and Uyen; Seth; Daniel; Ian; Paul; Antonio; Carlos; Lalo; Vidal and Pepe.

I want to acknowledge those who worked to help me with this, my first book. My learning curve was steep and they helped me through all of my mistakes. I give grateful thanks to my agent, Chip MacGregor at MacGregor Literary Agency, for walking me through the process of refining a manuscript and finding a publisher; Hannah Selleck, who took a very rough draft and turned it into an understandable manuscript, and the wonderful team at Charisma House: Ann, Barbara, Bill, Debbie, Jason, Joy, Leigh, Marcos, Rick, Steve, Susan, Tessie, and Woodley. Who knew it took such a big, hard-working, faithful, and kind team to put a book together? A special thanks to Jevon for her gracious patience and cheerful spirit in the editing process. And another special thanks to Jonathan for setting the whole thing up and going the extra mile, especially for favors outside of his job description. I am deeply grateful to you all.

Finally I want to express my gratitude to the real heroes of the church in the twentieth and twenty-first century; the tens if not hundreds of millions of unnamed brothers and sisters in China who have suffered, been imprisoned, and even died; yet have been victorious in following Jesus into the most powerful movement of the Spirit in the history of Christianity. Thank you for showing us in the West, and others around the world, the way the Spirit of Jesus is leading us forward in the building of His kingdom.

# ⭍ FOREWORD ⭍

*I* REMEMBER WELL THE bus ride home from San Pedro High School to our own Palisades High School in 1977. We had just won the city section water polo championship for the second year in a row. We were full of excitement and ready to celebrate our victory. From twenty or so miles away we could see some smoke rising on the hills in the direction of our homes, but we didn't think much of it...until we got closer. I will never forget pulling into the school parking lot at home and seeing a fire descend upon our own neighborhood. All the celebration stopped, and we were silent as we watched in awe. From a small little match a fire quickly spread, and in the time it took us to drive twenty miles it had become a raging wild fire.

I grew up in the canyons of Southern California. Each fall we would see the winds shift from blowing off the cool, moist ocean to coming off the hot and dry deserts. This fierce condition we refer to in California as Santa Ana winds is hot, dry, and always comes after the warm summer months that have already killed all the underbrush in the canyons, leaving dry, dead grass and lots of it. The results are fires raging out of control, often several at a time. My father fought to save his home as a young man from the Malibu fire. Dad was not a small man. Standing at 6 feet 3 inches with a trim, athletic body from years of swimming and surfing, he nevertheless felt small and weak as the flames roared over his head on the road to his house. The heat bearing down on him and the deafening roar in his ears left a sort of scar on his soul, and he would never forget it. The flames were shouting taunts against his seeming futile efforts to stop

xi

them. A lifelong duel began between him and the fires often recorded in his artwork. I remember hosing down the roof of my home with him in defense against the Mandeville Canyon fire instead of celebrating our water polo championship. We barely escaped that challenge with our home.

A few years ago, after a lifetime of battling these fires, my father finally lost his home, his lifetime of artwork and all his pets in the Sylmar fire. He would never quite be the same after that. The flames that taunted him as a young man returned to claim their victory.

It is strange that we can know why these fires happen, where the vulnerabilities lie and when they will start, but we are nevertheless powerless to stop them from coming each year. There is a force behind them that simply laughs at us as we try in vain to stop them.

What makes these fires so challenging is a "perfect storm" of conditions. The dry chaparral brush, dead from a hot summer, is the perfect kindling for the firestorm. The steep ridges of the many canyons form wind channels that accelerate the already fierce winds exploding off the desert. These same canyon ridges also make the acreage of kindling that much closer to the long reach of the flames. The flames spread, pushed by the strong winds with no regard for whatever lies in their path. The results are a fast-moving and rapidly spreading blaze that scorches the earth and all in its way. It can truly be both wondrous and devastating at the same time.

Every fall you will hear stories of fires raging in Southern California because of this perfect lineup of conditions that make it ripe for a firestorm.

In a similar way, there are also conditions that must line up to release a viral epidemic. What the enemy has meant for evil is also a lesson to us for good. We can learn about rapid movements from these scenarios.

Why is it that we will allow Satan to use movements to spread disease, lies, riots, fire, and immorality, but we tend to not tap into the principles of movement when it comes to the gospel and the kingdom of God? We must learn from the wildfires and the epidemics of the world if we want to release a real revival and see a transformative movement of God's kingdom.

It is clear that Jesus intended the kingdom to spread rapidly. He spoke of the kingdom of God starting small like a mustard seed and then growing rapidly to become the largest of trees. He spoke of the kingdom of God being like a little pinch of leaven dropped into some dough that rapidly transformed the entire lump. He spoke of a seed that bore fruit multiplying thirtyfold, sixtyfold and one hundredfold. The Book of Acts clearly lays out for us the story of a rapidly spreading viral movement that became unstoppable in the first century. Persecution, famine, and poverty couldn't stop it but only fanned the flames.

From my earliest days as a Christ follower, I desired to be part of a true movement that spread like a wildfire. I could never shake off this desire, in spite of the years of experiencing a Christianity that never spread at all. Only in recent years have I actually begun to see the sort of movement I had always dreamed about, but this is just the beginning. Like the wildfires my father fought throughout his life, such a movement is hard to stop when the conditions line up right.

I firmly believe we are about to see a movement like nothing seen since the first century. I see the conditions coming together to form the "perfect storm" for a viral move of God in this generation. As soon as the Spirit blows and fans the spark of the gospel in our dried-up lives, we will launch this movement and see it spread. Right now we are all cooking under the heat of a summer of global challenges. Our economical crisis, political futility, cultural moral decline, wars and rumors of wars, and even natural disasters are preparing us for something. The rise in technological advances, much like the steep hills of the canyons where I grew up, are bringing lives closer together so that the flames can spread and the Spirit's force can be accelerated.

The dry kindling for this coming wildfire are our own souls that are dying more and more every day and are being prepared to burn for something good. We are slowly dying to the things we once thought would bring us life, but now we see that these things are not at all life producing nor worthy of our faith. The fierce wind of the Holy Spirit coming out of the desert will fan the flame of the gospel and spread it from one willing soul to another until an unstoppable movement is born. I believe this and am willing to give my life for it. Are you?

Just as a wildfire can teach us about a rapidly spreading movement, so can the ideas behind a viral epidemic. While both a wildfire and an epidemic can be devastating, they share qualities that we can learn from when we consider the movement qualities of God's kingdom.

In this book, Ross Rohde presents clearly that the message, the vibrant new life, and the ongoing presence of Jesus are contagious and meant to spread like a beautiful, life-giving super-virus. From soul to soul, it can spread quickly from people group to people group, transforming entire cultures and society as it goes.

All movements begin small. Just as a virus is microscopic and starts with one contact point, a wildfire also begins with a single spark. The viral nature of God's kingdom also begins small and grows by spreading from one life to another. Like a viral epidemic, the redeemed life of a new Christ-follower spreads to others around him or her, each one becoming a carrier of the life-giving virus of Jesus. Soon a movement is birthed that is difficult to stop. Unlike a wildfire or a rapidly spreading epidemic, the results of a Jesus movement are not death and destruction but life and transformation.

I don't know about you, but I want to be a part of an unstoppable Jesus movement that spreads rapidly and uncontrollably and leaves behind people who are transformed into life-giving healthy followers of King Jesus. This book will take us all one step closer to the conditions necessary to see this happen in our day. My good friend and coworker Ross Rohde writes from his own experience both cross-culturally and in the United States. He uses real-life examples to illustrate each important principle explained in simple and uncluttered language. This resource is a valuable spark to ignite a new movement.

It is late summer. We are drying up. Fall is approaching. Are you ready for the wildfire? Let the winds blow.

—NEIL COLE
LONG BEACH, CALIFORNIA

Neil Cole is the cofounder of Church Multiplication Associates (www.cmaresources.org) and the organic church movement as well as the author of *Organic Church, Organic Leadership, Search & Rescue, Church 3.0,* and *Journeys to Significance.*

# ⋐ PREFACE ⋑

*T*HE YEAR IS about A.D. 107. Ignatius of Antioch, an apostolic father of the early church, is being marched through the tunnels of the coliseum of Rome. He can hear the roar of the lions in their holding pens below. He can smell their strong, musky stench. As he emerges into the daylight, he tracks through the sticky blood, soaked into the sand—the blood of his brothers and sisters killed moments before for the entertainment of the 50,000 murderous, overwrought, deafening spectators.

He had been captured in his homeland, Antioch of Syria, north of Israel, by the soldiers of Emperor Trajan. He has been brought to this point on a long and difficult journey. In his epistle to the Romans, chapter 5, he writes, "From Syria even unto Rome I fight with beasts, both by land and sea, both by night and day, being bound to ten leopards, I mean a band of soldiers, who, even when they receive benefits, show themselves all the worse."[1]

Ignatius didn't have to be here. He could have bowed before a statue of Trajan, sacrificed a little wine, declared his allegiance to Trajan as Emperor and gone his merry way. But he wouldn't and he didn't. Why? Instead, his life ended much as he had anticipated.

> May I enjoy the wild beasts that are prepared for me; and I pray they may be found eager to rush upon me, which also I will entice to devour me speedily, and not deal with me as with some, whom, out of fear, they have not touched. But if they be unwilling to

assail me, I will compel them to do so. Pardon me [in this]: I know
what is for my benefit. Now I begin to be a disciple. And let no
one, of things visible or invisible, envy me that I should attain to
Jesus Christ. Let fire and the cross; let the crowds of wild beasts;
let tearings, breakings, and dislocations of bones; let cutting off
of members; let shatterings of the whole body; and let all the
dreadful torments of the devil come upon me: only let me attain
to Jesus Christ.[2]

We will meet Ignatius again in *Viral Jesus*. Not everything we see
will be spotless, wonderful, and clean; but hopefully we will understand
Ignatius's unbending devotion to Jesus his Lord. And that is the point.
The backbone of Ignatius's life was based on two undeniable facts: Jesus
is Lord and Ignatius's life operated on a covenantal agreement with his
Lord, called the new covenant. Everything Ignatius did—how he lived
and how he died—was based on these two truths. Not truths in the sense
of correct ideas, but truths in the sense of the certitude of experience and
of how he lived his life and how he willingly gave it up.

The early church lived out "Jesus is Lord." The early church understood how to live every moment within their new covenant agreement
with Jesus their Lord. And because of this, the gospel spread like a wildfire through Greco-Roman society. Fewer than two hundred years after
Ignatius's death, Christianity became the most important religion in the
Western world. That too is a story we will explore.

The gospel is no longer spreading like a wildfire through the Western
world. And it is precisely because we don't really understand how to live
Jesus as Lord and within His new covenant agreement with us. We may
agree with these two truths as correct doctrines; but we live something
far different. In place of these living truths, we have human planning;
ministry as business; and human leadership, techniques, methods, and
strategic principles.

Professing to be wise we have become fools. We have succumbed
to the foundational principles of the world the apostle Paul warned us
about. And the end result is the kingdom of God stagnated in place, even
losing ground in the West. We have replaced the kingdom of God with
Christendom—a cheap and gaudy imitation.

I believe the gospel can once again spread like a beautiful, healthy contagion in the West. I believe the message of our King can become unfettered and thrive and proliferate like a living thing. I believe we can once again see the beautiful truths of the lordship of Jesus and His offer of a new covenant—in other words, the gospel—spread like the Jesus virus. And I truly believe Jesus can go viral again in Western society. I believe you and I can be part of this viral Jesus movement, but how? That's the question this book seeks to answer.

# Following Jesus
# Into a Viral Jesus Movement

ONNIE'S REQUEST TOOK my friend Vincent totally by surprise: "They tell me you are a Christian. Can you tell me how to be one too?" After all, it is not a request one hears every day, or every year, for that matter. Connie explained her problem: "My mother and I have been going to a big church in San Francisco for some time now. We figured they could show us how to find Jesus. But we really don't understand what they are talking about." That was reasonable. We Christians do have a tendency to get wrapped up in our own world and our own jargon. Sometimes what seems so comfortable to us is incomprehensible to outsiders. What seems to them like strange rituals and language can distance us even from people who want to know Jesus. If you scratch Vincent, he bleeds Jesus. So he did what comes naturally to him: he told Connie about the Savior he loves so much.

Vincent was one of the first participants in the first organic church planter's fellowship, which started in the Bay Area of California in June 2007. Within a few weeks, my friends and I had begun to follow Jesus into the harvest. We began to plant tiny fellowships of brand-new believers in homes, apartments, and restaurants. Vincent was hooked; he wanted to do the kinds of things he was hearing about. So, like the rest of us, he began to pray through Jesus's instructions in Luke 10:1–23. And like the rest of us, he began to pray that Jesus would lead him to a person of peace (Luke 10:6) who could introduce him to their friends, called a house or household (*oikos*) in biblical Greek. And that was exactly what Jesus did, at seemingly the most inconvenient time.

In many ways Vincent is a typical guy. However, there is one thing that makes Vincent stand out from the crowd here on the West Coast. It's his accent. He was New York City–born and –bred. Oh, and the fact that in his early years, before he knew Jesus, he was involved with... Well, let's just say we like to tease him about sounding like TV gangster Tony Soprano.

Vincent was pretty excited the next time our group met. He told us about Connie, and we were excited for him too. Vincent later took me aside and reminded me that Jesus sent out His workers into the harvest two by two. "I am try'n to get Connie to take me to her *oikos*. I think it will happen dis weekend. Why don't you come wit me?"

Vincent was right; Jesus did send workers out two by two. I'd have liked nothing better than getting in on the fun with Vincent. But I had an immediate check in my spirit. Probably the worst thing I could teach my friend was that there was power in the technique. Worse, what if Vincent thought I was some sort of expert; that my presence was the magic pill that led to ministry success? Jesus had actually given this fruit to Vincent, not me. Since I felt a check in my spirit, I declined. "No, sorry, Vincent, I don't think I should. Why don't you ask Bill? He would make a good partner for you."

"Yeah, but you've planted churches before. You done dis stuff. Why don't you come wit me, so you can lend your experience to da situation?"

If I have learned one thing in the last few years of ministry, it is this: there is no power in technique. There is power only in Jesus. Jesus may lead you to a technique. He may lead you to it time and time again, or only once. But the power comes when we are obedient to Jesus, not from the technique itself. My job was to obey, and Jesus was saying no.

Jesus had led some of us rather quickly from our contacts to their friends and family. Often we were able to plant a church rather rapidly. For some reason, it wasn't working this way for Vincent. Though Connie did come to Christ that day, instead of leading a willing Vincent to her network of friends, she went the other direction. Connie stopped talking about her friends. She didn't seem overly anxious to take Vincent to meet them. Vincent was beginning to wonder if he had done something wrong.

Finally about three weeks later Connie entered his office again. "Vincent, I want to be baptized." Vincent was excited. Jesus was moving Connie in the right direction. Then Jesus put a question in Vincent's mind. "Connie, if I'm going to baptize you, who are you going to invite to the baptism?" It turned out to be a very strategic question.

"Well, my dad just got out of prison; I'd like to invite him. My brother would come. My mom has a restraining order against dad, so they can't be in the same room together. But I'd love to have Andrea from work come."

Vincent gently inquired, "What about your old friends?"

"I don't hang with them anymore. They aren't a good influence on me." What Vincent had read as hesitation on her part and perhaps somehow failure on his was the Holy Spirit working in Connie's life. In this particular case, but certainly not in every case, Jesus knew that Connie needed protection from her old crowd. Because He is the Lord of the harvest and we are not, He had chosen a strategy that we might not think of. He had planned all along to take Vincent to people who needed to know Him. He had planned all along to do it through Connie. He was following His pattern in Luke 10, but He wasn't following our stereotyped version of it. Nor had He chosen me to be Vincent's partner, nor had He chosen Bill, who was my suggestion. Instead He chose Vincent's wife, Mary.

As Mary entered Connie's house Jesus put a conviction on her heart. She was to claim this house for Jesus. So she began to slowly walk through the house and quietly pray through spiritual warfare. "We've shown up in the name of Jesus. This place is ours now. If there are any evil spirits here I command them, in the name of Jesus, to leave. I'm not asking; I'm commanding in the name and authority He gives us. Holy Spirit, please come."

Vincent had another problem on his mind. He had a great plan in his head. He had dreamed about it a hundred times. He would show up. There would be a number of new people there. They would be interested. He'd quickly order a pizza, and then he'd get down to business. He'd turn on the disc in the boom box, teach them a few Christian songs, do a little gospel preaching, and they would all come to Christ.

Evidently Connie's friend and family didn't get the memo. The TV was blaring a baseball game. Larry, Connie's father, seemed more interested in the TV than in meeting Vincent and Mary. Lawrence, his son, was following his lead. Worse yet, the pizza parlor wouldn't deliver in Connie's neighborhood. Vincent's finely tuned plan was crumbling to dust.

"Well, Jesus, what am I supposed to do now?" It was a great question born out of frustration and desperation. Somehow, Jesus made it clear that the best thing he could do was take Connie with him and go pick up a pizza. On the way back, Vincent asked Jesus another question, "What should I do when I get there?" Jesus spoke directly to Vincent's heart. "Pray, then I'll show you what to do next." So Vincent arrived and set down the fragrant pizza. Larry and Lawrence turned off the TV and moved toward the smell of food. Vincent began to simply thank Jesus for the meal. As he was ending his prayer, he got his next directive, "Tell them how you came to know Me and what I've done for you."

So Vincent told the story of how he had been involved in a life of organized crime. How, in response to a subpoena, traveling to a court hearing, he met a person on a plane who led him to the Savior. Jesus had an immediate impact on Vincent's life. Instead of telling the district attorney a bunch of cleverly devised lies, he chose to tell the DA the truth, no matter what happened to him. The DA said, "Vincent, I knew this stuff all along. I was going to let you get caught up in your lies and throw the book at you. Since you are willing to tell the truth, let's go talk to the judge. I'm going to request that he let you off." And that's what happened. In short order Jesus had gotten Vincent out of a very difficult situation and given him a new lease on life, an honest life.

However, Vincent ended his testimony of Jesus's goodness with no new directives. Just as he was finishing, Lawrence, Connie's brother, interrupted: "That's what I'm talking about! My life's a mess. I'm strung out on drugs. I'm in the gangs, even if dad told me not to. I've got this girlfriend that dominates me. My life's just a mess. And now I see Connie. She's got Jesus. She's different. I want that."

About that time, Larry, Connie's father, told the story of how just a few weeks before he was released from prison he had found the Savior and how he was enjoying his new faith.

Just as he was finishing, Andrea told the group a story. "Vincent, when

I was a little girl, about ten years old, I was in an accident. I was in the hospital in a coma. I wasn't expected to live. Then I saw this man. He was in a bright white robe. He had sheep all around him. He had a stick in his hand. He came up to me and asked, 'Andrea, do you want to stay with Me, or do you want to go back to your grandma?' I told him I wanted to go back to Grandma. Then I woke up. That was Jesus, wasn't it?"

The next week, when we met in our church planter's fellowship, Vincent couldn't wait to share. "Guys, Jesus did it all. I didn't do nutt'n! I didn't do NUTT'N!"

## Peter and John Following Jesus Into the Harvest

Read through the eyes of a modern Christian, the behavior of the believers in the Book of Acts seems a bit strange, to say the least. They seem to do things we would never think of and be motivated in ways that mystify us. Let me give you an example of strange behavior that one just doesn't see in a "normal" church. Let's look at Acts chapter 3.

> One day Peter and John were going up to the temple at the time of prayer—at three in the afternoon. Now a man crippled from birth was being carried to the temple gate called Beautiful, where he was put every day to beg from those going into the temple courts. When he saw Peter and John about to enter, he asked them for money. Peter looked straight at him, as did John.
>
> Then Peter said, "Look at us!" So the man gave them his attention, expecting to get something from them. Then Peter said, "Silver or gold I do not have, but what I have I give you. In the name of Jesus Christ of Nazareth, walk." Taking him by the right hand, he helped him up, and instantly the man's feet and ankles became strong. He jumped to his feet and began to walk. Then he went with them into the temple courts, walking and jumping, and praising God. When all the people saw him walking and praising God, they recognized him as the same man who used to sit begging at the temple gate called Beautiful, and they were filled with wonder and amazement at what had happened to him.
>
> —Acts 3:1–10

Now come on, isn't that just weird? It does make a nice Sunday school story though. We even have a song about it. But we don't exactly teach our kids to team up in twos and go out gazing deeply into people's eyes, then command healing. As our British cousins say, it's not the done thing.

Actually, if you think about it, our whole interaction with the Book of Acts in particular, and the New Testament in general, ties us up in some pretty tight mental knots. We very rarely if ever act like the early Christians. They had incredible fruit; we don't. There must have been something wrong with them. Of course, we don't actually say there was something wrong with them; that would seem sacrilegious. What we do say is something like, "They had some sort of advantage that we don't have. That was a special age when the miraculous happened, but it doesn't happen now. Or, if it does happen, it happens in the Third World but not here."

Did they really have an advantage that we don't have? Was this a special, never-to-be-repeated time? Or are we making excuses for ourselves? Are we going through mental and theological gymnastics because we don't want to have to deal with the alternative? I think the answer is painful, but one we must face if we are ever to see a new and powerful culture-changing outpouring of the Holy Spirit.

## Vincent's Story Through a Different Lens

Actually, if you think about it, Vincent's story is a lot like what you see in the New Testament. It is not an exact copy, but there certainly is an underlying supernatural power that seems too often lacking in the modern church's ministry.

First, Vincent did not have some sort of technique where he went out and tried to convince people that they needed to become Christians. In fact, Vincent just prayed and they came to him. This was Vincent's "secret weapon": prayer not technique.

Second, what Vincent did was based on the ministry pattern Jesus modeled Himself and then taught to both His original twelve apostles and seventy-two others. We see this same pattern play out in the subsequent ministry of the apostles in the Book of Acts. This was not based on Vincent's extensive training. While he had a group of friends he periodically met with, the fruit came from his abiding relationship with Christ and through answered prayer.

In John 15:5 Jesus said, "I am the vine; you are the branches. If a man remains in me and I in him, he will bear much fruit; apart from me you can do nothing." For many of us, these have become just so many religious words. We agree on some philosophical level that this is correct. However, we actually put our confidence in our own effort, training, and ministry paradigms. We have much more confidence in the foundational principles of the world than we do in an abiding relationship with Jesus.

## Going Backward to Move Forward

It would be impossible for me to discern the individualized path that Jesus has for you. That is between you and Him. But I can take you back to the Scriptures to words you may have read a hundred times before and perhaps shine a new light on them. Perhaps we can ask a new set of questions together. Perhaps we can look at the Bible together in new ways, or better said, in ancient ways.

In order to do that, I'm going to have to shine some light on some pretty tangled knots. For the most part, they are the knots of Greek philosophy, the basic principles of this world and even sometimes Jewish and pagan religion. I can shine light on them, but you will have to untie them, or choose not to.

It is your choice. Jesus gives you absolute freedom of will. I can't take that away from you, and He won't. You may like some of the cords that bind you. They may give you a feeling of security. However, I will exercise the freedom Jesus has given me. I will share, hopefully graciously, that what many think of as a lifeline can become a noose. What you do with that information is up to you. I don't ask you to believe everything I say. For your own sake, I would ask you to evaluate honestly, even painfully, and ask Jesus to be your guide.

## Doing Ministry Jesus's Way

There is no doubt about it; the way ministry was done in the New Testament and the way it is done today are two very different things. I believe if we are ever to see a viral movement of the Spirit in the West, we need to recapture the spirituality and mind-set of our first-century brethren. We must learn to ask a whole new set of counterintuitive questions and make some culturally counterintuitive conclusions. For example, instead of saying, "They had incredible fruit, we don't. There must be something wrong with them," we should to learn to ask Jesus how we can bear fruit like that. Instead of assuming there was something special going on then that we can't access now, maybe, just maybe, we should ask Jesus to teach us how to walk in His special power. Instead of believing that the Holy Spirit limits Himself geographically to the Third World, perhaps we should ask how our beliefs, behavior, and theology are blocking the Holy Spirit here in the West.

I suspect strongly that we have sold Jesus and ourselves short. Instead of boldly going out on the limb of faith, we've learn to "theologize," squeezing the biblical record through a Western philosophical meat grinder, so that what comes out doesn't really look anything like what went in. Instead of learning to live in radical obedience to Jesus, we've learned to have a fascination with propositional doctrinal statements, disconnected from practical action. We can organize theology into complex systematic systems, yet our kingdom expanding behavior is anemic and halfhearted at best.

In fact, if we are really honest, we'd have to admit that most of our ministry is aimed at ourselves and has very little if anything to do with the expansion of the kingdom. Do we follow Jesus radically? How would we know? Many of us have no idea what His voice even sounds like.

## Hellenistic or Hebraic

I believe that we've become trapped in a nonbiblical cultural worldview. And we are so confused by it that we are not quite sure what radical obedience actually looks like. This trap is called the Hellenistic worldview of Western civilization. It is the way of thinking and understanding reality that we inherited from the Greek philosophers. We've all heard their names: Socrates, Plato, and Aristotle. It is the world of ideas separated from action. This dangerous philosophical mind-set was held to tacitly in the Middle Ages as a holdover from the Roman world. It was intentionally embraced again in the Renaissance, and brought to full maturity during the Enlightenment.

## Greek Dualism

One clear distinctive of the Hellenistic worldview is to classify everything in contrasting opposites without an understanding of how things are related to each other. This is commonly called dualism. Of particular interest is the distinction between body and soul. It also leads us to attempt to draw clear lines of separation between those people to whom we belong and others—us and them. Very little effort is focused on how the body and the soul are interrelated and how we are affected by and mimic our society. Of particular danger to believers is the tacit behavior of divorcing ideas from behavior. These rigid distinctions are made because dualism is very good at contrasting but not particularly skilled at integration.

For those of us who are Christians, there is a significant problem. This is pagan to the core. Yes, you heard me right; it is a pagan worldview. It is not the worldview of the writers of the Scriptures. It is not the worldview of Jesus. It has very little in common at all with the biblical worldview. As such, by thinking through its lens, we end up viewing reality in a very different way than the Bible does. It is dualism that allows the Hellenistic worldview to be highly speculative, focused on ideas divorced from life and action. Further, its excessive division between body and soul, human from divine, ended up separating our Christology away from practical action. We became obsessed with finely tuned distinctions about the nature of Christ's being without focusing on His life as a model of ministry and deep spirituality for our own lives. We became so focused on His divinity that His humanness could no longer impact how we live day to day.

Michael Frost and Alan Hirsch discuss the problematic nature of Hellenistic thought in *The Shaping of Things to Come:*

> Much of our Christology in the Western tradition was highly influenced by concerns relating to the Hellenistic-Roman context of Christendom with its focus on ontology. Ontology is the philosophical concern with the nature of "being" (ontos). As a result,

it is more concerned with metaphysics (a reality above or in back of the physical world) rather than physics and is therefore highly speculative by nature. Ontological Christology, therefore, focused on the nature of Christ's humanity in relation to his deity. It also focused on the preexistent role of the Logos in the Godhead, something the Bible only vaguely hints at.[1]

By focusing on speculative issues the Hellenistic worldview takes us away from the nitty-gritty of real life. It takes us away from the very things on which the biblical worldview focuses.

It is our contention that by focusing on development of the speculative doctrines, the early church lost the vital focus on the historical and practical implications of the faith. Mission and discipleship as such became marginal to theological correctness. Orthopraxy gave way to orthodoxy.[2]

Orthodoxy (right belief) is good. But when we become stunned by it, like a deer in the headlights and end up divorcing ourselves from the realities of living life correctly (orthopraxy), we have a serious problem.

## Hebraic Holism

This is far different from the Hebraic worldview in which the Bible and Christianity itself were given birth. The Hebraic worldview is holistic. It views life as a whole. It looks at our part in it and how all of this is connected to God. There is no separation of sacred and secular. There is no separation of thought from action. There is no separation between God and history or God and daily life. The God of the Hebraic worldview is not the deistic God who wound up the world and went on vacation. He is the God who not only made the world but is intimately involved in its daily reality and therefore its history. This is the God of life.

In John 10:10 Jesus offered us life, life to the full. Yet our life in a Hellenized Christendom is often marginalized, minimized, and takes place mostly in the mind. The Hebraic logic on which the Scriptures are founded offers us something far different.

We suggest that there is indeed a rather profound logic going on in the Torah, a logic that attempts to relate all aspects of life to

God. Therefore, everything—one's work, one's domestic life, one's health, one's worship—has the same significance to God. He is concerned with every aspect of the believer's life. Not even the mildew is insignificant.

While in the Western spiritual tradition, we have tended to see the "religious" as one category of life among many, the Hebrew mind incorporated "religious" existence into all of life. As such there is no distinction whatsoever between the secular and the sacred in the Hebrew worldview. All of life is sacred when it is placed in relationship to the living God. The Hebraic mind can draw a direct line from any and every aspect of life to the eternal purposes of God—this is the logic of the Torah.[3]

## Hellenism Separates Us From God

In the Hebraic worldview, not only is everything we do related to God, but God Himself is knowable. He can be experienced and loved. He is a God who not only loves us back but also interacts in every aspect of our lives. This is a God we not only talk about in propositional statements; He is a God we also encounter. The Bible itself is the story of mankind encountering God and God engaging mankind. The Hebraic worldview does not separate belief from action or us from God.

The Hellenistic worldview, on the other hand, is a humanistic and rationalistic worldview. It teaches or assumes that the highest expression of reality is man. It assumes that man, using his rational abilities, can understand the world and everything in it. That which man can measure or record exists. What he cannot measure or record is a phantasm, a figment of the imagination. Because this is a tacit assumption of the Hellenistic worldview, it puts barriers between God and us.

It is this Hellenistic separation from God that has had damaging effects on our daily lives. God, in the pagan Western worldview, is merely a God we talk about but don't encounter in practical, real ways. He becomes more of a "what" than a "who." We become more concerned with making propositions about the nature of His being than interacting with Him as a person. We give little attention to how His character can supernaturally transform our character. That's because there is little room for supernatural power in the Western worldview. In fact, from an extreme

Hellenistic point of view, God may not even exist. After all we can't measure Him, so His existence becomes a niggling doubt in the backs of our Hellenized minds. At best He is a God we can only talk about but not one with Whom we can have a real relationship.

That is not the God of the Bible. That is a God squeezed through a Greek philosophical meat grinder. What comes out the other side has very little in common with what went in. One of the most devastating aspects of this is that we end up losing the very thing God wants from us and what He created us for—a loving relationship.

Further, if we are disconnected from God in relationship, we become disconnected from His purposes. God's way, as we will discover, is to have a love relationship with us, and out of that relationship flows practical action. Out of this action flows God's purpose for His world. If we are disconnected from God in relationship, we not only miss the relationship, but we also miss the opportunity to participate with God in His wonderful purposes for His world.

We need to disentangle ourselves from the trap of Hellenistic philosophy, if the church is going to survive in the West. We need to embrace again the biblical worldview—a worldview that can connect us with God in deep relationship and at the same time reconnect us with His purposes for His lost and broken world.

## Disconnected From the Divine Operating System and Pledge of Allegiance

This Hellenistic thinking has disconnected us in another way. It has caused us to trust our own ability to understand the Bible and do what it says. This is humanism. Instead we will need to understand that God has a divine operating system for Christians called the new covenant. Just as computers have operating systems that govern how they function, so we have an operating system that governs how our Christian lives function. This operating system is based on the Spirit of God putting His law in our hearts and minds (Jer. 31:33; Heb. 8:10). He not only puts the law there, but also He gives us the power to obey. Life lived like this is supernaturally powerful.

Just as we have a divine operating system, we also have a divine pledge of allegiance which is intimately connected to our operating system. Our pledge of allegiance is "Jesus is Lord." This central, foundational truth must govern our every action. In the upcoming chapters we will see that in order to do things as God intended we must function in our correct operating system. And everything we believe and do must reflect our divine pledge of allegiance of "Jesus is Lord." If both of these things are not true then there is something wrong with what we are doing, thinking, or saying.

## Following Jesus into Passionate Viral Ministry

I have become passionate about doing ministry in a whole new way. In the process I have glimpsed and tasted of what Jesus calls new life, life to the full; fruit, more fruit, much fruit, and fruit that remains. I suspect that I'm not the only one who wants to live and experience this and not just talk about it. I suspect, in fact I know, there are many more like me.

If you are hoping that I'm going to give you the next new ministry technique, I'm going to disappoint you. If you are waiting for me to give you some hidden code to the New Testament only the Illuminati can decipher, you're going to be frustrated. However, if you long to live and bear fruit like the New Testament believers did, I may be able to point you in the right direction; or better still, to the right Person. I'm not going to tell you to do it just like me. I'm not going to tell you there is some generic path that everyone can take. There is only Jesus, always Jesus, nothing else but Jesus; and He will be enough.

## CHAPTER 1

# What a Viral Jesus Movement Looks Like

*I*MAGINE WITH ME for a moment walking down the street in San Francisco. You overhear a number of different conversations as you stroll through the financial district. Of those conversations, many people are discussing one of the hot topics, Jesus. "Then this guy prayed for Jesus to heal my sister and the tumor just..." "So, this dude tells me my ex-girlfriend's name and how she died. I asked how he could, know and he said Jesus had just told..." "Who do these people think they are, talking about Jesus..." "...and then I could feel a warm sensation, like warm honey. He told me that was Jesus." "I despise these Christians. Everywhere you go, they..."

No, I have not been smoking opium. And no, that is not currently happening in San Francisco. But it is currently happening in other places of the world and has occurred at various times throughout Christian history. The question is not whether this can happen in the West—it already has happened—but rather if and when it will happen again. That may depend on whether we are willing to follow Jesus into His harvest, as He has designed His harvest. The church as Jesus designed it in the New

Testament was designed to spread rapidly, to spread the message of Jesus like a virus.

## The Elements of a Viral Jesus Movement

If we are going to discuss viral Jesus movements we have to actually make clear what we are talking about. Every reader at this point probably has in his or her own mind a picture of what that would be. And many of those elements would be correct. But we must also acknowledge that it is difficult to get out of our Western Hellenistic Christendom mind-set. So it is probable that the picture we have created in our minds has some nonviral elements. This is true because we have probably never seen a viral movement of the gospel, if we are typical Western Christians, and because we've never questioned, or have not questioned enough, the models we have been given.

This chapter will try to lay out the essential elements of viral Jesus movements and see how they played out in Scripture. To do that let's look at what a first-century gathering actually looked like. It was unlike what most of us know as a "modern church service." This dissimilarity will highlight how far we have strayed from our first-century roots. It will also show how the very design of modern Christendom keeps us from becoming a viral Jesus movement.

## A First-Century Church Gathering

Our first-century brothers did things very differently from anything most of are accustomed to. We actually have Paul's description of what their gatherings were like. But they were poles apart from anything we normally see. These first-century gatherings were characterized by love, community, inclusion, and more than anything else a sense of spiritual power. They were also informal and unplanned. Listen to how Paul describes them.

> So if the whole church comes together and everyone speaks in tongues, and some who do not understand or some unbelievers come in, will they not say that you are out of your mind? But if an unbeliever or someone who does not understand comes in while everybody is prophesying, he will be convinced by all that

he is a sinner and will be judged by all, and the secrets of his heart will be laid bare. So he will fall down and worship God, exclaiming, "God is really among you!" What then shall we say, brothers? When you come together, everyone has a hymn, or a word of instruction, a revelation, a tongue or an interpretation. All of these must be done for the strengthening of the church. If anyone speaks in a tongue, two—or at the most three—should speak, one at a time, and someone must interpret. If there is no interpreter, the speaker should keep quiet in the church and speak to himself and God. Two or three prophets should speak, and the others should weigh carefully what is said. And if a revelation comes to someone who is sitting down, the first speaker should stop. For you can all prophesy in turn so that everyone may be instructed and encouraged. The spirits of prophets are subject to the control of prophets. For God is not a God of disorder but of peace.

—1 CORINTHIANS 14:23–33

The first thing we need to note is that there isn't an order of worship; there is no need. Actually what is happening here is that Jesus is leading the gathering. Spiritually sensitive non-Christians would note that as well. It seems strange that nowadays the phrase from this passage, "God is not a God of disorder but of peace," is taken to mean that we need some sort of man-made order of worship or things will erupt into chaos. Quite the opposite is being posited here. Paul is saying that you can tell when God is running the gathering because there is peace, not disorder.

Human intervention—in this case, prophets out of control—is what brings chaos. The solution is gentle inclusion, where no one feels the need to push an agenda. There is nothing worse for a pushy prophet than to have people weigh what has been said and decide that it was fleshly. In other words, be polite, wait your turn, and say something only if you believe it comes from God.

So in the first-century church we see incredible spiritual power, the presence of God, peace, and harmony. A spiritually sensitive outsider would love to be a part of such a supernatural encounter. That is not to say that these churches were attractional, they weren't. They were attractive, but not attractional. By attractional I mean trying to attract people to a "service." Evangelism went on mostly outside their meetings. They

3

did not have any illusion that they were supposed to doll up their meetings so that outsiders would want to come to them. They just did what they did and any outsider who happened to be there would be attracted to God, with Whom this community was having an encounter right before their eyes.

The vast majority of Christian churches nowadays have this completely backward. We often think we are supposed to put on an attractive show that will bring people in and keep them in—that is, if we even bother to try to attract outsiders at all. But what we really do is turn the outsiders off. We have, however, become highly proficient at attracting Christians from other gatherings.

So the first thing a viral Jesus movement looks like is that it is characterized by meetings of Christians that are attractive but that don't even bother to be attractional. They don't bother to put on a flashy show; they just are what they are. But since Jesus is in their midst, these gatherings end up being powerful and attractive. So now let's look at other characteristics of a viral Jesus movement.

## Characteristics of a Viral Jesus Movement

### It's "sneezable."

One of the first things we need to understand about viral movements is that they are, for lack of a better word, viral. That is to say they spread like a contagion. They are not and cannot be controlled by human intervention. In fact, one of the worst things we can do is try to control them.

This is the gospel set loose, the gospel moving so fast that we are not concentrating on preaching the gospel. Instead, we are focused on the issue Jesus actually told us to concentrate on: making disciples. Look at what Jesus actually said in the Great Commission:

> Then Jesus came to them and said, "All authority in heaven and on earth has been given to me. Therefore go and make disciples of all nations, baptizing them in the name of the Father and of the Son and of the Holy Spirit, and teaching them to obey everything I have commanded you. And surely I am with you always, to the very end of the age."
>
> —Matthew 28:18–20

In the original language the command is to make disciples. The other actions describe what that looks like. Jesus is the one in control here. He's the one with all the authority. We just play our part, which is to make disciples. We baptize them. We teach them how to obey everything Jesus commands, but we don't control what is happening. Every move we make is done in His power, under His direction.

Does this mean we don't preach the gospel? Of course we do. But the main focus of mature believers is on simple, straightforward discipleship. We will discuss what this discipleship looks like in a later chapter. There is, however, a really good reason mature Christians don't focus primarily on preaching the gospel. That is because we aren't doing the majority of it; the new Christians are. They are the ones newly infected with the Jesus virus, and they start to sneeze.

> This reference to sneezing is not just whimsical. We know from the study of ideas that they spread in patterns very similar to that of viral epidemics. We also know that in order to really take hold and become an "epidemic," they have to be easily transferred from one person to another. And to do this they need to be profound and yet simple—easily grasped by any person, and in many cases illiterate peasants.[1]

If we are to see a viral Jesus movement in our lifetime in the West we need to begin to practice a form of our faith that is sneezable. A good place to start would be to return to what we actually see in the New Testament, instead of religiously clinging to later nonviral additions from Christendom. Most of these additions come from later Christians copying the pagan society around them rather than following the biblical patterns laid out in the New Testament.[2]

## It's kingdom focused not church focused.

This kind of movement is focused on Jesus the King, not on the saints gathered. This is all about Jesus. The important thing is not that Christians have gathered, but that Jesus the King is among them. If Christians gather, you just have a group of Christians. When Jesus shows up, you have a church. Yet this is about more than about Jesus being among the gathered saints. It is about Jesus spreading virally through society. It is about Jesus using His saints to change society. It is about healing the sick and caring for the poor. Jesus wants to reclaim His world, not just have a bunch of religious meetings.

That is not to say that the church and churches are unimportant. They are very important, but they are not the center of attention. Jesus is. The gathering of the saints is a penultimate goal. We gather because Jesus told us to gather. We gather because new Christians grow while in relationship with more mature Christians who can guide them and be their examples. We gather because Jesus connects with people as whole communities, not with just individuals. We gather because Jesus enjoys our corporate worship. We gather because our faith cannot be fully expressed unless we do. Christianity is, by design, a corporate experience. We are Christ's body. He is our head. Since the whole Christian experience isn't about just being an eye or a foot, we need each other.

The kingdom is bigger than the church. It is deeply connected with the church, but its borders are much more extensive. When we give a cup of cold water to a child in Jesus's name, the kingdom is at hand. But that may not be the church. When my friends and I teach English to recent immigrants as an act of love, it is the kingdom, but it is not the church. Jesus uses us to plant churches because of this activity, but the language classes themselves are kingdom activity, not a church meeting. When we heal the sick we are showing Jesus's kingdom. When we get a word of knowledge for a non-Christian, the kingdom of God is at hand. When we shovel the sidewalk of our neighbor, motivated by the love of God and love for our neighbor, the kingdom is being expressed. Will the gospel be preached because of this? Sometimes it will. Sometimes we will be just planting a seed or watering what has already been planted. But it is through these simple acts, and many more like them, that the kingdom starts to spread like a virus.

## Its structure is organic.

The structure of this kingdom, and the church that results from it, can best be expressed with organic metaphors. I'm calling it organic because it is designed like a living thing to reproduce quickly. It should be noted that not once in the Bible is the church described as an institution. Human institutional structures are not even described. When we read the Bible, those of us who have been institutionalized tend to read an institution into the text, but it isn't really there. There is a very clear reason for this. The church that Jesus designed was based on a different structural logic than what we have become accustomed to. The best way to try to explain this structure is to do exactly what Jesus did when He described what the kingdom was like: use metaphors. And the best metaphors are the ones that Jesus used. I'll just borrow a few from Matthew 13.

> A farmer went out to sow his seed. As he was scattering the seed, some fell along the path, and the birds came and ate it up. Some fell on rocky places, where it did not have much soil. It sprang up quickly, because the soil was shallow. But when the sun came up, the plants were scorched, and they withered because they had no root. Other seed fell among thorns, which grew up and choked the plants. Still other seed fell on good soil, where it produced a crop—a hundred, sixty or thirty times what was sown. He who has ears, let him hear.
>
> —MATTHEW 13:3–9

Spreading the kingdom is like sowing seeds. They are going to fall among different hearts, just like seed gets sown on different soils. Note that the seed is spread abundantly. Humans don't control what kind of soil it falls on. Yet these seeds are so reproductive that even though only one soil is truly good, the seed sown will reproduce.

Can we really say that modern-day evangelism and the church as we know it resembles this? Every conventional church I've ever been a part of has sown very sparingly indeed. And they've tried to control what little gospel sowing happens. Further, would it be safe to say that the seed that reproduces abundantly would represent the Christians that remain in our churches?

> The kingdom of heaven is like a man who sowed good seed in his field. But while everyone was sleeping, his enemy came and sowed weeds among the wheat, and went away. When the wheat sprouted and formed heads, then the weeds also appeared.
>
> The owner's servants came to him and said, "Sir, didn't you sow good seed in your field? Where then did the weeds come from?"
>
> "An enemy did this," he replied.

The servants asked him, "Do you want us to go and pull them up?"

"No," he answered, "because while you are pulling the weeds, you may root up the wheat with them. Let both grow together until the harvest. At that time I will tell the harvesters: First collect the weeds and tie them in bundles to be burned; then gather the wheat and bring it into my barn."

—MATTHEW 13:24–30

The kingdom is not going to be like a perfectly groomed field. It will grow like a wheat field, but it will have weeds in it. Still, note that the servants don't do anything on their own initiative. Their plans to intervene were based on good intentions, but their strategy was way off.

In this we have a parable of the kingdom that represents church as we know it. I think it would be fair to say, in any congregation, of any size at all, we are going to have weeds. In fact, we probably have more weeds than we think. Yet despite all our efforts at keeping our doctrine pure, we still end up having people who really don't know Christ as much as they know how to look and act like Christians. Worse, they may not realize that being a Christian isn't about playing an appearance game. And it would be fair to say that organic church isn't different, at least in this aspect. We have some weeds too.

I do find it ironic, though, that church as we know it is so paranoid about having pure doctrine to keep the heretics out, yet it hasn't actually kept doctrine pure. Jesus didn't seem to be too concerned about this. He figured that by harvest time, it would be evident who was who. So the fakes could be gathered up and burned. Almost every pastor or priest of traditional churches who begins to hear about organic churches asks the same set of questions. One of the first questions is about keeping heresy out of the church. They do this without any sense of irony. They don't seem to note that they aren't doing such a good job themselves. When many so-called believers think that being a Christian is about going through church rituals and fitting within the accepted norms, we have a serious heresy on our hands.

Will organic churches produce heresy? Yes. Their track record in places such as China and India show that while they do produce heresy on occasion, they actually do a much better job of spreading true faith in

Jesus and discipling growing Christians than traditional churches do. But they won't do a perfect job. Paul's churches had problems. The church in Jerusalem had problems. But give me Paul's churches and Jerusalem any time, because despite their weaknesses, they will spread the gospel and teach new disciples to do everything that Jesus commanded. They'll have failures, but they will also spread virally. In other words, just like Jesus said, there will be weeds among the wheat. But at least they will spread rapidly and the majority of the disciples who remain will learn to reproduce and become disciples of Jesus Himself.

> He told them another parable: "The kingdom of heaven is like a mustard seed, which a man took and planted in his field. Though it is the smallest of all your seeds, yet when it grows, it is the largest of garden plants and becomes a tree, so that the birds of the air come and perch in its branches."
> —MATTHEW 13:31–32

So the kingdom is in some way like a mustard seed that is planted. Note here that it starts out very small but has the potential to grow so large that birds can perch on it. It does this in less than one season—in other words, very rapidly.

When was the last time you saw the kingdom grow rapidly like this? It goes from small to big in such a short period of time, it seems miraculous. Does this describe what we have become used to? Have you ever seen a traditional congregational church grow rapidly among non-Christians? Again, what we have become used to doesn't reflect what Jesus was talking about. Christianity isn't currently spreading rapidly anywhere in the West. That, in and of itself, is an indictment that we are not doing things Jesus's way.

I could go on and discuss other organic parables of the structure of the kingdom. But the point has been made. Church as we have come to know it no longer reflects what Jesus was talking about. The reason is that it no longer represents the design that Jesus intentionally built into it.

A point could be made that I'm confusing the kingdom with the church. However, the church is part of the kingdom, and as such it was designed with an organic structure. The church as Jesus designed it really is designed like a living thing. It reproduces according to its kind. Every

Christian can and does reproduce other Christians. If they don't, they are unusual and such lack of reproduction should be considered strange and a call for concern. Elders—that is to say, more mature Christians—reproduce maturing Christians who will later become elders. That is what discipleship is. Churches reproduce other churches. Networks of churches can start new networks of churches. Those with prophetic gifts will train up new prophets. Apostles will do the same, as will teachers.

> On that day a great persecution broke out against the church at Jerusalem, and all except the apostles were scattered throughout Judea and Samaria. Godly men buried Stephen and mourned deeply for him. But Saul began to destroy the church. Going from house to house, he dragged off men and women and put them in prison. Those who had been scattered preached the word wherever they went.
>
> —ACTS 8:1–4

It should be noted that this happened without the apostles. For some reason they stayed back in Jerusalem. But the early Christians were so fertile, they were so deeply infected by this contagious gospel, they preached the word everywhere they went. Persecution of organically discipled Christians is counterproductive. It spreads the seed more quickly. This is what Tertullian meant by his statement "The blood of the martyrs is seed."

### It's contagious.

In the Alan Hirsch quote above, Hirsch brought up the key point in understanding the difference between church as we know it and church as it was designed by God to be; it's "sneezable." It spreads just like a highly contagious disease spreads. He also makes another good point. In order for something to be contagious it has to be simple. Simple is not the same thing as simplistic. Simple means that it is clear, understandable, and uncomplicated. Simplistic means that it has been dumbed down. It removes anything that is hard to understand or tries to explain it to the last detail. Christianity is quite simple, but it is not simplistic.

What happens when someone begins to follow a Jesus he or she is actually encountering? What happens when Jesus begins to actually lead small gatherings of believers? What happens when they all start obeying, even when is seems foolish and counterintuitive, even irrational? What happens is that the gospel begins to spread like a contagion. It spreads easily because what is being spread is Jesus Himself, not a complex set of systematic doctrines. Yet what is being spread will be doctrinally sound because it is the Jesus of the Bible to whom new Christians are being introduced. It is His Spirit who inspired the writing of the Bible. He won't contradict His own writing.

New Christians in this type of simple viral gospel movement come to know Christ personally, often through experiencing a miracle, sign, or wonder. From that point on, Jesus is someone they expect to be super-[6] naturally powerful. They don't need to be convinced; they've already experienced a vital and viral Jesus. To encounter Jesus is a tremendous, wonderful thing. They are going to want to tell their friends. They don't need to be told what to do; Jesus is doing that by reigning in their hearts. That's why the gospel begins to spread like a virus. The new Christians are out sneezing it to all their friends.

Moreover, since Jesus is actually active in their lives, their lives are changing for the better. Their friends notice. In fact they will be asking what in the world is going on. That is what Peter meant when he said, "But in your hearts set apart Christ as Lord. Always be prepared to give an answer to everyone who asks you to give the reason for the hope that you have. But do this with gentleness and respect" (1 Peter 3:15).

Once a movement like this gets started, those of us who have more experience will have our hands full just teaching the new Christians how to obey Christ in community. We will need to teach them to distinguish which of their experiences is actually Jesus and which is the world, their flesh, or the devil. That is simple, but it won't be simplistic or necessarily easy. It will be a lot of hard but rewarding work. It will be messy. It will be taxing, and it will be exciting.

In the next chapter we will look at stability and control in a viral Jesus movement, like the one that began to break out of Jerusalem into the surrounding areas in Acts chapter 8. The lessons we will learn will be completely counterintuitive to all that we know from our previous church experience. Yet once we understand the logic of these movements, it will make sense; particularly if we keep in mind the most important doctrine of Christianity, our pledge of allegiance, Jesus is Lord, and we understand our operating system, the new covenant.

## CHAPTER 2

# Stability and Control
# in a Viral Jesus Movement

*P*HIL AND I were sitting in a coffee shop discipling one of the young men whom Phil had recently led to the Lord. We met there every Sunday morning to teach young Christians who had been led to the Lord through the ministry Phil and his wife, Lana, started in a migrant neighborhood in the Bay Area of California. To our surprise Emilio, one of our Christian language students, brought two other young men from the class to our table. Gerardo and Raymundo had recently moved to the United States from Central America looking for work. They had moved into the same apartment that Emilio lived in. Emilio wanted Phil and me to lead them to the Lord. We asked them to tell us their stories. We asked them to tell us about their new lives in the United States. Before long the conversation turned to Christ and we shared the gospel.

The next week Emilio, Gerardo, and Raymundo were back. Raymundo had had a dramatic conversion to the Lord that week as he pondered what we had talked about at the restaurant. He in turn encouraged Gerardo to accept Christ, and he did. They were both excited about their new faith and began to grow rapidly from our discipleship times in the restaurant. In fact, they started sharing their faith with friends and relatives. It looked as if we could soon plant a church among their sphere of influence. In fact we were excited because we were just beginning to embark on what could become the viral growth of the kingdom in this neighborhood.

However, within a few weeks Emilio had convinced the others that they needed to go to his "real" church, where a "real" pastor could watch over their souls and get them into a "real" singles group where they would learn how to be "real" Christians. Emilio did this with the best of intentions. He wanted to get them into a stable and controlled Christian environment where they would grow under the tutelage of official Christian leaders who did things the "normal" way. It wasn't long before Gerardo and Raymundo were told that they should concentrate on their real church and not go to the restaurant.

Let's fast forward the story about a year. I'm prayer walking the neighborhood. I bump into Raymundo. I strike up a conversation with him, but he is nervous and distant. It turns out that neither Gerardo nor Raymundo were attending church. None of their friends had come to Christ. Emilio had brought them into a "controlled" and "stable" environment to help them, but exactly the opposite of what he intended happened. This has become such a repeated pattern in our groups—experienced Christians taking new disciples to a "real" church where they are subsequently lost to the faith—that I am now very leery of mixing experienced, traditional Christians with new disciples.

Like many other issues in the kingdom, the issues of stability and control in a viral Jesus movement are counterintuitive to the way we've been trained to think. We have learned to think of stability as a good thing, something that provides continuity and allows a local gathering to have staying power, longevity. Control, on the other hand, has been given to Jesus as a theoretical concept, but not as a reality. We say that Jesus is the Lord of the church as a doctrinal statement, but the ones making actual decisions are usually humans, using human logic, training, wisdom, and positional power. This all makes perfect sense to us, raised as we were in the Greek-tainted humanism of the West. But it is not the way the kingdom is described in the New Testament. If we are going to again see a viral Jesus movement in the West, we are going to need to learn a couple of important lessons. We are going to need to learn to appreciate fragility. And we are going to need to learn to surrender actual control of the kingdom to its rightful leader, Jesus the King. After all, a kingdom is ruled by a king. That's why Jesus said, "All authority in heaven and on earth has been given to me" (Matt. 28:18).

## It's Fragile, Intentionally So

Jesus is head of the church, and Jesus has designed His church to be part of His organic kingdom, which in turn is designed to grow like a virus. The headship of Jesus must become much more than a theological statement; it must begin to control our behavior. When Jesus controls His kingdom, it grows virally. When humans take control, even for the best of reasons, the growth usually slows down or stops. Let me ask you some questions. How fast is the kingdom growing in the stable and controlled Christian environment of the West? Is it growing virally? Is it growing at all?

I once attended a very controlled church service with my father-in-law. Everything was planned down to the minute. Everything happened just as it was printed in the bulletin. My father-in-law leaned over and whispered, "What do you think would happen if the Holy Spirit showed up?" It was a very apt question for the situation. And I suspect the answer is that one of two things would happen. Either the Holy Spirit would interrupt and mess up the tight schedule and plan, or those who were really in control would wrest control back from the Holy Spirit again, for the sake of decency and order.

However, this is the wrong question for an organically designed church, a church designed by Jesus to grow virally. For such a church the right question is: What would happen if the Holy Spirit left? The answer is that it would be immediately noticeable. Jesus leads these gatherings. There is no order of service. People speak as they sense the prompting of the Spirit. And what they say is weighed for Spirit content by the others. There is order, but it is brought by the Spirit. If He leaves you would be left with silence, or more likely, just a few people in control of the agenda; which pretty much describes church as we have come to know it.

This viral, organic kind of church is very fragile. I believe it is designed by God to be fragile. Its structure demands the presence of the Holy Spirit to function. Further, our human tendency to try to control the agenda ourselves, the very essence of our sin nature, causes us to get off track. Worse, we think we are being wise, but it is only human wisdom, being wise in our own eyes. Isn't this the major story line of the Bible?

If the Holy Spirit isn't in control it should be absolutely obvious. If He leaves, it should be painful. Further, this type of movement is fragile. Again this is intentional. It isn't a kingdom without a king. The kingdom won't grow without His direction and lordship. In fact, as you will notice when we discuss evangelism and church planting in a later chapter, Jesus even leads us to the exact people we need to talk to.

This is not random evangelism or church planting. It is the kingdom expanding under the direct and specific orders of the King. Every detail is controlled by Him. We can only obey and cooperate. We do not control. If we do, the King will leave and the kingdom expansion will fall apart. Or, worse yet, it will be held together by human will, ability, and power. This feels comfortable to us, but as humans, we can only produce what humans are capable of. Wouldn't you rather have a supernaturally powerful King in control of the agenda? Wouldn't you rather see His power at work?

This fragility is a blessing in disguise. The essence of sin is to want to control ourselves, to want to do things our way, to want to make the decisions based on our own parameters and for our own glory. Sometimes we don't ever realize what we are doing. However, in doing so, we step out of the new covenant, in which the Holy Spirit puts God's laws and commands in our hearts and minds. Jesus is longsuffering. He is very patient. But after a while, He lets us do what we want and what we can accomplish in our own power. That, I believe, is the wood, hay, and stubble that gets burned up at the end of the age. As pervasive as sin is in our lives, shouldn't we rather want to know when we've taken control, so we can repent and surrender to the King again? We gain that kind of sensitivity only by living in the fragility of a weak organic system that is designed to fall apart outside the presence of the King. Rather than trying to control and preserve our institutions, we need to let Jesus be in control, and when He's not, things will fall apart naturally.

There are a number of ways to tell if one is involved with church as it

is described in the New Testament or church as we have come to know it.
One way is to look at its organizational structure. If there are hierarchies,
positional titles, and the ability to wield human power because of those
titles, we have a humanly organized church. This will seem hearty, stable,
and strong. It is so strong that when Jesus leaves, we don't even notice.
But this human-built stability gives us the ability to produce only human
results. We are trying to build the church for Jesus, as if He needs our
help. Jesus said in Matthew 16:18, "And I tell you that you are Peter, and
on this rock I will build my church, and the gates of Hades will not overcome it." If Peter couldn't build the church, neither you nor I can either.
That's a job for the King.

If we need an order of service to know what to do next, it is a sure bet
that the Holy Spirit is not guiding the church. He might show up every
once in a while, but it will be difficult to notice. If we need to prepare
some kind of lesson beforehand, what we are experiencing when we get
together probably isn't Jesus's leadership. Most likely it is human leadership. These things aren't necessary. What is needed are people who are
encountering Jesus on their own individually through an abiding relationship. They gather with Jesus corporately and wait to see what happens.

Have you ever gotten together with a group of Christians, perhaps for
a meal at someone's house and Jesus becomes the topic of conversation?
Soon you are quoting snippets of the Bible, or you look up a passage
and read it together. You pray for one another. You share concerns and
encourage one another. Godly advice is shared. Ministry just happens
naturally.

Awhile ago I met with a group of Christians over breakfast in someone's home. It was a planned meeting in the sense that we had intentionally gathered. After breakfast we met in the living room. I was perceived
to be the most experienced Christian present. Everyone looked to me to
get things rolling. However, I wanted them to learn to encounter Jesus
themselves. After all, Jesus had been the focus of our conversation ever
since people had arrived. Jesus was already present.

I suggested that they let Peter guide them in a more focused discussion, since he had been growing so rapidly in his faith. I needed to step
into the background. Peter was beginning to be recognized by others as
someone who was out ahead of the pack. I also felt Jesus led me to do this

as a demonstration of 2 Timothy 2:2: "And the things you have heard me say in the presence of many witnesses entrust to reliable men who will also be qualified to teach others."

The next thing you know, we were in the middle of a great dialogue. Everyone was animatedly discussing what they had been learning. Prayers were said. The Bible was read and passages were commented on. Sins were confessed, beginning with Peter. None of this was planned. The only rough spot in the whole morning was when I suggested that Peter teach something in a specific way. He responded by suggesting that I take over. The Lord convicted me and I apologized. From that moment on, it was a tremendous amount of fun and everyone participated. I would be hard pressed to say who spoke the most. Certainly everyone contributed, everyone felt as if they both learned and gave something important. And Jesus was in our midst.

To have a gathering like this is not complicated. It is simple. And that's just the point. As long as the Holy Spirit is in control, it is enough. The best way to destroy that ambience is for humans to take control. And when that happens, the wisest thing to do is to recognize it and stop.

## It Will Include the Ephesians 4:11 Ministries

I do not want to imply that Jesus does everything Himself. Quite the contrary, He does everything through us, but with His power. He chooses when and through whom. It is quite common for Him to choose more mature gifted individuals to accomplish specific tasks and ministries. These tasks are usually, but not always, based on the gifts mentioned in Ephesians 4:11–13. He also works through the entire body, not through the leadership of one or two gifted individuals.

In Ephesians chapter 4 Paul mentions five very important spiritual gifts that are foundational to a viral movement of the gospel.

> It was he who gave some to be apostles, some to be prophets, some to be evangelists, and some to be pastors and teachers, to prepare God's people for works of service, so that the body of Christ may be built up until we all reach unity in the faith and in the knowledge of the Son of God and become mature, attaining to the whole measure of the fullness of Christ.
>
> —EPHESIANS 4:11–13

These five gifts are the foundation on which the church is built in any new location. When these five gifts are used in the power of the Spirit, under the direction of the Lord of the harvest, the church will become a reality anywhere. Every gift is important. As Paul put it in 1 Corinthians 12, no one should say, "I am an eye. I have no need of you." These particular gifts do play a very important foundational role, yet they are not more important than mercy or tongues. Rather, it is that this cluster of gifts is designed for founding the church where it didn't exist before or where it is functioning at such a low level that it needs to again become viral.

The spiritual gifts mentioned in Ephesians 4:11 are foundational to any viral movement. Church as we know it has reduced these five gifts to a focus on two, teaching and pastoring, with an occasional tip of the hat to evangelism. Yet in Ephesians 2:19–21 we read:

> Consequently, you are no longer foreigners and aliens, but fellow citizens with God's people and members of God's household, built on the foundation of the apostles and prophets, with Christ Jesus himself as the chief cornerstone. In him the whole building is joined together and rises to become a holy temple in the Lord.

Church as we know it has not only left out two of the five foundational gifts for seeing a viral Jesus movement; they have left out the two that are the most foundational. Perhaps we need to see these five gifts in a new light.

## Apostles

The word *apostle* simply means a "sent one."[1] It comes from the Greek word, *apostolos*.[2] The Latin words related to the idea of being sent, *missio* and *mittere*,[3] are where we get the words *mission* and *missionary*. Jesus's twelve disciples are called His disciples until they are sent out on a mission. From that point on, they are called apostles. Note the italicized words below.

> He called his *twelve disciples* to him and gave them authority to drive out evil spirits and to heal every disease and sickness. These are the names of the *twelve apostles*: first, Simon (who is called Peter) and his brother Andrew; James son of Zebedee, and his brother John; Philip and Bartholomew; Thomas and Matthew the

tax collector; James son of Alphaeus, and Thaddaeus; Simon the Zealot and Judas Iscariot, who betrayed him. These twelve Jesus *sent out* with the following instructions...
—MATTHEW 10:1–5, EMPHASIS ADDED

To be merely a disciple is to be someone who is being taught by a master. However, the second someone is sent by God on a special mission, they become an apostle. We are all Jesus's disciples, if we allow Him to teach us. But some people are sent on a particular mission. Here's what God's sending looked like in Antioch.

In the church at Antioch there were prophets and teachers: Barnabas, Simeon called Niger, Lucius of Cyrene, Manaen (who had been brought up with Herod the tetrarch) and Saul. While they were worshiping the Lord and fasting, the Holy Spirit said, "Set apart for me Barnabas and Saul for the work to which I have called them." So after they had fasted and prayed, they placed their hands on them and sent them off.
—ACTS 13:1–3

We should note who is doing the sending here. It is not a mission board, a denomination, a local church, or the elders of a local church. The Holy Spirit directed this. While the church was involved in the send-off, it is really the Holy Spirit who is in control of the sending. Not every Christian is sent like this; it is a special calling. It doesn't make such a person more holy, powerful, or important. The person is just being sent on a special mission. The mission is special; the person is not.

The word *mission*, nowadays, can mean just about anything. I believe, however, those who are sent by God, with the apostolic gift, have a God-given drive to see the church founded among those who need to know Christ. That is far different from being a teacher, administrator, or pilot. Those are important things and are often done in support of the founding of the church. But I believe the word *apostle* should be reserved for those who are gifted and called to this special foundational ministry. God determines who they are and where they are sent. We can only discern that, not make it happen.

One of the characteristics of apostles is that they seem to be gifted by God to know what to do to get churches and church networks started.

They seem to have significant strategic insight. God seems to talk to them in strategic terms. They are leaders, but their leadership is focused on getting the church started among the lost. A mature apostle probably wouldn't have much patience leading a business meeting or a Sunday school class for adults who have been Christians for years—that is, unless he could teach them how to plant churches. The language of an apostle is strategy.

## Prophets

Apostles and prophets are mentioned together eight times in the New Testament. They are often also mentioned within a list of teachers, or teachers and workers of miracles. But the apostles and prophets are always placed together in the list. This is because prophetic work and apostolic work go together like a hand and glove. Though all five of the Ephesians 4:11 gifts are foundational, the gifts of apostle and prophet are the core of those gifts. Without these two gifts functioning together, the other gifts can't build a foundation for the church.

Prophets hear from God very specifically. They will be listening to God about where to go, what to do when they get there, and with whom to speak. It is not uncommon for them to receive a prophetic word from God for a non-Christian. That will get an unbeliever's attention. When the person responds, it is not uncommon for the apostle to use this God-given opportunity to plant a church among that person's friends. The language of a prophet is God-given symbols, such as images, impressions, visions, and words.

## Evangelists

The Ephesians 4:11 gifts are foundational. The core of that foundation is those gifted by Jesus to be apostles and prophets. However, all of these gifts are "to prepare God's people for works of service, so that the body of Christ may be built up until we all reach unity in the faith and in the knowledge of the Son of God and become mature, attaining to the whole measure of the fullness of Christ" (Eph. 4:12–13).

The evangelist isn't someone who does all the evangelism. Rather, he or she is someone who trains others how to evangelize. In a foundational situation of the church, it is the apostle who is doing the initial evangelism. However, any Christian can evangelize. And for that matter, any

Christian can plant a church. The apostle is sent especially to found a church when it needs to be started from scratch. This will involve evangelism, church planting, and church network development. It will also involve initial teaching and discipleship. This will be done in conjunction with prophetically gifted people. However, when churches start to group and networks start to form, the other three gifts come into sharper focus.

The work of an evangelist is to equip people to share their faith. That can be done any number of ways, but one good way is to take people along to assist as the evangelist shares the gospel. Then they can return and tell the church stories of what happened for the purpose of edification and community involvement. Later, the evangelist can give them their own opportunities to share the gospel. When they are mature, the evangelist can leave them on their own with instructions to train others, as we see in 2 Timothy 2:2. This is about life, not just information, so it is best learned in practice. It is also likely that new Christians are already telling their friends about Jesus. Since that is the case, the evangelist can give a few helpful ideas on how to be more effective. The language of an evangelist is the gospel.

## Pastors

This is not a positional title; it is a spiritual gift. The use of the word *pastor* as a positional title is not a biblical concept. This word, as a description of a Christian, is used only once in the New Testament, in Ephesians 4:11. In 1 Peter 5 the elders are exhorted to shepherd God's flock. This is a verb form of the same word. (*Shepherd* and *pastor* are the same word in Greek. This is true in other languages as well, for example, Spanish. So, when the Bible says the shepherds were watching their flocks at night in Luke 2, the word for *shepherd* is the same word as *pastor*. However, that is talking about real sheep, not sheep as a metaphor for Christians. Jesus also calls Himself the Good Shepherd in John 10.) But note that they are God's flock. They do not belong to any human. Further, this is an exhortation for the more mature to take care of the less mature. It is not giving a position of power to humans.

What do those who are specifically gifted by God to be pastors do? They equip the body, specifically when the body is broken, wounded, needs care or protection. These are the people who know how to mend broken relationships and broken emotions. The language of the pastor is the language of the heart.

### Teachers

Teachers have a God-given drive to make sure the whole counsel of God is taught. They love to teach the Bible and make sure doctrine is correct. They do this by being with people and listening for what God is doing in individual lives and what He is doing among groups. Teachers will listen to make sure heresy isn't springing up, but they will most often just make sure Christians continue to grow in understanding. In an organic setting, doctrine will probably not be taught as systematic theology. It will flow out of the situations that God is arranging in the lives of those who gather. Therefore teachers have to know the Bible, but they don't have to prepare lesson plans. The activities of God in lives are the lesson plans. The language of teachers is biblically sound doctrine.

# The Apostle as Jack of All Trades

Those who are apostolically gifted often need to function in all these ministry areas. This is because as founders of churches and church networks, they will be called on to listen to God (prophecy), preach the gospel (evangelism), heal the wounded (pastoral ministry), and teach (teaching). When the situation is foundational, it is the function of apostolic teams, which are often sent in small groups of two or three. Sometimes these teams are made up only of apostles.

When the church network starts to mature, there is opportunity for the more specialized ministry of teaching prophecy, a function of prophets; teaching evangelism, a function of evangelists; healing the wounded, an area for the pastorally gifted; and training in sound doctrine, the role of teachers. All these gifted people can be part of an apostolic team. It depends on how god sends out a group of people. Sometimes He sends out a group of apostles. Other times He sends out apostles teamed with prophets. A mature apostolic team might include all of the Ephesians 4:11 gifts. In any case, the apostles and prophets will certainly know whom they can call on to collaborate with them, if needed. In some situations, these gifted people may need to come strictly out of the harvest itself.

Finally, all of these gifted people reproduce after their kind. Apostles are always on the lookout for budding apostles to take with them and train. Mature prophets tend to look for less mature prophets to help them grow in their gifts. All of the Ephesians 4:11 gifted people do this, as should any especially gifted or mature Christian. We live to serve Christ and others. This is leadership.

## It's Done in Supernatural Power

Organic movements function in supernatural power. God's supernatural activity provides stability and control to the budding movement. As mentioned before, it is common in such movements for people to come to Christ as a result of a demonstration of God's supernatural power. Therefore it becomes natural for them to continue to expect and experience supernatural power. When Jesus sent out the twelve apostles in Matthew 10, Mark 6, and Luke 9, and when He later sent out an additional seventy-two in Luke 10, He told them to heal the sick, raise the dead, cast out demons, heal lepers, and preach the gospel of the kingdom. Supernatural power for its own sake is not sought. It is a means to an end and the end is Jesus. Jesus is also the source and He who controls.

When the kingdom is announced in conjunction with demonstrations of supernatural power, whether through healing, words of knowledge or casting out demons, it is done with much more authority and effectiveness than just preaching the gospel, no matter how doctrinally pure. Wherever organic movements of the gospel have broken out, they are accompanied by significant supernatural power and are bathed in a tremendous amount of prayer.

Experiencing God's supernatural power at work is part and parcel of being a Christian. Evangelism and church planting are done with supernatural power. Jesus is in control in such a context. Ministry in the church is done with supernatural power; ministry to nonbelievers is done with supernatural power. Jesus's power is providing stability. However, power for power's sake is not sought; it is just assumed that when Jesus wants to do something, He will give us the tools to do it. If a supernatural action is required, those tools will be provided by Jesus.

The supernatural power of God is encountered in obedience. While it is true that one can grow and mature in supernatural ministry, the main issue is obedience and trust in Jesus. He is the source and is in control of such power. He leads us to situations where His power will be needed. We should not expect demonstrations of power where there *a* is little obedience. We shouldn't expect God's power when humans are controlling ministry and doing it in their own ability. The supernatural power of God is reserved for those who are doing what they are being led to do. In fact, if there is a lack of supernatural power, it is often a sign *o* that ministry isn't being led by Jesus, or that there is a significant amount of unbelief. The goal is Jesus Himself and obedience to His leading, not supernatural power in and of itself.

Supernatural power is a fragile commodity just like the presence of the Holy Spirit—and for the same reasons. This is God's doing, not ours. His stability and control will be evident only when He is in charge. When we have a lack of God's power demonstrated, it may be a sign to us that *b* we need to get close to Jesus and pay attention to what He is asking of us. The best way to do that is through abiding, listening prayer, and prophecy. It is through prophecy that God guides His people. So it stands to reason that if we are off track, it is quite probable that He will use prophecy, among other things, to bring us back into obedience.

## Mariluz: Apostleship Through Prophecy

Mariluz, an apostolic friend of mine in Spain, was praying one day. She heard Jesus tell her to get up and go to a certain hospital. When she got to the hospital, she sensed God directing her to a specific room. As she entered a room, she saw a pregnant woman crying. Mariluz asked her what was wrong.

"The doctors tell me that I'm very sick. If they don't give me an abortion I may die. So tomorrow they are going to take my baby. I don't want to lose my baby."

Just at that point Mariluz heard Jesus speak to hear again. He said "That's not what I want to happen. Lay your hands on her and pray." So in obedience to the Lord of the harvest, she did as she was told. When Mariluz had finished praying, she handed the pregnant woman a card with her name and phone number on it and went home.

A few days later, Mariluz got a phone call from the woman asking her to come to her home. When Mariluz arrived, the apartment was full of people and the woman was still pregnant. So Mariluz asked her what happened.

The woman began to tell the rest of the story. "The following morning after you visited my room, the nurses came to prepare me for an abortion. The next thing I knew, the doctor was there checking me over carefully. Finally, he told me that he didn't understand what was going on. However, I was fine and the baby was fine, so I could go home."

Then the woman turned to the people gathered in her apartment. "This is the woman who healed me." "I didn't heal you." Mariluz interjected. "All I did was pray. Only Jesus can heal. Would you like to hear about my Jesus?"

And that was the beginning of a new church.

## It Is Led by Jesus Alone

In order for a viral Jesus movement to happen, the organizational structure of such a movement needs to be organic, not institutional. This is exactly the structure the kingdom parables describe. Organic ministry, organic churches, and organic church networks are focused on Jesus. His biblical titles give us some indication to at least some of the roles He plays in this organic context.

In Luke chapter 10 Jesus is called the Lord of the harvest. The harvest is His and He controls everything that happens. His presence provides stability. Just as He sent out apostles and prophets then, He is sending them out now, to announce the kingdom and found the church. He tells them where to go. He tells them what to do. He speaks to them in their language of strategy and symbols so they know exactly how He wants ministry done. When He begins to establish new Christians, churches, and networks, He calls in evangelists, pastors, and teachers to give this new work depth and solidity. But it is done under His direction and in His power.

We will talk more about how Jesus leads us into fruitful ministry in a later chapter. There, we will specifically focus on this Luke 10 passage where Jesus sends out seventy-two apostolic workers. We will also show the close relationship between this passage and Jesus sending out the twelve in Matthew 10, Mark 6, and Luke 9. These are key passages for understanding the foundational work of apostolic workers. But for now, the key understanding is that Jesus sends and superintends every detail and aspect of this type of organic ministry. He leads every step. So at every step apostolic teams need to be abiding, listening, praying, and obeying.

These are some of the key aspects of a viral Jesus movement.

- Apostolic teams found organic churches and networks that follow Jesus in every gathering. Yet every component, from individual Christians to networks, is easily reproducible and simple in design; simple but not simplistic.

- Viral Jesus movements are focused on the kingdom, not on the church per se. This is because they are focused on the King and His commands. The church is a product of kingdom work. Such ministry is fragile by its very nature, and that is good; in fact, it's essential.

- Viral Jesus movements are founded with the fivefold ministries mentioned in Ephesians 4:11.

- Viral movements, by their nature, are supernaturally powerful because they are under the authority and power of Jesus.

- Finally, viral Jesus movements are led by Jesus alone. He is the one who provides stability and control.

In a viral Jesus movement there is much human activity but it is actively focused on obedience to Jesus, not human insight, organization, leadership, and skill. All of this is true because we live in a new covenant relationship with Jesus. It is He who speaks His commands into our hearts and minds. Therefore, we have escaped the slavery of the old covenant law. We have also escaped slavery to human direction, will, ability, and power. These are the foundational principles of the world that Paul warned us about.

In the next chapter we will we be taking a hard look at our history. There might be some painful moments. We need to look at the human barriers that caused us to cease being a viral Jesus movement. We will see the church slowly, step by step, become entangled in the foundational principles of the world. We will name names and give dates. We do this not to criticize but to learn painful lessons together so we can soberly address our current state of affairs. These lessons will be important to us if we are to understand what a sustained viral movement of the gospel could look like in the West today.

## ⮞ CHAPTER 3 ⮜

# Supernaturalism
# in a Viral Jesus Movement

*I*HAVE PARTICIPATED IN the multiplication of the chicken and spaghetti. So I suspect I have a pretty good idea what the disciples felt like when they saw five loaves and two fish feed a multitude. Let me tell you my story. The rapid explosion of churches in Madrid had just gotten started. My friends had just won seven people to the Lord when I arrived at their apartment. The plan was to feed them and for me to begin to disciple them in the very basics of Christianity. My friend Mariluz had prepared a chicken, salad, and spaghetti dinner to feed them. In total there were the seven new Christians, Mariluz, her fiancé, Manuel, two of Manuel's roommates, and me. We had barely enough food for the twelve people who were there: two chickens, a large platter of spaghetti, a salad, two loaves of bread, and a couple of bottles of wine.

However, we had not counted on two crucial factors. First, our guests were hungry, and second the new Christians from the other churches decided to visit Manuel and Mariluz. The only polite thing to do was invite them to dinner. So as I spoke of salvation and the love of Jesus, I dished up the spaghetti and chicken. As they asked questions, they would hand me their plate and I would give them more chicken and spaghetti. Then as the discussion wore on, I'd do it again. Soon the apartment was full of visitors from the other new churches. Mariluz asked the people seated at the table to come to a corner of the apartment to have a discussion with Manuel while I fed the new guests. Eventually thirty-six people were fed, and I was serving the food.

It was God's grace that He did not allow me to realize what was going on until it was over. I was so absorbed in the dialog about Jesus and the new arrivals to the table that I wasn't paying much attention to those two chickens and the large plate of spaghetti. However, just as the last person was fed it was as if Jesus tapped me on the shoulder.

"Look at the chicken. How many were there?"

"Two, Lord, yet there is still chicken left. But I saw many people taking two and three pieces each."

"And how much spaghetti was there?"

"One plate full, Lord."

"How much is there now?

"There is still a half a plate left over, Lord."

A chill went down my spine that I will never forget. I was in the presence of the King.

## Supernaturalism and the Jesus Virus

Currently everywhere there is a Jesus movement there is also a powerful outbreak of God's supernatural power. Actually what we are seeing is a return not only to God's ecclesiology but also to His power. I don't think this is a coincidence. Church, as God designed it, was meant to be a demonstration of His love and His power, not merely a declaration of His love divorced from His power. When we return to our new covenant roots and allow Jesus to actually be Lord, we are leaving room for Him to act instead of trying to do everything in our own ability and power. The end result is that Jesus shows up, and Jesus is supernaturally powerful.

However, in the West, where we are still blinded by the Hellenistic thought of our Western worldview, we see little supernatural power. We need to return to a biblical worldview. The God of the Bible is supernaturally powerful. As believers around the world begin to trust Him to be who He actually is, instead of what rationalistic Western philosophy has made Him, He can again do as He did in the pages of Scripture.

> Coming to his hometown, he began teaching the people in their synagogue, and they were amazed. "Where did this man get this wisdom and these miraculous powers?" they asked. "Isn't this the carpenter's son? Isn't his mother's name Mary, and aren't his brothers James, Joseph, Simon and Judas? Aren't all his sisters with us? Where then did this man get all these things?" And they took offense at him.
>
> But Jesus said to them, "Only in his hometown and in his own house is a prophet without honor."
>
> And he did not do many miracles there because of their lack of faith.
>
> —MATTHEW 13:54–58

What we believe affects the way God acts among us. When we choose not to trust God, not to believe in His power, for whatever reason, we are choosing for ourselves not to be allowed to encounter His power. He did not do many miracles there because of their lack of faith (or in other versions, their unbelief). We have chosen, because of our rationalistic worldview, not to believe. If we are to get past this impasse in the West, we are going to have to return to the world as God sees it and as it is described in the Bible. Let's start with mysticism.

## Biblical Mysticism, the Foundation for an Encounter With God

Christianity, by its very nature, is a mystical faith—that is, if we truly understand what mysticism is and if we understand the new covenant. My spiritual formation was developed in a context in which mysticism was a bad word. In fact, in that context, in a theological debate, the quickest way to shoot down an argument was to accuse someone of being mystical. No one wanted to be seen as some kind of weird mystic. Frankly, I'm not sure most of us really knew what a mystic was. However, the word carried all sorts of negative connotations. In our minds, mystics were oddballs. Such people probably rolled their eyes around in their heads when they had a "mystical experience." Obviously they just weren't connected to rock-solid reality.

I think there is a problem with the view I grew up with. I suspect we didn't really know what mysticism was and therefore what a mystic was like. In order to clear up the confusion, perhaps it would be good to look at a nonmystical but reputable source to find out what mysticism really is. *Mysticism* is defined by the Merriam-Webster online dictionary, in its second definition, as "the belief that direct knowledge of God, spiritual truth, or ultimate reality can be attained through subjective experience (as intuition or insight)."[1]

By that definition, Jesus was a mystic when in John 5:19–20 He said, "I tell you the truth, the Son can do nothing by himself; he can do only what he sees his Father doing, because whatever the Father does the Son also does. For the Father loves the Son and shows him all he does."

Jesus was not only a mystic Himself; in John 16:5–15 He comforted the disciples, distressed by His statement that He was leaving, with a strange encouragement. It can be summarized as, "Don't worry about My leaving; I'll send the Holy Spirit to you, so you can all be mystics too."

If we truly understand what mysticism is we would realize that every time the Holy Spirit convicts us of sin (a subjective experience) we have become mystics. Every time we feel the Holy Spirit has given us insight into the Scriptures, we have become mystics. In fact, any interaction with God is, by definition, a mystical experience. This includes the Holy Spirit's writing the law on our hearts and minds, as the new covenant states.

Do you sense God is prompting you to pray about something? You are a mystic. Do you feel God teaches you when you read the Scriptures? You are a mystic. Now let's take it further. Do you think that prayer can be a two-way conversation? You are a serious mystic. Do you believe God can call you to a specific ministry? You are a dyed-in-the-wool mystic.

The problem isn't mysticism; the problem is the abuse of mysticism. Another of Merriam-Webster's definitions of *mysticism* is: "vague speculation: a belief without sound basis."[2] Can Christian mysticism be abused? Of course it can; and it is abused regularly in this manner. But since true Christianity is based on the Bible, and specifically the new covenant, we need to come up with a biblical cure for the disease. We should avoid wild overreaction to the problem.

# Biblical Prophecy

One of the most mystical Christian experiences is prophecy. It is also one of the most abused. As with mysticism, we need to understand what prophecy is. Again Merriam-Webster gives us a pretty good working definition.

1. an inspired utterance of a prophet

2. the function or vocation of a prophet; specifically: the inspired declaration of divine will and purpose

3. a prediction of something to come[3]

The idea of prophecy is that God speaks to specific people so that He can communicate His will for a specific situation. Some fear that such a thing impinges on the inspiration of the Bible, that such people are claiming their statements to be on equal footing with the Bible. There probably are such people and they are wrong. But most Christians who claim to be speaking prophetically do not make such claims. They believe that they have heard from God as to what He wants specific people to do in a specific time and place. This does not impinge on the Scriptures because the function of this kind of prophecy is very specific for particular people in a particular time and place. This is not the same as the general revelation of the Bible.

To further understand this, perhaps a couple of analogies would be helpful. If we play American football, we need to play by the rules. The rules, in this analogy, are the Bible. The Bible explains how Christianity was designed to be lived by our Creator. In the same way, the rules of football define how the game was designed to be played by the officials of football. However, each specific play in football is a specific decision based on the current reality of the game in progress. A coach can call in a play to his team. He can tell them that in this specific situation, against this specific opponent, in these weather conditions, he wants the next play to be a 21-X screen pass. That call from the sidelines is the analogy for prophecy. God not only gave us the rules of the game (the Bible) about how Christianity is to be lived, but He also wants to call in plays (prophecy) giving us specific instructions for our specific reality.

If all this is new to you, perhaps another analogy from Wolfgang Simson in his e-book *The Starfish Manifesto* would be helpful.

# GPS: God's Prophetic System

A few years ago some small devices started to revolutionize the way we drive our cars. Instead of a pile of city, county, state, and country maps that we consult to get from point A to B, many now have a small palm-sized minicomputer sitting in their car. These little navigational computers—or GPS (Global Positioning System)—can calculate, through a connection with a number of geostationary satellites and through triangular methods, the exact position of the GPS device, down to our exact location. Therefore, it becomes possible to navigate to any address or way-point, no matter whether we are on the move by boat, bike, car, or even on foot.

In this present prophetic-apostolic reformation, the prophetic gift has a similar role as the GPS-Systems for travelers. The current church scene (let alone the economic and political situation) has become a maze, at least for normal folks. It has become increasingly difficult to navigate spiritually, not knowing where we are on our journey, where exactly we are going, and whether we have to turn left or right at the next stop sign. To be on top of all this, we would have to look constantly at a million facts, developments, key players, and statistical developments.

Nobody knows any more what's going on—but God. And, instead of constantly going after the latest information (for many new ways of navigating are opening up), we are starting to look upward for help. Here we discover what God meant when He said: "I will guide you with my eyes." God speaks of a navigational system that He is offering to His folks. It has a horizontal and a vertical dimension. The horizontal is the Bible, the unchangeable, revealed Word of God that we can read and touch here on earth ("Your word is a lamp to my feet, and a light to my path." Psalm 119:105). The Bible is the map. The vertical dimension, straight from heaven, are prophetic insights, which may come in various ways: through visions, dreams, dialogs with God, angelic visitations, etc., that accentuate or temporarily lift out biblical truth, announce changes or are the symbolic red dot on the map that says: "You are here. Next left."[4]

So prophecy is God calling in His plays at a specific juncture of a game, or it is God giving us a divine GPS to let us know how to arrive exactly where He wants us to go. Can this be abused? Of course; and God anticipated this and gave us biblical parameters on how to deal with it. First of all, God wants us to prophesy. He is quite clear about that: "Follow the way of love and eagerly desire spiritual gifts, especially the gift of prophecy...I would like every one of you to speak in tongues, but I would rather have you prophesy. He who prophesies is greater than one who speaks in tongues, unless he interprets, so that the church may be edified" (1 Cor. 14:1–5).

God wants us listening to Him when He calls in plays. God wants us to use His GPS. Listening to Him and following His plays will strengthen us, encourage us, and comfort us. Prophecy is designed to let us know exactly what to do next. A biblical example of this would be the prophetic dream that God gave to the apostle Paul in Acts 16:

> Paul and his companions traveled throughout the region of Phrygia and Galatia, having been kept by the Holy Spirit from preaching the word in the province of Asia. When they came to the border of Mysia, they tried to enter Bithynia, but the Spirit of Jesus would not allow them to. So they passed by Mysia and went down to Troas. During the night Paul had a vision of a man of Macedonia standing and begging him, "Come over to Macedonia and help us." After Paul had seen the vision, we got ready at once to leave for Macedonia, concluding that God had called us to preach the gospel to them.
>
> —Acts 16:6–10

Note here that while in ministry these first-century church planters were paying constant attention to God's GPS. Were Paul and his companions to travel in Phrygia and Galatia? Yes. Were they to preach the Word in the province of Asia? No. When they followed the GPS to the border of Mysia, were they to continue on to Bithynia? Absolutely not; the Holy Spirit forbade it. The divine GPS took them to the port city of Troas, where God called in a significant play to Paul. The team was to go to Macedonia. He did this through a prophetic dream, and the team immediately responded in obedience.

Frankly, I can't understand why anyone would be uninterested in having this kind of specific guidance. This is God's biblical way of keeping us on His path, working on His time line, playing by His game plan. When we reject this kind of GPS, what are we saying to God?

First Corinthians 14 gives us further insight in how to correctly respond to prophecy.

> What then shall we say, brothers? When you come together, everyone has a hymn, or a word of instruction, a revelation, a tongue or an interpretation. All of these must be done for the strengthening of the church. If anyone speaks in a tongue, two— or at the most three—should speak, one at a time, and someone must interpret. If there is no interpreter, the speaker should keep quiet in the church and speak to himself and God.
>
> Two or three prophets should speak, and the others should weigh carefully what is said. And if a revelation comes to someone who is sitting down, the first speaker should stop. For you can all prophesy in turn so that everyone may be instructed and encouraged. The spirits of prophets are subject to the control of prophets. For God is not a God of disorder but of peace.
>
> —1 Corinthians 14:26–33

It should be noted that God's calling in a play or giving GPS instructions is to be expected when we gather together. In fact, I suspect everything happening in a Christian gathering is meant to be a mystical experience. This could be God's prompting someone to lead out with a song or share a teaching or instruction. But the divine interaction does not really end there. It is a divine mystical experience when someone gets a revelation that is a prophecy (v. 26) or when a tongue is interpreted (v. 5). If someone speaks in tongues in a gathering, it is to be interpreted, which turns it into prophecy. If there is no interpretation, the speaker is to not to speak further. Prophets are to prophesy in turn. They are to give each other a chance to speak. This is not meant to be a chaotic hodgepodge of people shouting out instructions from God. This, by the way, is what the decency and order injunction from Paul was about. It is not about having an order of worship or being boring and staid. Further, the whole church should weigh carefully what prophets say on each potential GPS download. This clearly implies that a prophet can get it wrong, or have a partial message, or be mostly correct but not entirely correct.

This may seem confusing. How are we to deal with such a situation? Should we just reject the whole thing as unpredictable, chaotic, and confusing? That is not God's answer. Instead we are to trust God to give us further insight as a group. This forces us to be intimately dependent on God as individuals and as a group. It also demands that we be humble enough to realize that we might not understand everything or always be correct. In this kind of context, if someone "prophesies" yet states something that is unbiblical, the others in the group are to weigh in. They should open the Bible and show where such a thing is wrong.

If a person is getting a revelation they believe is from God and that is within biblical parameters, it still may not be from God. Let's say for example that someone prophesies that they feel God is saying that the church should start an evangelistic ministry next weekend. There is certainly nothing unbiblical about that. It still doesn't mean that it is a good idea or that it comes from God. The church is to weigh what is being said. They are to continue to tune into God and sense from Him if this is correct or not. And perhaps God will give further refining revelation through another person. In that case, the first speaker is to stop and the other is to refine. This seems to be what verse 30 is referring to.

Finally, Paul makes it quite clear that the spirits of the prophets are subject to the control of the prophets. New Testament prophecy is not some experience where the prophet loses control. Their eyes do not roll to the back of their heads. They are quite aware of what they are saying. In fact, if someone makes such a claim, I would be highly dubious. We'll leave that to the séances depicted in movies.

The spirit of a Christian is still under their control when they prophesy. They may have seen or felt or heard something from God. But they are capable of stopping and waiting until later to share what they sense God is saying. They can analyze. They can submit it to the church for others' analysis. This is not the all-powerful prophets taking control of the lives of others with their pronouncements from on high. There should be no "thus saith the Lord." Arrogant prophets are dangerous prophets. Instead this is someone humbly submitting what they think they have heard from God to the others, who are also perfectly capable of hearing from God. Together they work with God to find out what He is really saying. In other words, as a community, they enter into a process of discernment with God as their leader.

Actually there is a good deal of prophecy going on even in churches that don't believe in it. God is still communicating. The problem is that since they don't believe in prophecy, they attribute it to themselves and therefore steal some of God's glory and honor. This is not a wise thing to do. Furthermore, since they don't realize it is prophecy, the important prophetic discernment process of 1 Corinthians 14 is bypassed or truncated. And because the process is truncated and in fact avoided, it is quite possible that much of what God wants to say is never understood or even stated due to the unwillingness to actually intentionally listen. All of this is rather unhealthy. Still, God is a gracious and patient God who is willing to communicate.

Therefore the biblical answer to sloppy prophecy is careful prophecy. It is not the avoidance of prophecy. This is true of all mystical experiences. They must be within the parameters of the Bible. If our GPS takes us off the map, our GPS has gone wonky. God would never call in a play that is against the rules of the game; after all, He wrote the rules of the game. This in and of itself keeps us fairly safe and keeps us from being led into evil from false or sloppy mysticism. But it doesn't assure that we are correct. For that we have to be careful with our mystical and prophetic experiences. We have to be humble enough to admit that no matter how much experience we have, no matter how much we have been right in the past, we may be wrong this time or we may not have the entire story. Good prophets are humble prophets. We should be willing to submit what we are sensing to other godly people who can discern with us. And all of this is in and of itself mystical.

God does not warn us away from prophecy. He tells us to do it well and then tells us how. God does not warn us away from mystical experiences; He expects us to weigh these experiences within the biblical parameters. God does not expect us to avoid prophecy, but He also doesn't expect us to abuse it. He expects us to hold His GPS downloads with humility and openly allow other godly people to examine them in community.

In this kind of context—where prophecy is carefully presented, compared with scripture, done in the community of mature believers, and discerned carefully—prophecy is safe. It still may not be entirely accurate, but it won't be dangerous. Let's go back to our example of someone who felt God wanted them to prophecy that the church was to start a specific evangelistic ministry the next weekend. Let's further say that this really isn't coming from God. The person shares this with the group. The first thing they would do is check to see if such a thing falls outside of biblical behavior. Is this sinful, or even questionable? There is no problem at this point. It is perfectly within the biblical parameters to evangelize on any given weekend. Now at least we are safe from sin. Next the group weighs in on whether they think God is really saying this. This is not an opinion fest; it is the rest of the group sensitively listening to God. In other words, it is further prophecy. Let's say that the group, perhaps in their evangelistic zeal, still misses what God is saying. The group approves. So the group goes out and evangelizes that weekend. Has something evil happened? No, but it may not have been God's best or even particularly effective. It might have been a waste of time and resources, but it wasn't wicked.

It should be noted here that those who believe in prophecy but sometimes get it wrong are at their worst participating in behavior that those who reject prophecy participate in all the time. They are living within biblical parameters but not necessarily listening to God correctly for specifics. At that point they may be functioning in the flesh. They could be trying to do God a favor but not ministering in His power or under His instruction. It is not a good idea, but it is not biblically evil, unless the intent is fleshly, rebellious, or sinful.

The most common expression of this in the current Western church is to replace the function of prophecy—i.e., knowing what to do next—with goals and objectives or authoritative positional leadership. Business methods and institutional leadership are human substitutions for divine guidance. Instead of actively listening to God and trusting He knows how to communicate to us, we trust our human ability to plan, make decisions, and utilize resources. This is the equivalent of trusting in horses and chariots in warfare instead of trusting God. (See Psalm 20:7.)

We need to be very careful we don't come so deeply under the sway of the humanistic foundational principles of the Western worldview that we think we as humans can and should make ministry decisions. The most effective tools of business are not helpful in ministry. Such tools are designed to maximize human decisions. Jesus did only what He saw the Father doing. Can we do better than Jesus in decision-making practices? Isn't Jesus our model of ministry behavior? Or should we believe, now that we have the genius of modern business, we have finally found a better way? Jesus told us that the Holy Spirit would comfort and guide us. Is this less effective than what some business guru can come up with? True biblical Christianity isn't people using the best resources to make the best human decisions. Let's let the CEOs and the CFOs do that. True biblical Christianity expects God to communicate and tell us what to do next. Can we actually trust in Him to do that?

## The Problem With Forbidding Mysticism, Prophecy, and Supernaturalism

To avoid mysticism and prophecy in particular is a nonbiblical response. It is not playing God's game by God's rules. Prophecy and a mystical connection to God are profoundly biblical. We should not avoid such things; we should do them well. After all, God made mankind to love us, be loved by us, and have fellowship with us. In other words, God made mankind to have mystical communion with Him.

One time a leader of a missionary team I was on prophesied that a car accident I was in was punishment for questioning his dictatorial leadership practices. This was done while my family and I stood injured on the side of a rural road. He then predicted that all sorts of other nasty things were going to happen to us; things, by the way, which did not occur. I'll let you decide if that was biblically handled prophecy or not. The response in my head at the time was to call for his stoning in reference to Deuteronomy 18:20–22.

Now, as I look back at that incident, I think we were both just a wee bit rash. But this does highlight a couple of issues. First, clearly in the name of prophecy, we can say anything we want and try to give it the authority of God Himself. This is carnal and dangerous. To follow such people is also dangerous. But just because a wonderful thing such as prophecy can be abused does not mean it should be avoided. It just needs to be done well. Do we avoid teaching because teaching can be abused? Do we avoid evangelism because evangelism is sometimes abused?

Second, my calling for such an abusive prophet to be stoned was also a bit off. I want to note here that I just thought this in my head; I didn't actually throw any rocks.

There is a difference between New Testament prophecy and Old Testament prophecy. This is because the prophetic act is being done under two very different covenants. Part of our new covenant heritage is that God puts His laws on our hearts and minds (Jer. 31:33; Heb. 8:10; 10:16). Another way of saying this is that God speaks directly to us and, through His Holy Spirit, shows us how to live. Every Christian, as a new covenant believer, has access to the Holy Spirit. This is a mystical experience because the new covenant is a mystical covenant. This allows us to weigh carefully what has been said in prophetic utterance (1 Cor. 14:29) since we all have access to the Holy Spirit.

The old covenant of the Law was not a guarantee that each believer could hear directly from God. They had the written law and were expected to obey it. They also had some prophets who did hear directly from God. But since this was a sporadic experience, and since not everyone could hear from God individually, they had to weigh what was said by a different set of parameters. First, they needed to check to see if what the "prophet" was saying was according to God's written law. They were to check to see if he prophesied anything God had not commanded. They were also to check to see if what was prophesied came about. If they did not pass this test the false prophet was to be put to death. This was a reasonable set of parameters given the circumstances. And so are the parameters set forth in the New Testament.

Neither God nor the Bible is being inconsistent. These are two very different circumstances that require two very different sets of behavior. Do you think it is wise to drive the same way on snow and black ice as one would on a warm summer evening? Different driving conditions require different driving habits. Different covenants, with completely different parameters for access to the Holy Spirit, require different prophetic behavior.

Why then are some Christians dead set against mysticism, prophecy, and other sorts of supernaturalism? I don't believe the answer is found in the Bible; it is found in a nonbiblical worldview. The Bible has supernaturalism happening on almost every page. This is no less true in the New Testament than in the Old Testament. As explained above, the new covenant, which we Christians are still under, is mystical and supernatural at its very core. It states that God speaks to our hearts and minds, which is a mystical experience and a form of prophecy.

The problem comes when we try to force the Bible through a non-supernatural cultural view commonly called the Enlightenment. Worse, most of the Christians who have this nonbiblical, nonsupernatural worldview don't even know that the Enlightenment controls their thinking. For them it is just the way things are. But in reality it is the worldview picked up from parents, school experience, friends, and perhaps church and seminary. It has been, after all, the worldview of Western civilization for about two hundred and fifty years. And the worldview before it, called the Renaissance, was just about as antisupernatural. So for about the last five hundred years, Western society, of which we are a part, has disdained supernaturalism as superstition.

What happens when someone takes the nonbiblical, actually antibiblical worldview of the Enlightenment, and reads the Bible through it? There have actually been two responses. The first is what has commonly been called Modernist theology. (This is a good title since the combined cultural epochs of the Renaissance and the Enlightenment are called the Modern era. The theological enemies of this movement normally call it theological liberalism.) This theology set out to debunk the Bible. Anything that the Bible stated that would not hold up to the Enlightenment worldview was thrown out as superstition. Hence all miracles needed to be explained as mass hysteria, superstition, or the backward culture of the time. Further, they subjected the Bible to a rigorous hermeneutic that expected the writers of the Bible to write it as a scientific textbook or be labeled as superstitious and backward. Or conversely they used their hermeneutic to cut out vast swaths of the text as not part of the original Bible or as later additions. It just so happens that not everything that is taken out squares with the Enlightenment worldview. To subject a text not written in the Enlightenment to the standards of the Enlightenment, expecting it to conform to those expectations, is arrogant, but then the Enlightenment isn't noted for its humility.

The second Enlightenment Christian response is what is often called the doctrine of cessationism. This is a doctrine common among non-Pentecostal or non-Charismatic evangelicals. This doctrine posits that everything the Bible says is true and it really happened in history. But sometime after the writing of the New Testament, the miraculous stopped. This is nothing more than forcing the humanistic Enlightenment worldview onto our own current lifestyle and the Bible. It is trying to find a way to believe the Bible is literally true while denying that what happened in the Bible could possibly happen today. There is no real credible biblical reason to believe this. It comes from the Enlightenment, not the Bible. (For a brief discussion of the philosophy, history, worldview, theology, and hermeneutics of cessationism see Appendix A.)

## Heal the Sick, Raise the Dead, Cast Out Demons, and Proclaim the Gospel

When Jesus sent out the twelve apostles (Matt. 10:1–16; Mark 6:6–13; Luke 9:1–6) and later the seventy-two others (Luke 10:1–23), He gave them a very specific pattern for how kingdom-advancing work was to be done. If we realize that supernaturalism is biblically viable today, then these instructions are perfectly reasonable. We won't go into all the instructions for Jesus's pattern here—that is covered in chapter 9—but we will focus on the supernatural elements. Each passage seems to focus on slightly different aspects of these supernatural elements. The instructions in Matthew 10:7–8 list them all.

> As you go, preach this message: "The kingdom of heaven is near."
> Heal the sick, raise the dead, cleanse those who have leprosy,
> drive out demons. Freely you have received, freely give.

The Mark 6 passage mentions only driving out demons and healing the sick and preaching repentance. The Luke 9 passage also emphasizes healing the sick, driving out demons, and preaching the gospel. The Luke 10 passage also emphasizes preaching the kingdom of God is near, healing, and demons. It also alludes to miracles, but it is not clear if Jesus or the apostles performed these.

I don't think the issue is exactly which kind of supernaturalism is allowed in kingdom ministry. The point is that it is part and parcel of kingdom ministry. And in fact, we see supernaturalism as an integral reality in the ministry of Jesus, in that of the original twelve apostles, and in the later apostolic work mentioned in Acts and the Epistles. Jesus doesn't mention in any of these passages that signs and wonders are to be a part of kingdom work, yet He multiplied fish and loaves twice when He preached the kingdom. Further, a significant sign and wonder was accomplished with Peter's shadow:

> Nevertheless, more and more men and women believed in the Lord and were added to their number. As a result, people brought the sick into the streets and laid them on beds and mats so that at least Peter's shadow might fall on some of them as he passed by. Crowds gathered also from the towns around Jerusalem, bringing their sick and those tormented by evil spirits, and all of them were healed.
>
> —Acts 5:14–16

We find God using handkerchiefs and aprons touched by Paul to expand the kingdom.

> God did extraordinary miracles through Paul, so that even hand-kerchiefs and aprons that had touched him were taken to the sick, and their illnesses were cured and the evil spirits left them.
>
> —Acts 19:10–12

Jesus used a prophetic word of knowledge with the woman at the well in John chapter 4. He asked about her husband and then stated that she had five husbands and was now living with another man who wasn't her husband. The end result was that Jesus reached many in that Samaritan village.

Peter had a prophetic vision that connected him to Cornelius. Cornelius himself had an angelic visitation. Jesus and Paul cast out demons. So did the twelve and the seventy-two. Many new converts spoke in tongues, even when it is doubtful that they knew what tongues were. The point is that we should expect supernaturalism in the context of expanding the kingdom and preaching the gospel. We cannot control when this supernaturalism will occur. Just like everything else in ministry, God directs.

It should be noted that the gospel-preaching ministry developed in the New Testament is a supernatural act. Just as Jesus could do only what He saw the Father doing, the apostles participated in only God-initiated work. For example, in Jesus's instructions in Luke 10, Jesus distinguishes between the special people called the man of peace and random people called the people along the road and those we find going house to house. He further gives instructions about how one is to distinguish a person of peace from a random person, by how the person responds to blessing (vv. 4–10).

The point here is that, as Jesus says, the servant is not greater than the master, nor the messenger greater than the one who sent him (John 13:16). If Jesus could do only what He saw the Father doing, we can do no more or less. This process of talking to only the person of peace and his household—a person God will indicate—or doing only what we see the Father doing is a supernatural process, not a natural human one. Therefore, evangelism done biblically is not a matter of randomly preaching on our own initiative to anyone who will listen. It is God setting up the circumstances for preaching, Peter (Acts 2–3). Or it is God setting up the circumstances for us to meet the man of peace, as He did when Paul met the Philippian jailer (Acts 16).

# Modern Stories of the Miraculous in Kingdom Ministry

In chapter 2 I told the story of my friend Mariluz healing a pregnant woman in a hospital through prayer. There are two subsequent encounters that led to two further churches being planted.

## A "chance" meeting on the metro

One day the woman Jesus had healed through Mariluz was riding on the Madrid Metro. We'll call her Maria. She sat down next to a pregnant woman in the seats reserved for those with special needs. The woman Maria sat next to was crying. When Maria asked her why she was crying, the woman responded that tomorrow she was to go to the hospital for an abortion, due to her troubled pregnancy. Maria responded to this news by shouting out, "Don't do it!" She then pulled Mariluz's card out of her purse and encouraged her new acquaintance to call Mariluz for prayer. This too resulted in a new church planted.

## Luke 10 over the phone

About three months after these two incidents, I was training leaders in the various churches that had sprung up in Madrid. Almost all of them had been planted through some sort of miracle or healing. I was training these new leaders on Jesus's pattern of church planting in Luke 10. As I did this one of the leaders, Roberta, said, "I think I have a Luke 10 story."

Roberta was originally from Brazil. Her husband, a practitioner of witchcraft, had many years before given her an ultimatum: give up Jesus or he would leave her and the children destitute. Roberta chose Jesus. In essence Roberta was left a widow. She read in her Bible that God would care for widows, so she asked for His provision. God did miraculously provide for her daily needs for many years.

After her children had left the home, Roberta decided to move to Spain, where she was hoping to find a job. Unfortunately, the service she used was a scam, which left her without a job or contacts at the Madrid airport. Yet God had not abandoned her. She bumped into another Brazilian person at the airport who invited her to stay with his family.

While staying with this new family, she met a young Brazilian woman named Adriana. It just so happened that Adriana was the daughter of a woman Roberta knew in Brazil. Adriana was pregnant by her married lover, who had paid to send her to Spain, where he intended to meet her. He never came. Instead Adriana was left destitute in Spain. Roberta preached the gospel to Adriana, but she was not interested. Somehow she blamed the ill treatment she received from her boyfriend on God.

Roberta lost contact with Adriana when Roberta moved to a nearby city to live with an old friend from Brazil named Mirelli. She wasn't a Christian; in fact Mirelli was bitter against the church of her youth.

Soon Roberta not only had a roof over her head but a job with a consistent income. One day Roberta was walking down the street and ran into Adriana. Somehow both of them had moved not only to the same city but also to the same neighborhood. However, life was not treating Adriana kindly. She was jobless, pregnant, sick, and living on the streets. Roberta took her home and started caring for her. Adriana's illness soon endangered the life of the unborn baby so she went to the hospital. In fact, Adriana was at the hospital while we were training the leaders of Madrid.

Just seconds after Roberta had finished telling us her story, she got a call on her cell phone. After a few minutes she informed me that the call was actually for me. It was Adriana, and she wanted me to pray for her. I had never met Adriana before. In fact, I didn't even know of her existence before Roberta told her story a few minutes before. Yet here I was on the phone with her. I thought to myself, *Where is Mariluz when you need her? She is the one who is good at praying for difficult pregnancies.* Yet I was the one to whom God had given this privilege. As I prayed for the health of Adriana and her unborn baby. I distinctly heard Jesus speak to me. He told me to tell Adriana how much He loved her. In detail I told her how much Jesus loved her, culminating with His intentional, sacrificial death on the cross so that she could have eternal life. I asked her, "Adriana, don't you want that?"

"Yes, Jesus, I want to be loved by You." Adriana became a Christian with me right there over the phone.

The next week at our weekly training time, I asked Roberta about Adriana's health. Roberta said, "Oh, she's fine and the baby's fine."

I thought that was a strange reply. When I had been on the phone a week earlier she was very ill and was in fear of losing her baby, perhaps even her own life. "What do you mean she's fine and the baby's fine?"

"Well, you are the one who prayed! Just after she got off the phone last week the doctor came in to check up on her. Her blood pressure had dropped so significantly that he immediately took her in for an emergency C-section since she was safe for surgery. Now she is home with the new baby. Like I said, she's fine and the baby's fine."

## How Adriana connected us to the real person of peace

A few weeks later I got a call from Adriana. She wanted me to come to the apartment and meet her new baby, Paulo. We arranged for a time that I could come by. When I got to the apartment, I was met at the door by Mirelli, the woman Roberta and Adriana were staying with. She said, "I've come to welcome the man of God to my house. It is a blessing to have you here. Roberta, Adriana, and the baby are in the living room. I'm going to cook for you."

I've never been comfortable with being called the man of God. It sets up two classes of people, those who aren't "men of God" and those who are. However, now wasn't the time to discuss issues like that, especially with Mirelli, a woman who didn't know Jesus. Roberta, Adriana, and I had a wonderful time playing with the baby while we talked about Adriana's new faith in Jesus. About forty-five minutes later Mirelli came into the living room and said, "I hate church, but I sure love what you guys are doing." I thought that was a strange statement to make to the "man of God." ˙

"Really," I responded, "what is it you don't like about church?" She proceeded to give me an earful. She didn't like the power and control of the clergy. She didn't like how disconnected it was from real life. In fact, she didn't like much of anything about organized religion.

"Since you seem to like what we are doing, would it be OK if I read a short Bible passage to you?" I asked.

"Sure," Mirelli replied, "that would be fine."

I read Luke 10:1–7 to her. "Mirelli, you know from Roberta that some of our friends are starting simple little churches in people's homes and apartments. In fact, what we do is just what you are doing with us. And if you will notice, Jesus sends out people like Roberta and I in pairs to start those groups. Do you remember the first thing you said to me when I came to your door?"

"Yes, I said, 'Welcome to my house; it is a blessing to have you here.'"

"Do you remember that Jesus said that when people like Roberta and I enter a house we are supposed to say 'Peace to this house'? That's a blessing. We are also supposed to watch how that blessing is received. If a person of peace is there, they will receive the blessing. If not, they will throw it back in our face. You not only received my blessing, you were looking forward to it. What else did you do?"

"Nothing, I just went off to cook a meal for you."

"Thank you so much for your hospitality, but I didn't actually come expecting you to fix me a meal. Did you notice what I am supposed to do when I come to a house? What does the Bible say?" I asked.

"Well, it says you are to stay there, eating and drinking whatever they give you."

"Right, so, I came to a house and someone I've never met before says that just coming to the house is a blessing. Further, you were so kind that you went to the kitchen and fixed a meal for me. Look at the text again. Who do you think you are?"

After reading the text again Mirelli said, "I'm the man of peace."

"I think you are right, you are the person of peace. Mirelli, what do people of peace do?"

"How should I know?" She asked. "You are the guy who knows the Bible. What do people of peace do?"

"Well, people of peace let us start a little church like this in their home and they invite their friends to come. Are you willing to do that?"

"Sure, I can do that. I'd be glad to do that." And that is how the last of the "baby churches" got stated in our network in the Madrid area.

## The Business Man

It is very easy to fall into the trap of thinking this stuff happens only in foreign countries. Of course anyone with experience in Spain knows that it is a much tougher spiritual environment that any place in the United States. In fact, after our return from Spain, I was impressed with just how spiritually wide open the San Francisco Bay Area was. But for the skeptics, I'd like to include a couple of stories from our ministry in Northern California.

One afternoon as I went out to check the mail, I saw a neighbor out tending to his lawn. "Hey, Ross!" he said. "We are going to have a Bible study tonight. Do you want to come?" I was a bit tired and was thinking that I'd just like to get some rest. "We are going to have some non-Christian couples."

My friend did know how to entice me. "Sure, I can come along." I replied.

We discussed the Bible study material that he would be going over. It was on John 1:1–17. However, it was very detailed and very theological. While it was good material for experienced Christians, I wasn't so sure that it would be helpful for non-Christians, so I mentioned this. My friend asked me what I would do. I told him I would just ask the Bible study participants four discussion questions and trust Jesus to do the rest.

1. What does it say?

2. What does it mean?

3. What are you going to do about it?

4. Who are you going to tell?

Further, I suggested that each question have a simple symbol by it to help them remember the questions. What does it say? was symbolized by a simple drawing of a book to represent the Bible. What does it mean? was symbolized by a question mark. What are you going to do about it? was symbolized by a light bulb. Who are you going to tell? was symbolized by a smile and an ear.

The first couple to arrive were wealthy business people. The man was a large, aggressive, muscular man. The woman was shy and retiring. The man was abusive toward his wife. He couldn't seem to say anything kind to her. His language was hostile and foul. In fact, I don't remember ever hearing anyone swear quite so much.

After a brief time eating snacks and enjoying the warm evening on the deck, we moved into the living room. Our host suggested that we all turn to the first chapter of the Gospel of John in the New Testament. He then announced that I would be leading the study. I simply gave the four questions and had someone read the passage. Then the discussion started. Who was the John mentioned in the passage? Was this the same guy who wrote the Gospel of John? Who are they referring to when it says "his own" in verses 11 to 13: "He came to that which was his own, but his own did not receive him. Yet to all who received him, to those who believed in his name, he gave the right to become children of God— children born not of natural descent, nor of human decision or a husband's will, but born of God." If they didn't receive Him, who did? What does it mean to be born of God?

Right in the midst of this, the businessman blurted out some expletives and said, "I want Jesus!" I was completely dumbfounded. I wasn't sure what to do. But I came up with a brilliant response: "Huh?"

"I said, I want Jesus."

For some reason, at that point, I felt compelled to stand up, close the distance between me and this man and actually put my face right in his.

"Do you really want Jesus?"

"I said I [expletive] did."

"But do you really want Jesus?" I felt a little bit like a Marine Master Sergeant.

"Yes, I do!"

I hugged him and said, "Welcome to the kingdom."

After welcoming him to the kingdom, I made a startling statement: "I want to start a church at your house. I want you to gather your friends who don't know Jesus. When are we going to do that?"

"Tomorrow at 5:00 p.m.," he replied. And that is exactly what happened. This church quickly resulted in a number of people coming to Christ and in fact started a daughter church where more people came to Christ. Both churches were in affluent neighborhoods of California, among very wealthy people.

You may be wondering what this has to do with supernaturalism. Without a doubt, the whole encounter mentioned above, and its timing, was set up by the Father. He used the host couple, he used me, and he used the businessman to later gather his friends. This, by the way, means the businessman was the person of peace mentioned in Luke 10:6. God directed all this. And just like Jesus, I could do only what I saw the Father doing.

However, there was another supernatural element. When the seventy-two went out on the apostolic journey with Jesus mentioned in Luke 10, they returned with this report, "Lord, even the demons submit to us in your name" (v. 17). My new friend had some serious problems with demons. In fact, over the next few weeks my church-planting partners and I had quite a few encounters with the demonic. They did submit to Jesus's name. I'd like to tell you that my new friend was completely cleansed, but that wouldn't be true. He made decisions after getting some initial relief that caused him to keep from getting complete freedom. Yet out of this a number of people came to Christ and began to follow Him. That was what the Father was doing.

## Tragedy and Rebirth in the Desert

Amado decided one Thursday that he would try to find a better life in the US. By Saturday he was on the US/Mexican border trying to cross. Unfortunately for him he chose the wrong "coyote" to help him. (A coyote is someone hired by undocumented aliens to facilitate border crossings into the United States from Mexico.) Instead of earning his money by getting Amado across the border and to safety on the other side, he dumped him in the desert with seven others and left. These immigrants were abandoned with no food or water in the Arizona desert in March. Soon members of the group began to die. Amado teamed up with one of the others in the group for encouragement. As Amado and his new friend wandered through the desert, they came across someone from another group who had been stabbed and robbed. He was lying dead in a dried pool of blood, his backpack hung on the branches of a tree. Amado was terrified.

But watching members of his own group die and finding murdered people in the desert were not his biggest problems. He was literally dying of thirst himself. If he didn't find water in the desert soon, he and his friend would surely die. Amado was not a religious man. His parents believed in God, but he wasn't too sure. However, in his desperation he called out to the God of his parents asking Him to spare his life.

Just then two joggers came running along a dirt path, seemingly out of nowhere. They ran right up to Amado and his friend and held out bottles of water. For some reason they had an address and phone number to a church on a piece of paper and somehow, despite the language difficulty, suggested that Amado and his friend make a call and the church would take care of them.

After drinking to their fill, Amado and his friend saw some houses in the distance and decided to walk toward them. When they reached a street sign, Amado's friend made a fateful decision. He decided to call the coyote who had stranded them, thinking somehow being stranded in the desert had been a mistake.

The coyote arrived in a car and took them to a beautiful home in an affluent Phoenix neighborhood. But instead of helping them, the coyote and his team kidnapped them. They beat them. They intimidated them. And they said they would never get out alive unless they contacted their families in Mexico to send money. To make their point clear, the head kidnapper took another victim who had been unable to pay, whipped off his belt, wrapped it around the neck of his victim and murdered him in front of Amado and his friend. Thankfully Amado's friend was able to convince some friends in Mexico to send money for both of them. They were again stranded but were able to make their way to California.

I met Amado in an English class for Hispanic day workers. Over time I began to develop a relationship with Amado. He was an outgoing, friendly guy. In fact, he had a magnetic personality. He made friends easily and knew how to keep them. One day when I left the building Amado was waiting for me.

Amado wanted to talk more about God. He was interested in God but wasn't quite sure which God to follow. I immediately felt the Holy Spirit tell me, "Don't disparage other religions or you are going to lose this guy. Lead him like you are catching a horse." Because I had grown up on a wheat and cattle ranch in Eastern Oregon, I knew about horses. If you want to catch a horse, you do not approach it or it will probably run away. No matter how fast you can run, a horse can run faster. Instead, you have to get the horse to come to you. You do this by offering it some grain or some other tasty treat. In other words, the Holy Spirit knew just the right metaphor to speak to me so I would know what to do next.

"Are all gods the same? How do you know your God is better? Is the God of the Catholics any different than the God of the Protestants?" He really wasn't asking questions as much as making statements to see how I would react. I told him I did think there was a difference in religions. But arguing over which was better wasn't something I was interested in. In fact, I wasn't particularly interested in talking about theology at all. Instead I suggested that if he was curious we could do a spiritual experiment. He could begin to talk to the God of the universe and ask Him to reveal Himself.

"I believe in God. I just don't know who He is." I didn't realize at the time that this statement was backed by a supernatural encounter in the desert of Arizona. I just knew that Amado was interested in God. "Good," I said, "Why don't you just pray to the God who created the universe and ask Him to reveal Himself?"

Amado had a big smile on his face, "I will do that."

"Great," I said. "But one last thing, Amado: I know my God. If you look for Him with all your heart, He will find you. You can count on it."

Over the next weeks Amado and I began to study the Bible together. We just read it together and used the four questions mentioned above to stimulate discussion. Amado enjoyed this. He continued to ask questions. I was careful to respond with qualifying statements such as, in my opinion... or I believe.... But I also told stories of my own encounters with God and suggested he be on the lookout for something like that. It didn't take long for Amado to become a Christian—a very serious one who began telling his friends about his Savior. Amado has had his ups and downs, like many new Christians do, but his journey isn't finished.

## Prayer Walking

Isaiah Hwang (my good friend who designed the cover of *Viral Jesus*) and Mike Kim were meeting in a Starbucks in Cupertino, California, near the intersection of Homestead Road and Stelling Road. They felt that God was asking them to prayer walk the area. As they did, they found themselves blessing the area and the people, specifically asking that they would find a person of peace. While prayer walking, they found themselves at a nearby bowling alley, so they prayed for that specific bowling alley.

A few weeks later Isaiah was invited to his cousin's birthday party, which happened to meet at that particular bowling alley. While Isaiah was standing outside the bowling alley, a drunk young man came up to him.

"Hey, aren't you Isaiah Hwang? Weren't you the guy who drove the Honda with the cool wheels? Yeah, that's you. You still doing that church stuff?"

Isaiah didn't recognize him. "Do I know you?"

"Yeah, I'm a friend of Calvin's. Calvin told me all about you and the stuff you used to talk about." Calvin was a young man whom Isaiah had known in a youth ministry he was involved in.

"Hey," the drunk asked, "What does the Bible say about drinking? How much is too much?"

This led to a conversation about the Bible and drinking and then deeper spiritual matters. "Hey, when I'm sober we're going to need to talk more. Here's my number. Call me tomorrow."

Isaiah figured that the young man wouldn't be nearly as open to such deep conversations when he called the next day, but he was wrong. Calvin's friend was eager to talk with Isaiah and discuss spiritual matters.

This developed into a discipleship relationship that led the young man to a close relationship with God. In fact, his life turned around so much that he ended up going to the university to study medicine.

In Isaiah's earlier Christian life, he would have been very reticent to go places where there would be smoking, partying, and drinking. He would have felt that it would compromise his testimony. But now he thinks, *These are the places Jesus would go. If we aren't going to those places to be light, who is?*

## Is It Always This Supernatural?

Jesus is the Lord of the harvest; we are not. He gets to decide what He is going to do, when He is going to do it, and how that will take place. Is it always supernatural? I think it would be more honest to say that supernaturalism was normal and expected in evangelism and church planting in the New Testament. My friends and I have also come to expect it to be part and parcel of our ministry. But we don't necessarily expect miracles every single time. We have no idea what will happen, when it will happen, or how. We don't know if five minutes from now, we will be in the middle of a phone conversation praying for healing. We don't know when we will be asked to lead a Bible study in an affluent neighborhood. We don't know when or how we will bump into a Hispanic day worker who has already met God in the desert. Nor do we know if the miraculous will be involved at all. Still, whatever happens will be supernatural, because God, who is a supernatural God, is leading the process.

We can only do what we see the Father doing. Jesus could do no more than that; neither can we. However, like Jesus in the Gospels, we can pray often, listen, and obey what we hear. That is the secret. There is no power in technique, but there is tremendous power in listening prayer and immediate obedience. I highly recommend it. When you start doing that, don't be surprised when you see God respond with supernatural power.

## Patterns and Practices Count

Patterns and practices count. Either they reflect the reality of Jesus as Lord and live within the operating system of the new covenant, or they don't. We can succumb to the Platonic philosophy that all that counts is the idea, the correct propositional doctrine; or we can have a biblical worldview. In the biblical worldview we demonstrate what we believe by how we behave. In the biblical worldview, Jesus has to be Lord of the way we gather as a church and the way we do ministry. He has to be Lord of every single thing we do, even the way we think. It is not merely a correct doctrine. It is a way of life. Only then, when we get the Greek philosophy out of our worldview and practice and start actually following Jesus as Lord, will we see a sustained viral Jesus movement once again in the West. It has been 1,700 years. Isn't that long enough?

# Conclusion

No first-century Christian hearing or reading any part of the New Testament would have believed that some of their brethren in later centuries would suggest that supernatural power was something that happened in the first century after Christ but then somehow ceased. They would be dumbfounded to hear that any Christian would believe that prophecy was a thing of the past, as were miracles, signs, and wonders. While the word *mysticism* was probably not part of their vocabulary, early Christians were mystics: all of them. They did not view mystical practices such as listening to God and obeying what they heard as strange. It was how the Christian life was lived. Every kind of supernatural experience mentioned in the Bible was normal for them. They expected power to be manifest when they gathered together. This was a normal part of life with the Holy Spirit. This was part of having a relationship with God.

The same should be true today. There is no solid credible reason, from a biblical point of view, to believe that what the first-century Christians experienced should be any different from our own experience. The felt need to "debunk" supernatural power within Christianity is driven by the Western worldview, not the Bible. This is a classic "weak and miserable principle" that Paul mentioned in Galatians 4:9. The answer to these worldly principles should be the same today as the one Paul suggested to the Colossians in Colossians 2:20: don't submit to its rules.

Instead we should have a vibrant, powerful, mystical, rich, and supernatural encounter with the triune God. This is part of our new covenant heritage. It is the normal reality for those who want to follow Jesus as

Lord. And if we are to see a viral Jesus movement in the West in our day, we need to learn to live in that heritage, not merely talk about it. That may take a lot of prayer, practice, listening, and obeying for many of us. We'll get it wrong as many times as we get it right, but we'll learn in the process. The learning curve will be steep, but isn't that the relationship with God we've always longed for in the deepest part of our hearts, whether we believed it was possible or not?

## CHAPTER 4

# The Early Church: The First Viral Jesus Movement

*I*T IS A sticky summer evening along the Roman road leading out of Nicomedia, August, A.D. 112. The smell of rotting flesh hangs in the air like a putrid miasma. Bloated dead bodies lie next to the wriggling, noisy, unwanted newborn babies who have been "exposed"—that is, left to die among the already dead. In the midst of this vile scene, the sounds of digging can be heard. The Christians have come to bury the dead with dignity. They have come to pick up the exposed babies, to give them a home where they would be loved and cared for. The Romans who could afford such luxuries either buried their dead or cremated them. However, the poor, slaves, criminals, and strangers were often thrown to the side of the road outside of the city. In the same way, unwanted babies, mostly little girls, were left to die among the rotting corpses.

It is in this unlikely and vile social scenario that Christians gained their first recognition, not as a new religion, but as a burial society. It was this unnerving tendency of the Christians to give love and dignity to the dead and unwanted that first brought them a small modicum of acceptance. From an unbeliever's perspective, most Christians might have been uneducated, poor, and decidedly strange, but at least they pulled the bloated bodies out of the sewers and the rivers. At least they buried the criminals, slaves, and poor left on the side of the roads leading out of the cities of the empire. At least they cleaned up the filth. This habit of taking living, exposed babies home to love them, to care for them as their own—well, that was just weird. However, one has to give grudging respect to any group that will clean up the putrid mess on the outskirts. Not that anyone in their right mind would do such a thing; but still, all in all, it was good for society.

# What the Early Christians Were Really Like

Our view of the first few centuries of the church is often clouded by romanticism, awe, and most of all, an institutional understanding of Christianity that keeps us from seeing clearly just how unlikely and phenomenal the growth of the church was. The early Christians didn't have a lot going for them, at least from a human perspective. They were mostly poor, having their greatest growth and numbers in the lowest classes of the Roman Empire, particularly among slaves. Still, it was true that followers of Jesus could be found in every social stratum very early on. But for the most part, they were disdained and ridiculed, at least when they were noticed.

They had no great organizational structure that held them together. At this early stage, they really didn't have leadership as we think of it. There were no clergy, no titular positions, just the recognition of who was trustworthy and how they were gifted. Not only were they usually poor, but they also had the counterintuitive habit of giving their resources away, even to people whom they didn't know and who could not advance their cause. For the most part, this generosity was disdained and ridiculed, sometimes even by the beneficiaries—that is, if the beneficiaries were alive or old enough to disdain their benefactors.

From a human perspective, the Christian church should not have grown, should not have prospered, should not have even survived, let alone become the favored religion of the Roman Empire by the early fourth century. It is this spectacular growth and the Christian's rise from obscurity to prominence that most modern-day Christians know about. This is indeed a spectacular story, and it is an undeniable fact of history.

However, it is not an easy story to piece together, particularly the account of the early years of the church. Early Christians were not exactly on the radar screen of the types of people whose writings tended to survive into the twentieth century. Christians were mentioned in passing every once in a great while. Their stories were usually associated with their brief skirmishes with Roman officials. Probably the most famous of these is described in an exchange of letters between the Emperor Trajan and Pliny the Younger, governor of Pontus and Bithynia, on the south coast of the Black Sea. This exchange of letters took place between the years A.D. 111–113.

In this exchange, we are going to learn a number of interesting things: How far had Christianity spread by the early second century? Who became Christians? How pervasive were Christians in a place like this on the edge of the empire? What was the attitude of the Roman government toward them? What about the surrounding society? How could the government determine who was a real Christian and who was just experimenting with the new religion? How were Christians punished for their "crimes"? What did the early practice of a Christian meeting look like? How egalitarian was Christianity? How willing were Christians to have leaders from the less respected segments of society? What could that tell us about how they chose leaders and how they viewed leadership? What kinds of problems was Christianity causing for traditional Roman society?

## Letter From Pliny the Younger to the Emperor Trajan

> It is my practice, my lord, to refer to you all matters concerning which I am in doubt. For who can better give guidance to my hesitation or inform my ignorance? I have never participated in trials of Christians. I therefore do not know what offenses it is the practice to punish or investigate, and to what extent. And I have been not a little hesitant as to whether there should be any distinction on account of age or no difference between the very young and the more mature; whether pardon is to be granted for repentance, or, if a man has once been a Christian, it does him no good to have ceased to be one; whether the name itself, even

without offenses, or only the offenses associated with the name are to be punished.

Meanwhile, in the case of those who were denounced to me as Christians, I have observed the following procedure: I interrogated these as to whether they were Christians; those who confessed I interrogated a second and a third time, threatening them with punishment; those who persisted I ordered executed. For I had no doubt that, whatever the nature of their creed, stubbornness and inflexible obstinacy surely deserve to be punished. There were others possessed of the same folly; but because they were Roman citizens, I signed an order for them to be transferred to Rome.

Soon accusations spread, as usually happens, because of the proceedings going on, and several incidents occurred. An anonymous document was published containing the names of many persons. Those who denied that they were or had been Christians, when they invoked the gods in words dictated by me, offered prayer with incense and wine to your image, which I had ordered to be brought for this purpose together with statues of the gods, and moreover cursed Christ—none of which those who are really Christians, it is said, can be forced to do—these I thought should be discharged. Others named by the informer declared that they were Christians, but then denied it, asserting that they had been but had ceased to be, some three years before, others many years, some as much as twenty-five years. They all worshipped your image and the statues of the gods, and cursed Christ.

They asserted, however, that the sum and substance of their fault or error had been that they were accustomed to meet on a fixed day before dawn and sing responsively a hymn to Christ as to a god, and to bind themselves by oath, not to some crime, but not to commit fraud, theft, or adultery, not falsify their trust, nor to refuse to return a trust when called upon to do so. When this was over, it was their custom to depart and to assemble again to partake of food—but ordinary and innocent food. Even this, they affirmed, they had ceased to do after my edict by which, in accordance with your instructions, I had forbidden political associations. Accordingly, I judged it all the more necessary to find out what the truth was by torturing two female slaves who were called deaconesses. But I discovered nothing else but depraved, excessive superstition.

I therefore postponed the investigation and hastened to consult you. For the matter seemed to me to warrant consulting you, especially because of the number involved. For many persons of every age, every rank, and also of both sexes are and will be endangered. For the contagion of this superstition has spread not only to the cities but also to the villages and farms. But it seems possible to check and cure it. It is certainly quite clear that the temples, which had been almost deserted, have begun to be frequented, that the established religious rites, long neglected, are being resumed, and that from everywhere sacrificial animals are coming, for which until now very few purchasers could be found. Hence it is easy to imagine what a multitude of people can be reformed if an opportunity for repentance is afforded.

## Trajan to Pliny the Younger

You observed proper procedure, my dear Pliny, in sifting the cases of those who had been denounced to you as Christians. For it is not possible to lay down any general rule to serve as a kind of fixed standard. They are not to be sought out; if they are denounced and proved guilty, they are to be punished, with this reservation, that whoever denies that he is a Christian and really proves it—that is, by worshiping our gods—even though he was under suspicion in the past, shall obtain pardon through repentance. But anonymously posted accusations ought to have no place in any prosecution. For this is both a dangerous kind of precedent and out of keeping with the spirit of our age.[1]

# The Epistle of Mathetes to Diognetus

Our other historical sources for this period are Christians responding to the complaints of the society around them. The content of these apologetic arguments tell us what society thought of the Christians, when they thought of them at all, and how Christians answered these complaints. These are important sources. What emerges from this scant data is a traditional Roman society that did not know how to respond to a rapidly growing group of people within their midst; a people who had a worldview that did not match their own. Sometimes the response of the people of the empire, particularly the government, was violent. Moreover, the Christians responded to their new worldview by living very different lives from the society around them. It should come as no surprise that Christians felt the need to explain themselves; if nothing else for protection. Here is a passage from one of the earliest apologetic writings, called *The Epistle of Mathetes to Diognetus.*

> For the Christians are distinguished from other men neither by country, nor language, nor the customs which they observe. For they neither inhabit cities of their own, nor employ a peculiar form of speech, nor lead a life which is marked out by any singularity. The course of conduct which they follow has not been devised by any speculation or deliberation of inquisitive men; nor do they, like some, proclaim themselves the advocates of any merely human doctrines. But, inhabiting Greek as well as barbarian cities, according as the lot of each of them has determined, and following the customs of the natives in respect to clothing, food, and the rest of their ordinary conduct, they display to us their wonderful and confessedly striking method of life. They dwell in their own countries, but simply as sojourners. As citizens, they share in all things with others, and yet endure all things as if foreigners. Every foreign land is to them as their native country, and every land of their birth as a land of strangers. They marry, as do all [others]; they beget children; but they do not destroy their offspring. They have a common table, but not a common bed. They are in the flesh, but they do not live after the flesh. They pass their days on earth, but they are citizens of heaven. They obey the prescribed laws, and at the same time surpass the laws by their lives. They love all men, and are persecuted by all. They are unknown and condemned; they are put to death, and miraculously restored to life. They are poor, yet make many rich; they are in lack of all things, and yet abound in all; they are dishonoured, and yet in their very dishonour are glorified. They are evil spoken of, and yet are justified; they are reviled, and bless; they are insulted, and repay the insult with honour; they do good, yet are punished as evil-doers. When punished, they rejoice as if quickened into life; they are assailed by the Jews as foreigners, and are persecuted

by the Greeks; yet those who hate them are unable to assign any reason for their hatred.[2]

As historical documents of the early church these letters are gold mines. What can we learn from these ancient sources, which are quite similar to the other extant sources of their type? First, these documents principally agree with each other. Pliny the Younger, a Roman official on the edges of the empire, encountered a new kind of inhabitant called a Christian. He found out about many of these people because they were denounced in a cowardly anonymous accusation, which listed names. Through interrogation he found that this group was rather nebulous. Some people used to be Christians but no longer were. Some of these "used to be Christians" date back to at least A.D. 88. True Christians were noted for their stubborn unwillingness to worship statues of the gods or curse Christ. Even those who used to be Christians asserted that the only thing wrong with Christians was that they met on a fixed day to sing a hymn to Christ as a god. They also bound themselves to an oath to avoid fraud, theft, adultery, or going back on their word. Further they swore to be trustworthy in their dealings with others. They then ate an ordinary meal together. However, they gave up these communal meals when Pliny published an edict forbidding such gatherings.

Some of these people were Roman citizens (who were duly transferred to Rome, for further interrogation, per Roman law, if they refused to renounce Christ). However, there were others who were not citizens. If these refused three times to renounce Christ, they were executed. Since they were not citizens, this execution would have been anything but swift. Most likely they were crucified like their Lord. At least two of these Christians were slaves. However, both of these slaves were women and leaders (deaconesses). Even under torture and threat of death, these tough women didn't crack. They simply told the truth, which Pliny regarded as depraved, excessive superstition.

Pliny is so concerned by what he has found that, as governor, he felt the need to write to Emperor Trajan, due to the number of people involved. He noted that people of every age and rank and of both sexes "are and will be endangered." The contagion seemed to be spreading, spreading like a virus. He then tries to cheer up the emperor with good news. The long-neglected pagan religious rites were once again being resumed, including the purchase of sacrificial animals, whose purchase was previously neglected. The clear implication is that the "multitude" of Christians were beginning to repent of their crimes and practice official paganism again. This was no doubt due to Pliny's diligent effort with torture and execution. Once a politician, always a politician; spin is everything when it comes to politics and when dealing with a powerful man like Trajan.

However, Pliny was probably an honest, objective observer of the Christians. He is noted for his descriptive prose and objectivity. In fact, his description of the eruption of Mount Vesuvius in A.D. 79 was so accurate that the same type of eruption is called a plinian eruption to this day.[3] Naturally he wrote from his cultural perspective. As a pagan Roman official he was charged with upholding the laws of the empire and immediately nipping in the bud anything that could threaten the social order. And of course he carefully spun his participation in starting up the long-neglected rites and the magnanimous opportunities for repentance he afforded.

Christians were indeed strange people from a pagan Roman point of view. They seemed to have no decorum in distinguishing who should associate with whom. Roman citizens, in fact people of every rank, were eating meals with slaves. Worse, these mixed-gender groupings allowed female slaves to serve as leaders. In the hypocritical Roman culture, which respected marital fidelity, yet was noted for its wild sexual practice of every type, these mixed-gender groups met regularly but did not engage in any immoral act. In fact, they didn't commit any crime other than refusing to worship the gods and to offer incense and wine to the emperor. Rather, they took oaths to avoid adultery and other crimes. They even vowed to be trustworthy in all their dealings. So Pliny, from Trajan's point of view, did the right thing. He tortured the ones he could torture (the noncitizens), he executed the recalcitrant, and he allowed the rest to repent. Emperor Trajan's only advice was to avoid allowing anonymous accusations, which would be a dangerous precedent.

In comparison, from a historical point of view, the statements of the writer of *The Epistle of Mathetes to Diognetus* make absolute sense. Basically he says we Christians are everywhere. We look like you but we behave ourselves. We marry, but we don't expose our children. We eat together, but we don't sleep together, except with our spouses. We obey the laws of the land and even exceed the laws by our exemplary lives. However, we consider our citizenship in heaven. We are treated poorly, but we don't return evil for evil. We are persecuted even to death, yet those who hate us can't come up with a good reason for their own behavior.

It doesn't take much reading between the lines to realize what was happening by the year 113, even in places such as Bithynia and Pontus, the very edges of the empire. Pontus was the region where Aquila of the famous couple Priscilla and Aquila was from. (See Acts 18:2.) Bithynia was the Apostle Paul's destination before he was forbidden by the Holy Spirit to travel there in Acts 16. In utter obedience he went to Macedonia instead. We don't know exactly how or when the gospel got to this region. We do know it happened very early. (See 1 Peter 1:1.) Yet by the time of Pliny's writing, there were so many Christians, in every social stratum, that the pagan rites were being neglected. Even at this early date, roughly eighty years after Pentecost, the Christians were significantly changing the society in an area where we have no record of a visit from the first generation of apostles.

Even from a pagan Roman perspective, the everyday Christians lived exemplary lives, except in one issue, they worshiped only one God, Jesus Christ. They would worship no other, even to the point of torture and gruesome execution. In fact, even the pagan governor recognized the best way to tell a real Christian from a false one was to try to force them to worship idols, burn incense to the emperor, and curse Christ. A real Christian just wouldn't do that. Second-century Christians lived by a simple creed: Jesus is Lord. They would willingly give honor where honor was due, but only the Lord Jesus controlled their lives.

And that is why they grew. That is why they became a social force which, in some ways, conquered the empire in about two hundred and eighty years. The secret to their success was not incredible organizational structure. It was not a clever human strategy of pandering to the powerful and rich. It was not adhering to a common-sense practice of allowing the educated and trained to be their leaders. Often even slaves and women led them. Nor was it blending in so much that one couldn't tell the behavior of a Christian from a pagan. One most certainly could. Their lives were different in ways that really counted. They may dress the same, but they didn't have the same morals. They may speak the common language, eat normal food, and marry just like everyone else, but they were faithful to their spouses and loved children, all children, even the children thrown away like garbage by their own parents. In fact, they were known for loving all men, even those who reviled them. The secret of their success was simple; they obeyed Jesus and Jesus only. Disobedience to the Lord was, for them, a fate worse than death.

## Ampliata Visits Our Elder Board Meeting

I was just out of graduate school feeling like a newly minted penny; well, maybe a dime. This was my first paying job on a church staff. I had my own office, my own desk, and a typewriter that corrected spelling. Obviously I knew my stuff and couldn't wait to prove it. I had studied the paradigms. I could do church-growth surveys. I could read graphs. I was so hot I sizzled. I was hired to help the church grow through evangelism. My bookcase was full of books with good ideas. I read case studies of big churches that knew how to grow. And I was in a church that was cool. The church was so cool; it even had a personal computer for the secretary. This baby had a nine-by-nine-inch screen that glowed phosphorescent green. It looked like something out of a science-fiction movie, only smaller.

I was attending one of the first elder's meetings as a new staff member. But being the cautious participant observer I was, I already knew who got their way and who didn't. Obviously, I was low on the pecking order. After all, I was young and from out of town. Not only was I from out of town, I was pretty much a country boy, even if I had gone to a fairly prestigious Christian college. My place was to sit down and shut up.

There was one elder who knew how to sway a crowd. Let me rephrase that: He knew how to bully the elder board. He was loud, forceful, and opinionated. Negative energy came off him in waves. One of his favorite ways to start a sentence was, "Well, I don't know..." just before he disagreed with a positive statement—any and all positive statements. People were truly intimidated by this man, and I'm pretty sure he liked it that way. I clearly remember a new woman on the board bursting into tears and rushing out of the room during one of his harangues. He wasn't even talking to her.

Our church building was near a freeway. Our steeple stuck up high enough that people hitchhiking along the freeway could see it. For those needing more than a lift to the next town, it was like a beacon saying "free eats." I had a great idea. If the church could spare a little out of the deacon's budget I could take these people out to a nearby fast-food restaurant and share lunch with them. I could also share the gospel with them. After all, I was a hired gun, a sizzling hot hired gun. Have gospel, will travel—all the way to McDonald's.

So I prepared my little speech to the elder board. Who knows, I probably even drew up a little budget. At the next meeting we opened with a brief prayer, and we ticked off the meeting items one by one. When my turn came, I presented my idea. Then there was a deep rumble from somewhere near the head of the table. "Well, I don't know. I think this could cause all sorts of problems with our insurance policy. If we allow those types on our property, we could get sued." It was short, not so sweet, and just as fatal as Pliny the Younger's sword. I didn't say a word after that. I knew my place, which was to sit down and shut up.

Looking back, I wonder what would have happened if one of those deaconesses from Bithynia had been there—one of the Christian slaves martyred by Pliny. Yes, I know it is impossible, but play along with me for a moment. For fun, let's call this slave Ampliata, the feminine form of Ampliatus, a name found in Romans 16.

Ampliata is sitting in her customary rags. Out of habit she would have sat wherever she felt was the lowest place in the room; probably on the floor. She would not have said much, probably nothing at all. Women did not speak in second-century Roman churches. However, her silence would have come from her status as a woman, not as a slave. I wonder what she would have thought about my idea of getting the church to pay for feeding these needy poor who came to our doorstep. Would she have wondered how deep my pockets were and why I was reluctant to cough up the money out of my personal funds? I wonder what she would have thought of my cowardice. Would she wonder what a Christian college was? I wonder what she would have thought while we blithely found cheap excuses to ignore the poor. I wonder what her reaction to His Grumpiness, Lord of the Elder Board, would be.

True, Ampliata was a slave, used to being subservient to her master. She was probably quite aware of the statements of Paul in his letter to the Ephesian church that slaves were to be obedient to their masters, as if they were serving Christ. But she was also a second-century Christian used to being loved and respected in a church setting. Her daily life was a life of poverty and disrespect. Yet in the church she was someone else. In church she was loved like family by everyone, even wealthy Christians. She was a deaconess, someone noted by her lifestyle of service. Unlike now, in the early church service and leadership were the same thing.

This was the kind of ministry where she had played a leadership role, where she was respected, where she was loved. Even Pliny knew she would know everybody and know the answers he was looking for. In other words, she was a mature Christian. And she did know the answers he was looking for. Pliny just didn't understand what she was saying. Nor was she about to give up the names of her fellow Christians. Betrayal of her beloved Christian family would have been awful; betrayal of her Lord—unthinkable.

Would she have fingered the nail marks in her wrists where Pliny the Younger had her nailed to a cross in the hills outside Nicomedia? Would she think back to searing pain mixed with devotion to Jesus, agony and humiliation mixed with unbroken love? Would she remember the look of horror on Sylvania's face—a look of horror based on seeing Ampliata nailed to the beams before she was? Sylvania was her beloved sister in Christ. She was closer than a sister, really—a fellow deaconess and fellow slave. Sylvania didn't crack under Pliny's interrogation either.

Would a tear roll down Ampliata's cheek thinking about a lost opportunity to the poor? What would she have thought about trading a hamburger for a gospel presentation? What would she have thought about our strange concern for insurance policies? What would she have thought about our building? How would she feel about trying to keep "those types" off of "our property"? Would she be confused by the way we handled this business meeting? Would she know what a business meeting was? What would she have thought about our little opening prayer? Would she have been impressed by the way we followed Jesus our Lord? Would she even think of us as Christians? What would she have thought? I wonder. I wonder.

## How Did We Get From There to Here?

It is important to grapple with the very real historical issues that got us from there to where we find ourselves now. By "there" I mean what someone in the first and second century, like Ampliata, would have experienced. By "here" I mean what most of us in Western Christianity have experienced. This is the story of a viral Jesus movement becoming Christendom. I do not use the word *Christendom* in a positive way. It is contrasted with Christianity, particularly Christianity that is being used by God to sustain a viral movement of the gospel. The word *Christendom*, as I am using it here, is the historical aging process that Christianity went through. The older it got, the less fit it was to spark or sustain a viral Jesus movement. Soon it became so aged and cracked that it could no longer contain such a movement. Christianity, as I'm using the word here, is the real thing. It is the body of Christ, the church. However, it can be anything from a viral Jesus movement, which is how Jesus designed it to be and what we see in the New Testament, to a wineskin so old, stiff, and cracked that it can no longer contain new wine.

We don't want to tear anything down for the mere sake of being critical. Nor do we want to destroy, without trying to build something much better. However, if we are to experience a viral Jesus movement in the West, we must know what is impeding our progress and why. The Christendom we have now is not, will not, and cannot start or sustain a viral Jesus movement.

## A Further Amplification of the Wineskin Metaphor

Let's embark on a further investigation of the old wineskin. We have much to learn together for those of us who want to see a viral Jesus movement in our lifetimes. I think a review of Jesus's insight about wineskins would be helpful.

> And no one pours new wine into old wineskins. If he does, the
> new wine will burst the skins, the wine will run out and the

wineskins will be ruined. No, new wine must be poured into new wineskins. And no one after drinking old wine wants the new, for he says, "The old is better."

—Luke 5:37–39

The new wine of a viral Jesus movement cannot be contained in the old wineskin of Western Christendom. In fact, to attempt to do so would destroy the old wineskin. The new wine would be lost. It would be destructive without being constructive.

Further, those who are accustomed to the old wineskin love the old wine. Many in Christendom know Christ. If they love the old wine and are truly spiritually nourished by it, let them continue. However, Jesus is making new wine in our day. Some of us are hearing His call to live in a new wineskin.

We should note that Jesus never disparages the old wine in the old wineskin. All He says is that old wineskins can't hold new wine. To merely pour new wine in the old skin bursts the wineskin itself, losing the new wine. Christendom is the old wineskin, not Christianity or the church. It is the set of nonbiblical traditions that make up Christendom that makes it unfit as a wineskin for the new wine Jesus is pouring out in our day.

### The aging of a beautiful wineskin

So let's look at how we got from Ampliata's day to ours so we can make sure we don't just build the same old wineskin over again. Or, to use Jesus's metaphor, let's look at what a new wineskin fit for new wine looks like. Further, we need to look at what the aging process of an old wineskin, which can no longer hold new wine, looks like. To be honest, even by Ampliata's day the aging process of the wineskin had already started. Following are some key events in this aging process along with some approximate dates.

I am concentrating here on issues of structure and leadership, not on theology. What we will see is the very early church change from a new covenant structure, something organized in an organic way (something organized like a living thing) to a human organizational structure like an army, government, institution, or business. The new structure is based on a completely different logic (hierarchical logic) than the new covenant structure modeled by Jesus and the first-century apostles in the

New Testament (organic logic). The different logic makes doing ministry based on the New Testament example impossible or extremely clumsy and truncated. This brings us right back to new wine in old wineskins. New wine needs new wineskins because it will burst the old wineskins (structures). The historical issues below will show the important events as the new wineskin of the New Testament church aged into a human structure based on human logic.

| APPROXIMATE YEAR | |
|---|---|
| About 97 | Apostolic succession |
| Between 98–117 | Single bishop |
| Before 225 | Concept of clergy first appears in writing |
| After 313 | Hierarchical leadership |
| Around 327 | The church building |
| Around 347 | Service with order of worship and sermon |
| Before 373 | Ordination |

The change of the historical ecclesiology of the church, as stated above, is based on human logic. This human logic can be called hierarchical or institutional. It is the way that all human social groups and institutions organize themselves. Tribes have chiefs. Businesses have bosses, department heads, and team leaders. Armies have officers of various ranks. Political entities have presidents, dictators, and all sorts of other hierarchical leadership structures. Even families, in all their worldwide cultural variations, have those who have more power and those who have less. The larger and more complex the social group, the more complex the hierarchical power structure and institutional forms. The human logic behind this structure is human power, organization, and leadership. Humans, if they are to make lasting decisions and function as a cohesive unit must, by necessity, organize themselves this way. Somebody has to make the final decision. Somebody must have enough power to coordinate others in work. The other human option is chaos. Given our human nature, chaos often leads to bloodshed.

# Two Exceptions to the Rule

There are two significant exceptions to this rule of humans being organized by the human organizational structure of human hierarchical power.

### Israel at the time of the judges

The first is the structure of the nation of Israel from the Exodus to 1 Samuel 8. This first structure of Israel is a theocracy, a nation ruled by God Himself. God, as He has always done, worked through men He appointed. This structure intentionally forced the nation of Israel to seek God. The structure itself was not humanly sustainable. There was no standing army and often there was no assigned leader until the people came to God and clamored for one in the midst of a crisis.

This all changed when, for their own sense of security—a security focused on their own human ability to protect themselves—Israel sought to become a kingdom—a hierarchical political structure like the nations around them.

> And the Lord told him: "Listen to all that the people are saying to you; it is not you they have rejected, but they have rejected me as their king. As they have done from the day I brought them up out of Egypt until this day, forsaking me and serving other gods, so they are doing to you. Now listen to them; but warn them solemnly and let them know what the king who will reign over them will do."
>
> —1 SAMUEL 8:7–9

The thing to note here is fundamental. To seek human leadership is to reject God. As God said, "It is not you they have rejected, but they have rejected me as their king." God wants to lead His people. We humans want to control everything ourselves. We are much more comfortable with the human logic of hierarchies than God's organic structure. God's organic structure will hold up only if He is involved, which is why Israel continually fell into chaos in the theocracy phase. It was not that God was a poor leader; it was that an organic social structure could not work without God. The chaos was caused by the people of Israel trying to live apart from their God's leadership.

## The early church

Above I noted that there are two significant exceptions to this rule of people being organized by the human organizational structure of hierarchical power. The second exception is the early church, as long as it lived in the new covenant. There was no decisive moment when the church, like Israel, chose to follow human leaders rather than God. Instead it was the gradual process outlined above, which took about three hundred years.

The decisions the church took in those centuries, as we went from an organic wineskin to an institutional wineskin, were each logical in and of themselves. But they were all based on a basic human logic that denied the need for God. People were succumbing to *stoicheia*, the foundational principles of the world. This was an unconscious process, not an intentional one. Influential leaders tried to fix the problems they had. They used the best human reason and logic they had in an attempt to create a safe and secure structure that people could understand and run. These series of steps, based on the foundational principles of the world, slowly changed a church led by God and characterized by obedience to God into a human institution with all of the inherent problems of an institution.

When the church, under this system, has godly leaders, we do OK; not great, but at least OK. But we are always one human decision away from disaster. I am by no means saying that God has left the church. He didn't leave Israel and He hasn't left the church, even in her darkest moments.

The human decisions outlined above have had huge consequences in the way we do ministry and in how we bear fruit. Jesus was absolutely correct: old wineskins cannot contain new wine. Once the wineskin passes a certain point, it cannot hold new wine. It doesn't have the flexibility to do so. The wineskin becomes unyielding, fit only for the old wine.

Once the church, like Israel, became an old wineskin, it could no longer hold new incoming Christians. This is what has happened to the church in the West. We have become compromised Christendom, rather than the vibrant church of the early centuries. Now, particularly in light of the significant social changes of postmodernism, we can no longer hold the new wine Jesus wants to give us.

In the following chapter we'll look more in depth at the key historical events in the ecclesiology of church history between roughly A.D. 100

and A.D. 400. We'll look at the strategic consequences of these events and show how they resist new covenant ministry the way Jesus and the early apostles modeled it. It will be important to note how the decisions build on one another until a completely new system based on human logic and power develops.

# ⌒ CHAPTER 5 ⌒

# The Crumbling of
# a Viral Jesus Movement

*C*AN A PERSON be a hero and an unintentional problem at the same time? I believe they can. And in fact this bittersweet reality is far from rare in the history of the church. Let's look at the story of one of the early church fathers, Ignatius of Antioch, as an example of how good people with the best intentions can introduce ideas that have unintentional, long-lasting, and devastating consequences on the kingdom of God.

Ignatius (not to be confused with Ignatius of Loyola, a much later church leader who founded the Jesuit monastic order in the sixteenth century) died during the reign of Emperor Trajan. He was the third bishop of the city of Antioch in present-day southern Turkey. He was martyred for his outspoken devotion to Jesus his Lord. He was taken willingly toward his ultimate destination, to be eaten by lions in the Coliseum of Rome.

> I write to all the Churches, and impress on them all, that I shall willingly die for God, unless you hinder me. I beseech of you not to show an unseasonable goodwill towards me. Suffer me to become food for the wild beasts, through whose instrumentality it will be granted me to attain to God. I am the wheat of God, and

am ground by the teeth of the wild beasts, that I may be found
the pure bread of God.[1]
—IGNATIUS' LETTER TO THE ROMANS, CHAPTER 4

On his journey he wrote letters to six local churches to encourage
them and give instruction.

There is no doubt about his unswerving devotion to Jesus. There is no
doubt about his desire to promote the kingdom of God. For this he should
be respected as a hero of the early church. However, at the same time
Ignatius introduced some ideas to the early church that also impaired the
viral kingdom movement we are calling the viral Jesus movement.

I exhort you to strive to do all things in harmony with God: the
bishop is to preside in the place of God, while the presbyters are
to function as the council of the Apostles, and the deacons, who
are most dear to me, are entrusted with the ministry of Jesus
Christ, who before time began was with the Father and has at last
appeared.[2]
—LETTER TO THE MAGNESIANS, 6

In this one brief passage Ignatius had introduced a number of ideas that
played havoc with a rapidly spreading viral movement of the kingdom
where Jesus and only Jesus is Lord. Let's look at these ideas.

• Bishops (he is using the word to represent elders)
  "preside"—that is, they occupy the place of control,
  acting as president, chairman, or moderator.
• They do so "in the place of God."
• They do so in a new hierarchical structure with "the
  bishop" exercising this control over "presbyters."
• These various hierarchical functionaries are entrusted
  with the business of Jesus Christ.

Where do these ideas come from? Not from the New Testament.
Ignatius, perhaps with the best intentions, is borrowing ideas from the
worldly structures around him. These ideas came from his non-Christian
cultural value system. But by introducing worldly ideas, Ignatius, along
with other early Christian leaders like him, opened up Pandora's box.

# Opening Pandora's Box by Rejecting God's New Covenant

The Pandora's box these leaders opened up was something Paul, in both the books of Galatians and Colossians, warned us about. This Pandora's box is to rely on the wrong operating system, instead of God's operating system, His new covenant. (See Jeremiah 31:31; Luke 22:20; 2 Corinthians 3:6; Hebrews 8:8.)

What I'm calling using the wrong operating system, Paul calls relying on the foundational or basic principles of the world. The Greek word for these foundational or basic principles is *stoicheia* (stoy-KEY-uh). In turning to these foundational principles of the world, we have changed from Spirit-controlled, new covenant Christianity to human-controlled Christendom. We are trusting in man and the strength of our flesh rather than trusting in God. We are turning from God's leadership and His lordship and relying on the leadership of men.

> Formerly, when you did not know God, you were slaves to those who by nature are not gods. But now that you know God—or rather are known by God—how is it that you are turning back to those weak and miserable principles? Do you wish to be enslaved by them all over again? You are observing special days and months and seasons and years! I fear for you, that somehow I have wasted my efforts on you.
>
> —GALATIANS 4:8–11

There are two interesting things going on here. First, Paul is stating that there are foundational principles of the world, which keep us in slavery. Secondly he states that by going back to keeping old covenant law (observing special days and months and seasons and years), one is in essence going back to these foundational principles.

Paul warned the Colossians about something similar: "See to it that no one takes you captive through hollow and deceptive philosophy, which depends on human tradition and the basic principles of this world rather than on Christ" (Col. 2:8).

Just like following the old covenant law was returning to miserable foundational principles, so was adding Greek philosophy to the mix. To do so would be to be taken captive, to become slaves, just as he warned the Galatians.

> Since you died with Christ to the basic principles of this world, why, as though you still belonged to it, do you submit to its rules: "Do not handle! Do not taste! Do not touch!"? These are all destined to perish with use, because they are based on human commands and teachings. Such regulations indeed have an appearance of wisdom, with their self-imposed worship, their false humility and their harsh treatment of the body, but they lack any value in restraining sensual indulgence.
> —COLOSSIANS 2:20–23

Returning to the old covenant law, just like turning to Greek philosophy, was to turn to the basic principles of this world (*stoicheia*). Such things appear to be wise, but in fact are actually incredibly foolish.

It is one thing to claim that going back to a noncovenant relationship with God would be functioning under these miserable principles. This is what the Colossians did by trying to add the "wisdom" of Greek philosophy to the new covenant. But why is functioning in a covenantal relationship, albeit the wrong covenant, as the Galatians did, still going back to the foolish foundational principles? And why is that slavery? To put it simply, either going back to the old covenant of the Law or relying on the human wisdom of Greek philosophy is to rely on human abilities and human structures. We are no longer functioning in the new covenant of the New Testament where God puts the law on our hearts and minds through His Spirit, but we are now functioning on human ability. We are following the Old Testament Law in our human ability or following our own human wisdom. Both amount to the same thing and both reject Jesus's lordship.

## The Strategic Consequences of Historic Changes

The early church was a vibrant movement of the Spirit of God. It had an organic structure unlike anything the world had ever seen before. Israel, however, before it rejected God for human leadership was, like the church, led by God Himself. In the previous chapter we saw that just as Israel rejected God as her king, the early church also ended up forsaking divine leadership for human leadership. However, unlike Israel's decisive rejection of God's leadership in 1 Samuel 8, we see the church making small incremental steps. Yet it ended up having the same devastating effect.

In this chapter we will look at these incremental steps in closer detail and struggle with their damaging strategic implications. We will also grapple with how these historic steps continue to inhibit a viral movement of the Spirit in the West today. We will look at these steps roughly in the historical order of their emergence. Each step is important, yet each step is small and seemed to make sense at the time. However, their cumulative effect was monumental and devastating. Below are some of the incremental steps the church took as it slowly morphed from a vibrant movement of the Spirit into human-controlled institutional Christendom.

## Single-Bishop Rule

With this early step, we have a small but distinct change in the power dynamics of the church. Ignatius of Antioch (A.D. 35–107; Ignatius's date of death is a matter of historical debate) exalted the status and authority of one man above others. He wrote in his *Epistle to the Ephesians*, "It is manifest, therefore, that we should look upon the bishop even as we would upon the Lord Himself."[3] This small step is the first planting of a seed that eventually sprouted into Roman Catholic priests and Protestant pastors.

This is actually the first small step toward hierarchical structure. However, at this point the structure is small and simple. It is also sporadic. This idea didn't catch on right away. Viola and Barna write, "At the time of Ignatius, the one-bishop rule had not caught on in other regions. But by the mid-second century, this model was firmly established in most churches. By the end of the third century, it prevailed everywhere."[4] There is a good reason this didn't catch on immediately. It is distinctly foreign to New Testament thought.

With single-bishop rule, we have set up a priest in the pagan and old covenant sense of the word. The key concept was the introduction of the exclusive priesthood back into a faith in which all were priests. The New Testament idea of priesthood was that everyone has equal and direct access to God. (See 1 Peter 2:9.) With this change we have a special person who stands between God and the average person. Humans—not Christ, the head of the church—are making leadership decisions for others. The fundamental principle of the new covenant has been violated.

What congregational church doesn't have a priest or pastor? In some structures, these leaders are more accountable to others; in others, they are less. In all they have power over the lives of others. In all they end up "presiding in the place of God," as Ignatius put it. And in all they unintentionally circumvent the lordship of Jesus Christ by clinging to the foundational principle of human leadership rather than following the Spirit-controlled operating system of the new covenant. In doing so, many have become like Ignatius, a person of heroic intention but also an unintentional problem. The problem is in the human structure itself, not merely in the hearts of men. Worse, good people of pure intentions can create unintentional problems just by participating in a structure that reflects the foundational principles of the world instead of God's organic new covenant structure.

## Levels of Leadership

Ignatius of Antioch is also the one who introduced the idea of levels of leadership. "For Ignatius, the bishop stood in the place of God while the presbyters, or elders, stood in the place of the twelve apostles. It fell to the bishop alone to celebrate the Lord's Supper, conduct baptisms, give counsel, discipline church members, approve marriages, and preach sermons."[5] The key strategic concept here is the beginning of multilevel leadership.

The hierarchical structure of a human power pyramid is endemic to all human-controlled leadership, but it is a direct contradiction to the new covenant and our pledge of allegiance, Jesus is Lord. We don't need ever-more complex levels of human leadership. We need to learn to trust the Spirit, who puts His law in our hearts and minds. This is the same as trusting Jesus our Lord. At the same time we need to learn to live in mutual accountability to other Spirit-controlled Christians. We listen to His Spirit individually, and we learn to listen and confirm in community. We are Spirit-led under the new covenant, and our community is

Spirit-led. This is not independence; it is dependence on Jesus as individuals and as a community. It is also interdependence on each other as Jesus leads the community. It is trusting Jesus to speak to us as individuals. He does this as He speaks to our hearts, and He does it through our Spirit-filled community. In every instance He is the Lord; He is the leader. Sadly the discernment skills of listening to the Spirit and seeking His confirmation have largely been lost to the Western church. In its place, we fall back on human-controlled leadership, human power, human plans, and human results.

## Apostolic succession

Clement of Rome (late first and early second century) came up with the idea that one leader got to appoint another who would succeed him in ministry.[6] He invented the idea out of thin air. It is not found in the New Testament. The key concept here is that special power is derived from other men. Now the function of who leads and when has been taken from Christ and placed in the hands of people.

From where do our leaders derive their positions and power? Does it come from the denomination? Does it come from the elder board? Does it come from the board of directors? Does it come from Rome or Colorado Springs? The Roman Catholic Church openly practices apostolic succession. The various expressions of Protestantism practice a functional equivalent covertly or without even knowing it. In every case humans are giving power to other humans. In doing so they circumvent the new covenant and Jesus the Lord.

## Laity

Clement of Rome was also the first known person to use the concept of "laity" in Christian writing.[7] It comes from the word *laos,* which simply means "people." We now have two kinds of people defined, not merely the bishops and the rest, but the bishops and the other folk, who have their own term, "laity." There is an underlying logic in the distinction of these two terms that is clearly human in origin.

The key concept here is the demotion of status and significance of those who did not have official titles or position. This leads to those who "do ministry" and those who are "ministered to." This is completely distinct from the New Testament concept of an organic body where the eye cannot say to the hand, "I don't need you" (1 Cor. 12:21). It also disrupts the interactive relationship of the body ministering to each other through the prompting of the Spirit as we see it described in 1 Corinthians 14:26–32. With this change we are seeing a significant perversion of how Christians relate to one another.

Again the problem is not merely in the hearts of people; it is in the way we have organized ourselves. The organizational structure we take for granted does not reflect the new convenient structure of the New Testament or reflect the lordship of Jesus. How many churches that have "laity" (i.e., congregational members) have 100 percent of their body functioning in their spiritual gifts—or 50 percent or even 20 percent? How many "lay members" are able to use their spiritual gifts in a church service in a given week or month? How many actually do use their gifts weekly or monthly outside of a church service? How many even know how God has gifted them or what God's call on their life is? How many lay people feel that their function is to be ministered to? How many are passive? How many are spiritually weak? All of these issues are the unintentional consequences of what Clement pulled out of thin air.

## Clergy

Tertullian (born 160) was the first person known to use the term "clergy."[8] It is first used in his work *On Monogomy*,[9] which was written about the year 217.[10] The use of the term notes a clear change in thinking. The term *clergy* is derived from the Greek word *kleros*, which means "a lot, a share, or an inheritance." The New Testament never uses the word *kleros* for leaders. It rather uses it for the whole people of God. The division of laity and clergy was also slow to be adopted and not universally accepted. This is because it is a clear violation of Jesus's teaching on leadership.

With the introduction of this title, we have a special "class" of people. That is to say, the church is beginning to think of the clergy as a distinct group with special power, privilege, and status. The key concept here is class division. Each class has its own name: clergy and laity. Clergy are defined not merely by the title "bishop" but also by their class distinction as a whole group. This is mirroring the religious concepts of the pagan religions prevalent in Greco-Roman society. The idea of clergy also mirrors the normal human power structure of all societies. Note how one small step builds on another.

Clergy is a spiritual class distinction, one that is not reflected in the language or the history of the New Testament itself. How many people do we know who are willing to follow their "spiritual leaders" rather than listen to Jesus Himself in the context of community? How many feel that to do so is fidelity to God Himself? How many mistakenly believe that such people are above them spiritually and in status? How many clergy feel that it is their responsibility or right to "rule over" or lead the laity? How many Christians do you know who have been spiritually wounded by those who had positional power over them in the church?

Again the problem is in the hearts of people while at the same time being built into the structure. Lay people tend to become spiritually weak and shallow. They do so because the system tends to disconnect them from their Lord by replacing Him with higher-status humans. While this system harms the laity, it is also very dangerous to the souls of those who are given special status, power, and control. When leaders take for granted their right to decision making, power, status, and control, they unintentionally usurp the lordship of Jesus. This is extremely dangerous spiritually. At least sometimes this usurping is unintentional. Unintentional or not, they have sinned and their souls are damaged by a non–New Testament system.

## Civil Religion

After the Edict of Milan in 313, we rather quickly adopted the Roman government's multilevel human leadership hierarchy as our model. This is because the church began to think of itself as the officially sanctioned religion of the Roman Empire.

In pagan Roman society, religion was not merely spiritual. It played a civil role, deeply intertwined with the culture and officially connected to the state. Christianity began to adopt this role. This was initially an underlying, unstated attitude, but it eventually became official state policy. The Edict of Milan only began the process of the "civilization" of Christianity; however, over time, we became strongly identified with the Roman state and its structure.

Christianity began to model the governmental structure, even to the point of taking pagan names from the pagan religion, for example *Pontifex Maximus*. "The *Pontifex Maximus* was the pagan high priest of the Ancient Roman College of Pontiffs. This was the most important position in the Ancient Roman religion, open only to patricians until 254 B.C., when a plebeian first occupied this post. A distinctly religious office under the early Roman Republic, it gradually became politicized until, beginning with Augustus, it was subsumed into the Imperial office."[11] The title *Pontifex*, meaning priest, was first used by Pope Damasus I, Bishop of Rome from 366 to 384.[12] Much later *Pontifex Maximus* was used, as it is today, by the Roman Catholic Church to mean the highest priest of the hierarchy, namely the pope.

A serious and dangerous line has been crossed here. The church was not only organizing itself based on a pagan governmental structure but also borrowing titles from a pagan religion. It saw itself associated with the pagan government in the same way the pagan religion had been related to it. This was not only an organizational principle; it also tied the church to pagan thinking, religion, and government. We were now wallowing in the foundational principles of the world. This was done for the sake of the power and prestige and perceived protection that the government could bestow on Christendom. This same government, just a few decades before, was murdering Christians for not bowing to the emperor and idols as gods. The church was clearly looking for legitimacy and power, but it was thinking about power and legitimacy from the wrong source. The church, just like Israel before it, had untied itself from God and tied itself to kings (or emperors).

The connection of religion to governmental power and authority has never been good for the spirituality of those involved. Further, the church no longer tacitly assumed that clergy is somehow superior to laity. We explicitly took on titles for such people and gave them official power. These titles specifically referred to priests, ones who stand between men and God. The separation between clergy and laity had become explicit.

How many Christians in the West today view their faith through a political lens? How many allow that political orientation to cloud how they respond to political and social issues, viewing them through the thinking of a political party or ideology rather than what the Bible says?

How many Christians are sad because we no longer pray in schools, for example? How many look to Christian political clout to accomplish a moral agenda, rather than relying on the vibrant testimony of a holy people living holy lives? How morally different are the lives of Christians from the lives of non-Christians around us? Is our divorce rate distinctly different? Are our marriages distinctly better?

This connection of the church with political power is a legacy of Christendom's marriage to the Roman state. Since that time Christianity has been viewed as the state religion of the West. We have been viewed as the moral arbiters of society. Many of us still consider Christendom's role as moral arbiter of society as Christianity's birthright. Western society no longer wants Christianity to play that role. If we insist on playing that role when society no longer seeks it, we risk losing the privilege of being heard, not only about politics and morals but also about the gospel itself. Are we going to view this as a loss or an opportunity to be distinct and beautiful to the society around us?

## Ordination

Bad ideas began building on each other rapidly. Because the church modeled itself on the Roman governmental structure, we took on a Roman custom of appointing men to an office. This governmental process was called "ordination." The church has become fixed in its pagan thinking, with some people appointing others to "offices." Those who are appointed to these offices are thought of as the holy men of God.

How many clergy have we seen who believe that their role as the "ordained" gives them special privileges and rights? How many times have we considered sacraments such as baptism and the Lord's Supper the exclusive estate of the ordained? Does a sixteen-year-old Christian have the right to baptize someone he led to the Lord? Can the nonordained give out communion? What do the Scriptures say about these things? What does this pagan idea of ordination do to those who aren't ordained? Worse yet, what can it do to the ordained?

# Church Buildings

The concept of meeting in specified buildings has had a significant effect on our ministry practice. We began to think of buildings first as a holy place where ministry is done at predetermined times and later as the only right place for ministry to be done. Further, the layout of the building heightens the power distinctions between clergy and laity. Those with power stand at the front. Those without power sit facing them. Ministry became stuck in space and time. Apostolic ministry, as taught by Jesus and as practiced in the New Testament, became nearly impossible. In its place, we developed parishes. Parishes are local territories associated with a local church building.

This logic of the holy place where ministry is carried out is also reflected in current ministry practice. Ministry has become an indoor sport with special hours. At best we can now be what Frost and Hirsch call "attractional": "an approach to Christian mission in which the church develops programs, meetings, services, or other 'products' in order to attract unbelievers into the influence of the Christian community."[13]

Strategically this is no small thing. We are no longer going out; we are trying to somehow convince others to come to us. Jesus commanded us to go. More accurately, He assumed that we would go, saying in Matthew 28:19, "As you go, make disciples..." (author's translation). He never assumed or implied that we should set up shop and try to get unbelievers to check out our cool programs and certainly did not command us to do so. The forefront of Jesus's strategy is apostles. He sends them. That's what apostles are: "sent ones." Apostles are people appointed by God and sent by God. Church buildings completely disrupt and destroy the flexibility and outward movement of that kind of ministry. It should come as no surprise that Christendom has stopped talking about and practicing apostolic ministry as designed and taught by Jesus.

# Service With Order of Worship and Sermon

The gradual emergence of the religious service is intertwined with the concepts of a clergy or priestly class and the idea of a sacred space or temple. The church devolved into a mirror image of the pagan religions around them, which happened to mimic the structure of Judaism. There is a special priestly caste and a common caste that need the priests to connect with God. There is a holy place where these priests do their bidding for us. There is a holy ritual; this is called the service or the mass. If we want to help someone know Christ, we must somehow convince them to come to this "special" place with "special" people hoping that somehow they will get something out of this "special" ritual. Attendance at this ritual somehow is expected to do something spiritual for us as well. At least that is the hope. The ritualized service itself has devolved into an ordered, rigid, structured event. Often these rituals are symbolic and their meaning is not necessarily clear to us. So we end up expressing ourselves in "special" jargon that we don't completely understand and those who don't know Christ can't possibly understand.

How many of us equate attending a church service with going to church? How many of us confuse attendance and perhaps passive participation in a church service with actual spiritual life? How many of us equate listening to a sermon with being taught and singing songs with worship? What would happen if the Holy Spirit wanted to do something distinct from what was printed in the bulletin? How does allowing a controlled, ritualized church service potentially disconnect us from God? How much does the New Testament talk about "church services"? The intentional gathering of Christians is described only once in the New Testament (1 Cor. 14:26–32). How does this compare to what we commonly do today?

## Adopting the Logic of the Times

As society changed around the church, the church adapted to society. This is not entirely bad. We do need to communicate to the society around us in ways that are understandable. But when we adopt the elementary principles of the age in which we live, we become enslaved by them (Col. 2:8). It is one thing to adopt customs such as dress, music, or figures of speech. (Obviously moral discretion needs to be observed in these issues as well.) It is entirely another to accommodate ourselves to values and principles. We have noted in some detail how the early church succumbed to the foundational principles of the Roman Empire. This was not the last time we became enslaved to deceptive philosophy and human tradition.

These changes through the ages have slowly but surely disconnected us from our biblical roots. They have also disconnected us from God Himself. The behavior of the early church was far simpler and yet much more profound. It was based on the new covenant. The Spirit of Christ lived in every believer in an abiding relationship. He spoke to them and they obeyed Him because He was their Lord. This loving obedience was lived out in every aspect of life both individually and in loving community.

Clergy creates a barrier to this new covenant behavior because now "laymen" need leadership or perhaps even permission from clergy to function within the church system. Some even feel they need the clergy to access God.

The special buildings and services keep us from abiding and obeying all day long. We tend to feel we need to go to a special service at a special time in a special place. We've come to rely on the special program, event, or project as the best way to minister to our non-Christian friends. Furthermore the service is not based on listening individually and in community to God. It is based on a scheduled, planned, programmed, and timed agenda. Where is there room for the Holy Spirit to do something different? What happens when He wants to do something not previously programmed?

Christianity has become knowledge and ritual/event/project/program based. It is no longer new covenant/abide/listen/hear/obey based. Or, more succinctly, it is knowledge based not obedience based, human based not Jesus based. We have been disconnected from the God of the new covenant by the system. At the very best, we can know and abide in Christ in spite of the system.

The most dangerous disconnection of all that the Christendom system perpetrates on Christians is our disconnection from Christ Himself. In Christendom, Christ can no longer easily function as the Head of the church who is intimately connected to all parts of the body, which in turn are connected to each other. The system itself distances us from our Lord.

Paul's extended metaphor in 1 Corinthians 12 is an organic metaphor based on God's design of His creation. And in this structure, He is Head and absolute Lord. He controls everything. There are no human lords and no mediators between God and man. That is Christ's function (1 Tim.

2:5). The whole new covenant structure is based on the Spirit of Jesus in us and working through us. He does this individually and corporately.

What then does new covenant life look like? For individuals it looks like the abiding relationship in John 15:1–17. We are so closely connected with Jesus that we are like the vine (Jesus) and the branches (us). As individuals, we are so deeply connected with Jesus that it is impossible to tell where the vine ends and the branch begins. The abiding relationship is marked by deep intimacy.

First Corinthians 14:26–32 is shared new-covenant lifestyle in action. We don't need to copy this as though it were an order of service. Paul is merely mentioning what kinds of things happen when Christians get together and the Spirit of Jesus leads them corporately. Each and every Christian plays spontaneous roles based on his giftedness, maturity, experience, and most of all the leading of the Holy Spirit.

This is new-covenant Christianity expressed in new-covenant wineskins. It has no clergy. This Christianity has no order of service, because it doesn't have services. There are no special buildings; it can be done anywhere that seems fit. There are no special hours or days, no sacred time. It can meet weekly if that seems to be what the Spirit wants, but it will probably also just be a group that hangs out together and meets spontaneously all together or in smaller subgroups, all through the week.

This type of Christianity was not expressed only in the first few centuries of the church; new communities like this are springing up all over the world, including the West. The wineskin of Christendom cannot contain Christianity of this kind. There are too many historical incrustations that block immediate abiding access, listening, hearing, and obeying. These believers realize that the wineskin of Christendom actually distances them from God. It keeps them from fully encountering and obeying Christ. The negative consequences of Christendom are certainly not intentional on anyone's part, but we must be honest with ourselves. Ignoring these ramifications will not help anyone connect with God on the deepest level.

## Political Correctness and Blocks
## to a Viral Jesus Movement

It is currently politically correct in many ministry circles to say that the form of the church really doesn't matter. What matters is if the church is the kind of church that has correct doctrine. Whether a church has organic structure or institutional structure is just a matter of personal preference or ecclesiastical taste. While I appreciate the kindness, love, and openhandedness this view expresses, I believe it is utterly wrong.

Such a view betrays an Enlightenment mind-set that says that all that counts is the propositional facts of doctrine. Doctrine is important. However, the way we express doctrine betrays what we really believe. The fundamental doctrine of the early church was "Jesus is Lord." Pliny the Younger slaughtered Christians because they would not waiver from this doctrine. To hold to such a belief, not only as a propositional fact but also as a matter of life and death, was important to early Christians. It was important enough to die for.

We live in a world that separates belief from behavior. From a biblical point of view, this is bizarre. This way of thinking comes from pagan, Platonic philosophy that treats ideas as an "ideal" out there, not something that necessarily controls our behavior. Note that the words *idea* and *ideal* are related. The strange dichotomy between what we believe and how we behave is what James was dealing with in James 1:22–25 and again in 2:14–24. James makes it clear that the way we treat the rich and the poor matters. Our every behavior matters. True heartfelt belief and behavior are deeply interrelated.

Unlike the Enlightenment, the biblical worldview is not based on pagan, Greek ideals. It is based on an organic way of thinking in which everything is connected in a cohesive whole. This is the way the Hebrews thought. This is the way Jesus thought. And this is the worldview in which the New Testament was written. It is not a Greek conceptual document; it is a divine document written in a Hebrew context from a holistic point of view. It was written in the Greek language, which was the *lingua franca* of the time, but its conceptual framework is Hebrew. Therefore, what someone believes, truly believes, will be played out in the way he lives. We can give lip service to anything. We can even fool ourselves into thinking we believe something but then betray what we truly believe by how we act. Belief without consequent behavior is worthless, like a dead body. It has no life; it is just an empty shell.

This being so, we need to think carefully not only about what we believe about propositional truth (which is important) but also about how we act; and what our behavior says about what we truly believe and who we are. James, for example, clearly points out that if you have the propositions right about salvation (faith) but don't live it out, something is wrong. He goes on to state the most important proposition in the Old Testament, the Shema: "Hear, O Israel: The Lord our God, the Lord is one" (Deut. 6:4). The amazing thing is that even demons know that as a propositional fact. However, their behavior is based on something else. In fact, the Shema just makes them shudder in fear.

When we live out the ecclesiology of Christendom, we are giving legs to things we may not actually believe on a propositional level. Nevertheless, we are acting out something that can be contrary to what I've called the Christian pledge of allegiance: Jesus is Lord. The Old Testament Shema, the Jewish pledge of allegiance, told us that God is one. Our pledge of allegiance tells us who He is.

The behaviors we have inherited from Christendom have had devastating effects on our ability to participate in a viral movement of the gospel. These inherited behaviors continue to be roadblocks to a viral movement of the gospel today.

The early church was a viral movement of the Spirit. It was designed to be so by God Himself. It wasn't until men, with good but mistaken intentions, stepped in that our faith slowly stopped fulfilling its kingdom purpose and living in a new covenant wineskin.

In this chapter we have seen how early viral Christianity became the old wineskin Christendom. It was Christendom that killed the very first viral movement of the gospel in the early fourth century.

In the next chapter we will see how time after time God gave us opportunity to break out of the Christendom mold and become viral again. We will see example after example of how our wrong thinking took potentially viral movements and killed them in just a few decades. Prepare to be excited by what God did, even in the most difficult wrongheaded structures. Then prepare to be saddened as Christendom time and time again suppresses the kingdom of God.

## CHAPTER 6

# The History of Partial Viral Jesus Movements

$T$HE YEAR WAS 1801, August, to be exact. Wagons were rumbling down the dusty roads of rural Kentucky to converge at a place called Cane Ridge. It was in this obscure destination that one of the most fascinating yet little known events in American Christian history took place. Some estimate the size of the crowds that gathered to be as large as 25,000 people. Twelve thousand would be a rather conservative estimate. Probably about one eighth of the nonslave population of Kentucky eventually gathered in this newly made clearing in the virgin forest. The rough, tough woodsmen of that area had gathered earlier to fell the trees, make benches out of logs and build at least seven raised preaching stands. Over the next days and weeks powerful and unusual manifestations of God were witnessed here. Thousands came to Christ. As a result, hundreds of churches were planted. Dangerous men and women of questionable character were converted, and US history was changed, all because of what happened in that wooded clearing.

Perhaps it would be best to describe what happened there through the words of the participants themselves.

To this meeting I repaired, a guilty, wretched sinner. On the Saturday evening of said meeting, I went, with weeping multitudes, and bowed before the stand, and earnestly prayed for mercy. In the midst of a solemn struggle of soul, an impression was made on my mind, as though a voice said to me, "Thy sins are all forgiven thee." Divine light flashed all round me, unspeakable joy sprung up in my soul. I rose to my feet, opened my eyes, and it really seemed as if I was in heaven; the trees, the leaves on them, and everything seemed, and I really thought were, praising God. My mother raised the shout, my Christian friends crowded around me and joined me in praising God; and though I have been since then, in many instances, unfaithful, yet I have never, for one moment, doubted that the Lord did, then and there, forgive my sins and give me religion.[1]

A noise was like the roar of Niagara. The vast sea of human beings seemed to be agitated as if by a storm. I counted seven ministers, all preaching at one time, some on stumps, others in wagons...Some of the people were singing, others praying, some crying for mercy in the most piteous accents, while others were shouting most vociferously. While witnessing these scenes, a peculiarly-strange sensation, such as I had never felt before, came over me. My heart beat tumultuously, my knees trembled, my lip quivered, and I felt as though I must fall to the ground. A strange supernatural power seemed to pervade the entire mass of mind there collected...Soon after, I left and went into the woods, and there I strove to rally and man up my courage.

After some time, I returned to the scene of the excitement, the waves of which, if possible, had risen still higher. The same awfulness of feeling came over me...I saw at least five hundred swept down in a moment, as if a battery of a thousand guns had been opened upon them, and then immediately followed shrieks and shouts that rent the very heavens. My hair rose up on my head...I fled into the woods a second time, and wished I had stayed at home.[2]

What we would call "manifestations" in the vernacular of the day were called "exercises." These exercises were common at Cane Ridge and in subsequent meetings of what came to be called the Second Great Awakening.

I have seen more than a hundred sinners fall like dead men under one powerful sermon, and I have seen and heard more than five hundred Christians all shouting aloud the high praises of God at once; and I will venture to assert that many happy thousands were awakened and converted to God at these camp-meetings. Some sinners mocked, some of the old dry professors opposed, some of the old starched Presbyterian preachers preached against these exercises, but still the work went on and spread almost in every direction, gathering additional force, until our country seemed all coming home to God.

In this great revival the Methodists kept moderately balanced; for we had excellent preachers to steer the ship or guide the flock. But some of our members ran wild, and indulged in some extravagancies that were hard to control....

Just in the midst of our controversies on the subject of the powerful exercises among the people under preaching, a new exercise broke out among us, called *the jerks,* which was overwhelming in its effects upon the bodies and minds of the people. No matter whether they were saints or sinners, they would be taken under a warm song or sermon, and seized with a convulsive jerking all over, which they could not by any possibility avoid, and the more they resisted the more they jerked. If they would not strive against it and pray in good earnest, the jerking would usually abate. I have seen more than five hundred persons jerking at one time in my large congregations. Most usually persons taken with the jerks, to obtain relief, as they said, would rise up and dance. Some would run, but could not get away. Some would resist; on such the jerks were generally very severe.

To see those proud young gentlemen and young ladies, dressed in their silks, jewelry, and prunella, from top to toe, take the jerks would often excite my risibilities. The first jerk or so, you would see their fine bonnets, caps, and combs fly; and so sudden would be the jerking of the head that their long loose hair would crack almost as loud as a wagoners whip.[3]

# What We Have Not Learned From History

George Santayana once said that "those who cannot learn from history are doomed to repeat it."[4] The church has taken this quote to heart in all the wrong ways. We honestly don't seem to learn much from history, even our own. This should come as no great surprise. By their nature institutions tend to be conservative and resistant to change. Make that institution a religious one and you have something that normally changes at glacial speed. Yet once the changes are made, they become set in stone—the cold rigid stonework of tradition. The church tends to look at history more as a depository of tradition, not as a textbook for mistakes to be avoided.

Jesus had a few things to say about keeping traditions, but not anything that warms a traditionalist's heart.

> "Isaiah was right when he prophesied about you hypocrites; as it is written: 'These people honor me with their lips, but their hearts are far from me. They worship me in vain; their teachings are but rules taught by men.' You have let go of the commands of God and are holding on to the traditions of men." And he said to them: "You have a fine way of setting aside the commands of God in order to observe your own traditions!"
>
> —Mark 7:6–9

Let's face it; we have a long history of nullifying the Word of God by focusing on the usual conventions. So we misuse history to uphold extrabiblical traditions but don't learn from our mistakes. And there are a lot of mistakes to learn from. In this chapter I want to focus on some of the most tragic mistakes in our Christian history, when men snuffed out partial viral movements. This was always done for the sake of traditions—traditions so ingrained that they were not questioned or even noticed.

## The Waldensians

About the year 1170 a rich merchant from Lyons, France, named Vaudes or Valdes (much later he was referred to as Peter Waldo) had a powerful religious experience based on reading Matthew 19:16–21. It was the story of the rich young man who fails to follow Jesus due to concern for his wealth. Valdes was particularly struck by the Lord's injunction to sell all, give to the poor, and follow Him. This is exactly what he did, after arranging for the care of his wife and daughters. He also paid some clerics to translate the Bible and quotes of the early church fathers into the local dialect. Then he embarked on a lifelong preaching expedition. Those involved with this early movement didn't call themselves "Waldensians" but rather the "Poor of Lyons", "the Poor of Christ", or "the Poor in Spirit." Often they simply called themselves and each other brothers.

There were three key characteristics of the ministry of Valdes and his early followers: they interpreted the Bible literally, they lived in poverty, and they preached the gospel. These characteristics survived until they were subsequently absorbed into a later movement, the Reformation. The Reformation flew in the face of the Catholic church of the time, which was controlled by a clergy that came from the higher classes and lived in splendor. Euan Cameron commented on the response of the hierarchy to the Poor of Lyons.

> The priestly hierarchy, in the period, c.1177–c.1183, was asked to accommodate the enthusiasm of a group of lay people who had no proper place within the estate of the "clergy" and whose insistence on poverty must have appeared a standing reproach to the clergy's own prosperous condition.[5]

The Catholic clergy preached in Latin, a language the common person couldn't understand. When they bothered to interpret the Bible for the masses, it was more about philosophy than telling the stories of Jesus and the early church.

Valdes was not trying to start his own church. He just wanted to get the Catholic church to go back to the model of Christ and His truth. Valdes himself went to the Third Lateran Council where he gained partial approval for his work from the pope. His own document, called the "Profession of Faith," was orthodox from the Catholic point of view.

His problem stemmed from the fact that he received only a partial approval from the pope. The pope's approval was subject to the approval of local church authorities. One particular enemy ended up being the archbishop of Lyons. We can imagine why. Valdes and his followers acted pretty much like Christ. The local clergy, including the archbishop, did just the opposite. Since Valdes was technically orthodox in his preaching, it was easier to address Waldensian behavior. They were labeled and excommunicated as schematics rather than heretics. They were viewed as a group that divides rather than a group with wrong doctrine. Despite being excommunicated, they continued to preach and have great sway with the common people of the day, particularly in Southern and Central France and Northern Italy as well as in Eastern Europe.

In 1215 they were relabeled heretics by the Fourth Lateran Council. By 1231 they were openly persecuted by the church, which tended to target public preachers rather than their followers. This significantly curtailed one of the hallmarks of the Waldensians: public preaching. The response of the Waldensians was to curtail public preaching and focus on their own institutional survival. They were no longer growing significantly by conversion growth. They had ceased being a partial viral movement.

The Waldensians were later absorbed into the Reformation movement and became one more denomination. But they had long since ceased to be a partial viral movement. They survive to this day in small pockets, mostly in the valleys of Northern Italy.

They had never been a full, sustained, viral movement. There is a clear reason for this. Despite their preaching to the poor, which was a direct imitation of the ministry of Jesus and the early church from the Bible, they still retained some elements of a distinction between clergy and laity, between the regular folk and the preachers. They ended up focusing on becoming congregational churches, which limited their ability to spread like a virus. Finally, because they thought institutionally, they focused on institutional survival in the face of persecution, instead of focusing on the proclamation of the message of the kingdom. In doing so they saved the institution but ended up no longer spreading the kingdom.

## The Anabaptists

The Anabaptists have a history similar to that of the Waldensians. However, they appeared later in history, so they ended up enduring the wrath of not only the Catholic church but also the Early Reformation churches as well.

Much like the Waldensians, the Anabaptists spread through the work of public preachers—and their preachers were very effective. Some areas of the local population contained at least a majority of Anabaptist sympathizers, if they were not all outright Anabaptist. Even their detractors feared that the majority of some populations were becoming Anabaptist.

They shared not only the Waldensian style of mission but also its inherent weaknesses. But the real problem for the Anabaptists was a non-biblical idea shared by the Catholic church and their Reformation detractors: the marriage of church and state. It is not that the Anabaptists believed in this; it was that the rest of the church around them did. Imagine sending out highly effective street preachers in areas, both Protestant and Catholic, where the predominant idea of evangelism was to convert the prince so that he would determine the religion of the country. This is what the Thirty Years War was fought over: which expression of the faith, Protestant or Catholic, controlled which area. When religion is intrinsically linked to political power, roving preachers become a serious nuisance.

Early on the Protestant reformers were all for liberty of conscience, unlike the Catholics. But they later changed their tune, just about the time they started having political power and converting princes. By the 1520s it became a capital offense to be an Anabaptist in both Catholic and Protestant areas.

The lesson to be learned here is similar to what we learned from the Waldensians. If we rely merely on public preaching of a specially trained class, our missionary methods are inadequate to withstand persecution and create a sustained viral movement of the gospel. To initiate and spread a viral movement, we must encourage everyone who becomes infected with the Jesus virus. If our missionary activity is focused on street preaching in a social-political climate where the state's power is abused to control religion and murder the preferred religion's enemies, we have a context in which the gospel of Jesus cannot become viral.

## The First Great Awakening

The initial sparks of the First Great Awakening in the United States can be traced to the preaching of Solomon Stoddard in 1679. But the awakening really began to hit its stride with the preaching of Jonathan Edwards. Within a few decades religious fervor and conversion was spreading all over the English colonies in America. The first preachers mainly preached in churches, using their pulpits to spread the good news.

Later preachers such as George Whitefield and John Wesley took their messages to the streets.

There were a number of impediments that eventually slowed this first dramatic spiritual awakening in the New World and eventually stopped it. First was the extreme expression of Calvinism of the day. New World Puritanism could be called exaggerated Calvinism. In the Calvinistic view, why would one bother preaching the gospel? Either a person was elect, in which case they would become a Christian, or they weren't, in which case they would go to hell no matter what one preached.

It is interesting that Edwards's early preaching reflects this Calvinism. The important issue that distinguishes Edwards from his contemporary clergy was that he was preaching the gospel. And the people who heard it, in an age of corrupted and impotent Christianity, were hungry for it. When Edwards preached about subjects such as it's not being impossible to "press into the kingdom," he was referring to God's power to save whomever He chooses. But not surprisingly, in a social context dominated by the Enlightenment, where man's ability is emphasized, what his congregants heard was there was a chance they could achieve election, if they sought for it. In other words, Edwards was misunderstood. Those who came to Christ, especially under his early preaching, did so despite his Calvinist understanding, not because of it.

A second issue that kept the First Great Awakening from becoming a sustained viral movement was this same Enlightenment understanding of the general populace. While it was wonderful that Edwards's listeners misunderstood the fine points of what he was trying to convey, they ended up misunderstanding Christian spirituality in general. The main point of the Enlightenment was that man is in control of life. He can figure anything out for himself, and if there is a God or gods, they are distant and superfluous. Edwards was right—God can do anything—including start a movement of the Spirit in a hostile environment. But to say that the predominant worldview doesn't affect how people respond and live their lives, including the life of faith, is naive. And the Enlightenment has proven to be an extremely hostile environment for Christian spirituality.

People were impacted powerfully by such godly First Great Awakening preachers as Stoddard, Gilbert Tennant, Edwards, Whitefield, and Wesley. But this didn't end up being a viral movement of the gospel because so

much emphasis was placed by society on rationalism and human ability.
This is precisely one of the predominant problems the evangelical church
has today. It was born in the Enlightenment and is more concerned with
human technique and models, business planning and human leadership,
than it is with listening to and obeying God Himself.

A third issue was the same problem that the Anabaptists ran into,
although in a much gentler form. Religion was married to the state, particularly in the upper classes. The First Great Awakening was not uni-
formly accepted in all areas of the colonies. For example, in the tidewater
area of Virginia where the established Anglican church of the established classes predominated, the awakening had little impact. The typical
person in this area, at that time, had just enough religion to keep him
immune from the real thing. The local clergy could use their governmental connections to keep the itinerant preachers at bay. But in areas
such as the Piedmont, the Appalachian Mountains, and the Shenandoah
Valley, where the settlers were mainly Scotch-Irish and German and of a
much lower social class, there was much greater receptivity.

The standard ecclesiology of the day did not allow for a rapid spread
of the gospel. We have mentioned such issues as the clergy/laity distinction before. In this case, as in the case of the earlier European movements, the church was viewed as an institution of which one became a
member, an institution that had a clear class distinction between clergy
and laity. There was an emphasis placed on joining a new church, where
one learned to be a layman—in other words, a passive congregant. The
preachers took the gospel to the streets, but they led the converts to
buildings, where they learned to sit under the teaching of leaders with
official titles and power. This is not exactly a replay of Acts chapter 8.

There is a further contrast between the First Great Awakening and the
movements of the Waldensians and the Anabaptists: the severity of persecution. None of the leaders of the First Great Awakening, or common
folk impacted by it, were burned at the stake, beheaded, or torn asunder.
At worst, the leaders would be thrown out of town and the common folk
would be scorned. This would seem like an advantage, and it did have its
advantages. But the end result was that the clergy/laity distinction was
greatly reinforced.

It should be noted that there were significant signs of God's power being displayed publicly in the First Great Awakening. True, it wasn't the preachers (actually acting as truncated apostles) who showed God's power through the behavior mentioned in Matthew 10:8: healing the sick, raising the dead, cleansing those who have leprosy, and driving out demons. Instead, it was the people who were at times overwhelmed by the presence and power of the Spirit, evidenced by such manifestations as cries, groans, bodily convulsions, and fainting. Sometimes the newly converted even started running around. It is true that some of the Great Awakening preachers such as Whitefield could be powerfully enthusiastic. But others, such as Edwards, were actually quite inhibited, even boring. The real show of God's power was in the response of the listeners, which, even though weird by our standards, brought new listeners in by the droves.

Edwards wrote to Reverend Thomas Prince of Boston on December 12, 1743, describing instances of the second wave of the Great Awakening. The events Edwards mentions took place in Northampton, Massachusetts.

> The months of August and September were the most remarkable of any this year, for appearances of conviction and conversion of sinners, and great revivings, quickenings, and comforts of professors, [Edwards is using the word "professor" here as one who has professed Christ, i.e., a convert] and for extraordinary external effects of these things. It was a very frequent thing to see a houseful of outcries, faintings, convulsions, and suchlike, both with distress and also with admiration and joy. It was not the manner here to hold meetings all night, as in some places, nor was it common to continue them until very late in the night; but it was pretty often so that there were some that were so affected, and their bodies so overcome, that they could not go home, but were obliged to stay all night at the house where they were.[6]

## The Second Great Awakening

If the First Great Awakening was a heavy rain, the Second Great Awakening was a flood. It was a flood of God's power and salvation on the new American Republic that has had repercussions on our religious culture to this day. American evangelicals can all trace their spiritual heritage back through the Second Great Awakening, yet few actually know of its impact on their faith. Many don't even know it happened.

The Second Great Awakening, starting about 1799, was quite similar to the first, yet it was far larger in scope and impact. It had some of the same characteristics, and it had some of the same inhibitors to the viral spread of the gospel as the First Great Awakening. However, there were some differences of emphasis and degree. First it had less famous names and leaders. Most Christians who are aware at all of their history have heard the names of Jonathan Edwards, George Whitefield, and John Wesley. Most have never heard of Peter Cartwright, James McGready, or Barton Stone. These men were no less powerful or spiritual than the leaders of the First Great Awakening; they are just less famous.

There was a greater emphasis placed on preaching in the open air in the Second Great Awakening as is evidenced by the Cane Ridge Camp Meeting. Finally there were more supernatural manifestations than in the First Great Awakening. Again, this is a matter of degree since there were significant supernatural demonstrations in the first. These supernatural expressions were experienced by the preachers and those in attendance. Some were individual and others were mass demonstrations of God's power. Peter Marshall and David Manuel describe some of these powerful manifestations by giving a few examples of what happened at Cane Ridge.

> Among the preachers present were Methodist John McGee and his Presbyterian brother William. The latter would sometimes exhort after the sermons, standing on the floor, or sitting, or lying in the dust, his eyes steaming, and his heart so full that he could only cry out "Jesus, Jesus." His brother John, who had been so used by God at McGready's meeting at Red River the summer before, described the awesome scene at night: "The camp ground was well illuminated; the people were differently exercised all over the ground, some exhorting, some shouting, some praying, and some crying for mercy, while others lay as dead men on the ground."
>
> There were many instances of hard cases and scoffers falling at the continual services "as suddenly as if struck by lightning," sometimes at the very moment they were cursing the proceedings.

One tried to prove that the fallen were faking their experience and began prodding them with a nail on a stick, but to no avail. Frustrated, he went and purchased several cupfuls of whiskey, then returned and shouted that he, at least, would not fall. The words were scarcely out of his mouth before he found himself flat on his back. When he regained his speech the first words out of his mouth "acknowledged himself a great sinner, and hoped for pardon through Christ."

The meeting continued all night long and into the next day and the next night. As people were converted they would spell the preachers, giving their own testimonies in the most vibrant terms. More fell, and all manner of manifestations were given vent, but the most unaccountable—and moving—to chief preacher Barton Stone was the "singing exercise." With a sublime countenance, the individual "would sing most melodiously, not from the mouth or nose, but entirely in the breast, the sounds issuing thence...It was most heavenly. None could ever be tired of hearing it."[7]

It should come as no great surprise that there were powerful manifestations of the Spirit of God. What must have been surprising for the trained clergy was that it did not represent anything taught to them by their teachers or in the seminaries of the time.

The Second Great Awakening, despite its lack of famous leaders, had a much longer-lasting impact on American society. Some would argue that the American penchant for evangelical religion, particularly in what is commonly called the Bible Belt, is a direct outcome of the Second Great Awakening. This would show a social impact of about two hundred years. That does not mean it was a sustained viral movement of the gospel for two hundred years. It was never a completely viral movement, but it was clearly a move of God that had a tremendous and positive impact on American society.

Though the First and Second Great Awakenings were similar, there was a much greater participation by untrained or what some would call undertrained participants. Note in the quote above that the recently converted would spell the exhausted preachers, often to great effect. This gave tacit permission for "laymen" to preach the gospel. It could be argued that this tendency of laymen to preach the gospel is played out in the emphasis American evangelicalism puts on "lay witness." Not that many current evangelicals actually witness, but some do and this is probably a heritage of the Second Awakening.

There was also a stronger tendency in the Second Awakening to engage in public worship and evangelism rather than containing it in an established church. This tendency is probably attributable to the fact that the Second Awakening began in the American West (Kentucky) and had its greatest impact in frontier areas, eventually making its way to the big cities of the Eastern seaboard. The emphasis on open-air evangelism, particularly with the participation of the recently converted, undermined but did not eliminate the powerful role of the clergy.

Still, the Second Awakening eventually moved from the clearing to the cloister, so to speak. Eventually the converts were herded into buildings and tacitly trained to be passive laymen. Within a generation or two the damage was done. Once the work was contained in a building, with its pews and pulpits, the domination of the clergy could come to the fore. This was not by some great design or plan; rather it is built into "doing church" in this manner. But doing church in this way inevitably hindered the Second Great Awakening from ever becoming a viral movement or even a sustained movement of the Spirit. The long-term impact was a social/cultural one particularly affecting the evangelical subculture of the South.

## Latin America

I lived and ministered in Latin America from the late eighties to the mid-nineties. I witnessed firsthand what God was doing in Latin America. Granted, my time in Mexico and Guatemala did not occur at the most powerful, dramatic moments of their particular awakening, but I did see some of what happened with my own eyes; even if it was a mere afterglow. Further, I heard many firsthand accounts from highly credible witnesses who had been in Guatemala in the late seventies and eighties.

By all accounts it was an exciting time. Yet it was over in about a decade. My own extensive church growth research documented that the growth had gone from 3–4 percent of the population of Guatemala to roughly 20 percent in about fifteen years. But by the time I completed my research, the growth had stopped. Why?

At the time I would have said the problem was that the clergy were not seminary trained. Now I would be more likely to say that the problem is what the Latin American church inherited from sincere people like me, North American missionaries. There is no doubt that the gospel spread much faster in Latin America once it was out of the hands of us missionaries and into the hands of normal folk.

In Latin America the normal course for the gospel was to flow through lines of relationship to friends and family. That is pretty similar to what happened in Acts 8 and the early church in general. The problem was that we missionaries came along and made new believers feel inadequate if they didn't have some sort of formal training and official title. Again, giving training is a good thing, in and of itself. It is the inadvertent and tacit messages that go along with it that can be deadly to a movement of the gospel.

Let me lay out some of those inadvertent, normally unspoken messages. A church isn't real until there is a building. A real church building has a pulpit and pews, no matter how crude. I've personally seen many Latin American churches without walls; but I've never seen one without pews, pulpit, and usually a high-octane sound system. A real church has a pastor or two. Real pastors have some sort of formal training with associated titles. Real pastors know that for the good of the flock they must protect them by leading them. Particularly in Latin America this means making all the important decisions. And all the decisions are important.

No one tried to thwart the gospel. No one tried to teach Guatemalan Christians bad habits. It was simply the way church was done. But the end result was that a movement of the Spirit was largely contained not by bad doctrine but by unspoken traditions.

## Korea

By any measurement Korea has been a bright spot on the map of modern missions. I don't want to throw cold water on what our Korean brethren have done in a relatively short period of time. One of the outstanding characteristics of Korean Protestantism is the huge emphasis placed on fasting and prayer. Korean Christians are noted not merely by fasting but also by sustained fasting and prayer both individually and in large groups. They have gone to the point of spending a considerable amount of money in developing "prayer mountains" with what can be best described as hermit huts for extensive prayer and fasting. Picture the entire side of a mountain covered with prayer huts, paths, and even restaurants that specialize in helping people safely come off of prolonged fasts. The only prayer mountains I know of in the West were built for and run by Koreans and are mostly used by Korean expatriate Christians.

Considering this emphasis on personal prayer and piety by many Korean Christians, even those who are not considered clergy, we should not be surprised that the Lord delights in answering their prayers and has given them a significant movement of the Spirit in South Korea and in their worldwide expatriate community.

What the Koreans excel at is prayer, personal spirituality, and holiness. These have served them well. They have also developed slight adaptations in ecclesiology that further augment their numerical growth. One characteristic of many Korean churches is the megachurch model. But it is somewhat distinct from the Western megachurch. The bread and butter of a Western megachurch is a high-powered preacher. The preacher mostly brings in Christians from surrounding churches. This is called church growth. The bread and butter of Korean megachurches are small cell groups. These cell groups are usually led by nonseminary trained leaders, often women. And these cell groups are most often in homes or at least away from the church building. The best of these cell groups take on the life and behavior we see in 1 Corinthians 14:26–33. In fact in many Korean churches cell groups are where the main ministry is done. The larger meeting is only seen as a nice get together, a large celebration, on the weekend.

What the Koreans have, then, and what hasn't actually been shown in the other stated examples, is a deep experiential spirituality among normal Christians based on personal prayer and fasting. They also have an ecclesiology of the small. Sometimes they have an ecclesiology that emphasizes the small and the nonseminary trained.

Still the Korean movement has not been a sustained viral movement of the gospel. It has been a relatively healthy movement, but it has not become viral. And it has not become viral for all the same reasons as stated in the other examples. The Korean church may have a theology of the small, but they also express all the Christendom traditions of every other movement that traces its roots back to Western Christianity. Korean Christianity is still marked by hierarchical leadership and leaders with positional power, titles and status, as well as by denominations and buildings. They just do church with an East Asian twist and heartfelt prayer, for which they are to be respected and admired.

# Conclusions

What does all this show us? I believe it clearly demonstrates that there are unintentional but very real consequences to the way we "do church." This isn't due to the evil design of power-hungry clergy and denominational leaders. Nor is it the fault of lazy laity. It is built into our traditional ecclesiology. The very ecclesiology that the modern Western church inherited from the Catholic church and later the Reformers inhibits growth and prevents any movement of the Spirit from becoming viral.

It is a telling fact that there has not been one truly sustained viral movement of the Spirit in the West since the signing of the Edict of Milan in A.D. 313. Nor have there been sustained viral movements in any area dominated by Western missionaries. Obviously there have been movements of the Spirit since then. They just did not become sustained and viral, as was the growth of the early church in the Roman Empire and as is the growth of the church in China today. In the next chapter we will take an extensive look at a current viral movement of the gospel in China, which has had a sustained movement of the gospel for more than sixty years. It continues to be a rapidly growing, multigenerational movement of the Spirit to this day.

## CHAPTER 7

# China: A Current
# Viral Jesus Movement

*T*HE YEAR WAS 1975. I was a young Christian attending a leadership conference in a camp in the forests of Western Washington. While there, I met a Christian who had a completely different view of the world than I did. He was a young Chinese American. But instead of the small view I had of Christianity, he had a view as large as the world. In fact, he had an intense desire to go to Communist China to preach the gospel.

## The Persecution of the Chinese Church

What he was suggesting was unheard of, strange, and more than a little dangerous. He was talking about a China in the grips of the Cultural Revolution. He was talking about a China where the state encouraged children to denounce their parents as enemies of the state. He was talking about a China where violent bands of state-sponsored bullies, called Red Guards, roamed the countryside intimidating at will. Their tactics included beating, rape, torture, and murder. There were even sporadic reports of cannibalism. Even Chinese government officials admit the deaths from their beatings reached in the tens of thousands. Many believe that a more accurate figure would reach into the hundreds of thousands, if not more. This does not include the people hounded into suicide. This violence was not discouraged by the state; it was encouraged. The chairman of the Chinese Communist Party, Mao Zedong stated, "This man Hitler was even more ferocious. The more ferocious the better, don't you think? The more people you kill, the more revolutionary you are."[1]

The Cultural Revolution was not a good time to be a Christian in China. At one point there were only two officially permitted churches, a Catholic congregation for foreign diplomats and a Protestant congregation for the same purpose. Both were controlled by the government, and Chinese citizens were not allowed to participate in either church. To have a Bible at this time could be a death sentence. Some of the few Christians who had Bibles buried them, afraid even to take them out, let alone read them regularly. To preach the gospel, something my Chinese American friend wanted to do, would be a death sentence, if one were caught.

As my new friend discussed these issues with me two things stood out. The first was that I had lived a very privileged life in which I took my freedom for granted. The worst that could happen to me was to be mocked, which frankly rarely happened. My brothers and sisters in China were tortured to death for things I avoided out of laziness or simple embarrassment. The second thing that stood out was my friend's deep sadness, perhaps horror is a better word, at the destruction of the church in his ancestral home. At that time it was not known how many Christians had survived the systematic destruction of the church. This was a persecution more widespread, brutal, and systematic than anything the Romans ever unleashed on Christians. Frankly, my friend despaired of finding any Christians in China; that is, if he could find a way to get there.

If you walk down the streets of Shanghai today perhaps as many as one in ten people you see in the teeming crowds knows Christ personally. The same might also be true in Beijing. The average Christian in China is not a nominal Christian more emotionally linked with a denomination or church body than to Christ personally. They are Christians who are clear on who Jesus is and what He has done for them. No one knows exactly how many Christians there are in China. Estimates run from the ridiculously low, 4 million Catholics and about 10 million Protestants in the year 2000 (the Chinese government); to the exuberant 150 million total Christian population. The most conservative yet somewhat realistic estimate is about 50 million. The truth probably falls somewhere between 50 million and 100 million, perhaps closer to the higher number. There tend to be much higher concentrations in some areas and provinces, particularly the East Coast and the South. Other areas, particularly the West and extreme North, have very few Christians. There tend to be high concentrations in some rural areas and in the largest cities. We know that since 1949, by far the greatest growth of the church was in the unregulated underground church, not the formal organized church. We know that in that time the Protestants have greatly surpassed the Catholics in total numbers. We also know that there has been a sustained viral movement of the gospel for more than sixty years, which has endured incredible persecution and grown not despite the persecution but because of it.

Further, this sustained viral movement of the gospel is of incredible historic proportions. The population of the Roman Empire at the time of Constantine (A.D. 306 to A.D. 337) was roughly 56 million people, counting both the Eastern and Western Empire.[2] So the Chinese church in about sixty years roughly equals the total population of the entire Roman Empire when the church was around 270 years old. The growth of the early church needs a further comparison to the Chinese church.

Gradually over the next 250 years, Christianity won a growing number of converts. By the fourth century, about 10 percent of the residents of the Roman Empire were Christian, and the new religion had also made converts elsewhere in the Middle East and Ethiopia.[3]

So it took the early church about 250 to 300 years to grow to about 5 to 6 million people. The underground Chinese church grew to 50 to 100 million in about 60 years. Both suffered sporadic persecution. However, the Chinese Christians have suffered more systematic and severe persecution.

What we are seeing in China is the most rapid and robust movement of the gospel in the history of Christianity. The nongovernment-controlled church in China is remarkably orthodox in doctrine, despite the inability to have seminaries. It is characterized by the zeal of its adherents despite persecution. It grows rapidly despite the lack of financial resources. And more than anything else, it stands in stark contrast to the Western church from which it was birthed, both in growth and spiritual vitality. In order to understand this contrast, we need to understand the Chinese church's history.

## The Strangling of the Church

Before World War II there were very few Christians in China. In the small church that existed, Catholics far outnumbered Protestants. With the takeover of the government by the Communists in 1949, after years of war and civil war, the small Christian church entered a tense, confusing, and dangerous period.

The new Chinese government was officially atheistic. As a matter of policy it set out to destroy all religion. In the case of the Christians, it intentionally used the institutional nature of the established church against itself. One of the first things the Communists did was expel all foreign missionaries, both Protestant and Catholic. Next they organized all Christians into two broad groups, the Chinese Catholic Patriotic Association (CCPA) and what later became known as the Three Self Patriotic Movement (TSPM), the sanctioned Protestant church. Both of these groups were controlled by the government. Both had their leadership handpicked by the government. This tended to divide both Catholics and Protestants into two camps: Christians who would be faithful to Christ (or at least Christianity) as long as it didn't get them in trouble, and those who chose to follow Christ even at great personal expense. This latter group, both Protestant and Catholic, went underground. Next the government slowly but surely tightened down its control of Christians. Those who were in the official churches had more and more restrictions put on them. Those who were outside of the CCPA or TSPM were officially persecuted.

At first those in the official Catholic church and those in the official Three Self Protestant church had relative freedom. Slowly, however, more and more church buildings were confiscated or simply torn down. There were fewer and fewer places for Christians to legally meet. There was a growing restriction on who was allowed to pastor churches or be a priest. There was control of the seminaries, related both to what was taught and who was allowed to have a seminary education. Fewer and fewer were allowed to enter seminary, yet formal training was required to be a pastor or priest. At the same time, it became increasingly clear that even officially sanctioned Christians were not well thought of by the government.

The three main mechanisms used to intentionally control the official churches were social stigma, control of leadership while slowly decreasing their numbers, and the eradication of church buildings. However, while this was undoubtedly very traumatic for the Chinese believers, they can also be understood as God's dismantling Chinese Christendom so that His gospel could flourish in this difficult situation.

In the early part of this persecution the government turned the church against itself. Any Christian who would not attend the official church was reported to and punished by the very government agency that was in charge of official Christianity, the Religious Affairs Bureau. This was done in conjunction with various police agencies. The Three Self Patriotic Movement (Protestant) leadership intentionally used their connections with the Religious Affairs Bureau to have house church leaders thrown in jail, which often meant torture and even death.

The nonofficially sanctioned Christians rapidly became what is now called the Chinese house church movement. At the same time the sanctioned churches were being slowly strangled through purging of membership, church buildings, and leadership. This situation reached its lowest point in the aforementioned reality of having only two legal churches in China toward the end of the Cultural Revolution, neither of which the Chinese could attend.

Here is a story from that period:

> During the early phase of the Cultural Revolution, all church windows were smashed, the pews burned, and the crosses taken down. Every pastor had to "walk the street," wearing a placard around the neck detailing one or more "crimes," and often wearing a tall hat similar to a dunce's cap, people were paraded as a means of revealing their offenses against the revolution. Many Christians were humiliated, and one woman was beaten to death. Communist cadres and Red Guards searched every house for Bibles, hymnals, and other Christian literature. They gathered over twenty YMCA and YWCA secretaries and forced them to kneel in front of a pile of burning Bibles, surrounded by the watching crowd. A large

crowd stood around the great spectacle. As the flames intensified and radiated their heat toward them, they cried out because of the excruciating pain. It was a pitiful sight. Tormented by their extensive burns, most of them, including the general secretary of the YMCA, committed suicide by jumping from high buildings. These were the same progressive secretaries and pastors who had supported government policies in the 1950s and who praised the party for having attained what Christianity had failed to do in a hundred years. Strangely enough, a few of the older faithful pastors who were "struggled against" previously were exempt from the torture, and the younger men of faith survived the ordeal. After the Cultural Revolution, there were no more open church meetings.[4]

This was a bleak situation. However, as dire as the situation was, and it was indeed dire, God was doing much below the surface. Here is a typical story taken from an interview of a Christian from the Fujian province during the Cultural Revolution.

During that time, the Christian brothers and sisters met secretly for fellowship. Some of them were able to meet in a semiopen way, in family gatherings or private home visits. Sometimes in Gulangyu, meetings were held with as many as twenty or thirty Christians. But these had to be preplanned. Ways of escaping were thought out ahead of time, in case of an emergency.

Excuses for holding house meetings included social occasions such as weddings and funerals, thereby avoiding attracting undue attention. For example, when the mother of one Christian sister died, visitors came for two or three days afterward. While there, they would pray, have fellowship, and give thanksgiving to the Lord. But in this way, the "churches" became very family oriented, because this was the way that meeting and sharing was most convenient in those days.

Besides the suppression of public worship during the Cultural Revolution, there was also widespread suffering. One sister, a teacher, went through years of deprivation. After her husband died during the Cultural Revolution, she was dismissed by her school. But she had four children to support. In a letter which I recently received from her, she said that she has now been able to resume her job. Her four children are now grown, and two of them have done well in their higher exams.

Q: What is the general situation in Fujian now?

A: Let me give you an example. A truck driver accepted Jesus in Amoy after hearing the witness of a Christian brother there. When the truck driver went back to his home in Xinmin, he told his whole family and brought them to the Lord. So the gospel is spreading in ways like this.

Some Christians there believe that the number of full-time and part-time preachers in Fujian now is probably more than the number of pastors [This term in the Chinese house church context can often mean what other house church movements would call apostles. However, it can also mean an elder or even sometimes a full-time pastor in the Christendom sense.] that were there before 1949.[5]

So what do we learn of the condition and the behavior of the underground Chinese church from this story? First, while it was both illegal and dangerous for Christians to meet, they continued to have fellowship in secret. These groups could be as large as twenty or thirty believers, though most were much smaller.

There were planned fellowship meetings, which sometimes used normal social occasions such as weddings and funerals as an excuse to meet. This avoided attracting attention from police and government officials. One characteristic of these preplanned meetings was to think through escape routes and hiding places ahead of time. Implied in the concept of the large meetings needing to be preplanned is the idea that other meetings were much more spontaneous. This goes back to Jesus's statement in Matthew chapter 18 that when two or three gather together in His name He would be in their midst. (I am aware that this statement in Matthew 18 is stated in the context of church discipline. Nevertheless, Jesus is in our midst when we gather, even in small numbers. I believe this is both a statement of promise to bless and guide church discipline and a statement of the spiritual reality of Christ being among and ministering in gatherings of believers, no matter how informal.) In fact, one of the major networks of Chinese house churches, the Little Flock, didn't conduct any organized house worship. What did these meetings look like? This story of the persecution of a Christian woman may indicate what some of them were like.

> They made a board for her and a tall hat for her to wear. They gave her a gong and told her to walk and beat the gong. On the hat they had written four characters: "God Blesses." At the time, she was thinking in her heart, "God, why don't you bless me?" but when she put on the hat and saw the characters, she said, "Oh, 'God blesses!' What do I have to fear?"
>
> So she put on the tall hat, beat the gong, walked down the street, and truly thanked the Lord. Afterwards, all the people in the area where she walked knew that she believed in Jesus. So later, all who believed in Jesus came to her house looking for her. Thus, when the brothers and sisters were struggled against, it was really an opportunity given to them by God to give a testimony to bring about the repentance of many and lead them to a belief in God.[6]

Most of these meetings were personal visits at home, or believers would meet while at work or as they walked along the road. The meetings often consisted of no more than two, three, or four people. The Christians would encourage each other, pray, and perhaps share a Bible story or teaching spontaneously. These were not church services. They did not have a specific order. Usually no one prepared any kind of teaching or lesson. Yet they were the most common type of meeting, and tremendous ministry happened in these spontaneous and casual encounters. Note how similar these Chinese meetings are to the meeting Vincent and Mary held in Connie's house, mentioned in the Introduction.

Another thing we learn from these stories was that the house churches became very family oriented. Does that mean that they were based on a nuclear or extended family? Or does it mean that the interaction between members was characterized by the way a family treats each other, rather than the more stilted and shallow way that people tend to treat each other in a more formal setting? The answer is both. In a context where one has to be careful about with whom one is seen, it is much more natural to gather with one's family. However, that does not mean that these groups became totally insular. The Christians knew who each other were.

They met in small groups spontaneously. And when they met, they loved each other like family members.

Since these groups didn't have formal membership, individuals would end up being taught, encouraged, and prayed for by many different believers. They in turn would do the same for others. So though the gatherings were small and unplanned, not only did tremendous ministry happen but also information spread quickly and all the true advantages of large groups (with the exception of large-scale worship) could take place. Furthermore, as Paul described in 1 Corinthians 14, each person contributed, not just a select few.

We also learn that the gospel was not thwarted by the church being forced into these small spontaneous meetings. As the story of the truck driver attests, Chinese believers were still preaching the gospel, and those who were infected with the virus spread the contagion.

During the Cultural Revolution, and in fact in the official persecutions before and after it, many Christians were thrown into prison, particularly for preaching the gospel. How did this end up affecting the spread of the gospel?

> Another sister, who was born in Guangdong, was arrested in 1958. She continued to preach the gospel in prison. I have personally met her. She was imprisoned along with all kinds of prisoners: corrupt officials, robbers, immoral persons, political prisoners, etc. There was one prisoner who gave everyone a hard time. Not even the prison warden could do anything about her. She would not wash her face, brush her teeth, or comb her hair. Whenever she got a chance she would open her mouth to scold others. No matter what the warden did to her—and he applied all sorts of punishments to her—still it was useless. The Communist prison keepers then asked the Christian sister to talk to this hopeless prisoner. "Alright, I'll try," replied our sister. Sister Chen then lived together with the other woman prisoner. She prayed for her. Gradually the woman changed. She bathed herself, changed her clothes, and even combed her hair. The prison warden was greatly surprised and asked, "How did you change her?"
>
> "I had no strength to change her. I prayed for her, and I believed that God could change her."
>
> The transformed prisoner expressed her desire to receive

Christ as her Savior and Lord of her life. Many other prisoners in the same prison also came to believe in the Lord. They all said to the sister, "In the past we did not understand you. Now that we have lived together with you, we have discovered that you are different from others. Through you we have come to understand what it means to believe in the Lord."

After Sister Chen was released from prison, she told me that formerly the Lord has used her in public meetings to preach the gospel to others or to lead revival meetings. She was glad when she saw so many people attend her meetings. Now the Lord is using her to do personal work, on a one-to-one basis, and she also sees great significance in this.[7]

Christian witness has not been stopped in China by throwing Christians in prison. In fact, Chinese prisons are often a place where the gospel effectively spreads. Since significant Christian leaders tend to be thrown into prison in times of persecution, it becomes a leadership training camp for them as they network with other leaders and train new believers. It is not uncommon for Chinese leaders to refer to their prison experience as going to seminary.

While the outward form or ecclesiology of the church in China was significantly changed due to persecution, its ability to minister deeply to believers and to spread the gospel was not hindered. In fact, it was this shedding of the later encrustations of Christendom that greatly enhanced the ability of the Chinese brethren to minister to one another. They no longer tended to worry about having formal meetings. They were no longer constrained by an order of service or a weekly schedule. They just ministered to one another. They did not wait for the official clergy to plan, call, and run a meeting. They often didn't know with whom they were going to gather and when they would have an opportunity to fellowship. Therefore, when they did gather, they ministered to each other without respect to title or position. The end result was that most believers tended to mature quickly and learn to minister to one another.

The Chinese believers learned in this context that buildings were an expensive and wasteful luxury that did not enhance the spiritual growth of believers. The important thing about fellowship, teaching, mutual prayer, and every other kind of ministry is not where it happens, just that is does happen and is of good quality. The quality comes from the presence of other believers and most importantly from the presence and guidance of God Himself.

The Christians in China learned something else. As long as a church is in the grips of Christendom but endures persecution, the church buildings themselves become a dangerous liability. If Christians believed they needed special buildings to worship and minister in, their enemies needed only to wait outside the buildings to identify the believers. Furthermore, the destruction of buildings could be used to control, discourage, and disorient Christians. This was done to the Chinese believers. It was through enduring this kind of persecution that the Chinese Christians learned losing their buildings was a blessing.

In heroic response to persecution many believers shared their faith, met, prayed, encouraged, taught, and trained boldly despite the potential dangers. And in response, the government sent the most noticeable leadership to prison. Besides using this government-sponsored gathering of Christians as a training and gospel-sharing opportunity, this also set the standard for what Christian leaders were like. Women and uneducated peasants significantly and often fearlessly expressed Christian leadership in the Chinese church, as they still do today. Young men and women responded to the absence of their older leaders and stepped into gaps caused by the jailing of established leaders. They learned that Jesus Himself was their greatest leadership resource and that one becomes a leader by who one is and how one lives. And who one is and how one lives doesn't depends on education, sex, title, or age; it depends on an abiding relationship with Jesus Himself.

These were not cloistered individuals. They were people who were living Christ in their average, everyday lives. They were people who relied on their relationship with Jesus to give them the courage to obey Him, despite the circumstances. They were people who endured public humiliation, found ways to take advantage of adversity, and in many other ways showed just how bold and brave Christians can and ought to be.

In effect, one became a respected Christian leader not by going to school and having an impressive knowledge set; one became a leader by fearlessly living a relationship with Christ in harsh circumstances. Persecution has a way of showing who is really serious about their faith.

The behavior and practice of faith that evolves from persecution of this kind becomes a standard to follow. This, for the underground Chinese church, is what leadership looked like.

Are all the believers in China so heroic? No, this is certainly not true. As in any other situation, there are mature believers and less mature ones, cowards and heroes. There are those who deny their faith and those who endure unbelievable hardship in order to testify to their faith. And there is everything in-between. Chinese Christians are just as human as everyone else.

But the persecution of the church in China did tend to refine it. It tended to separate the wheat from the chaff. It tended to heighten the influence of those who truly lived their faith in daily life, not merely those who had gained an education, title, or position. Certainly there was no social status associated with being a Christian leader. Quite the contrary. Being an influential Christian invited hardship, possibly even death. It certainly invited social stigma and humiliation. Persecution taught the Chinese church that all believers can minister and should minister. It taught them how to be involved in significant, life-changing ministry without clergy, curricula, or even planned meetings.

The persecution of the Chinese church freed Christians from anything that wasn't absolutely necessary. What ended up being shed, like a lobster shedding its shell, were the historical encrustations of Christendom. And in this shedding, the Chinese church once again learned how to live like the church we see in the New Testament—a rapidly growing viral movement, under the headship of Christ. It expanded when it was persecuted and even when it was not persecuted.

A church that doesn't need clergy in order to grow becomes much more flexible. Of course the fear is that heresy will break out in such circumstances. And indeed it has, but not as severely as is often feared. The Chinese house church movement is much more orthodox in its doctrine than Western Protestantism. They've had the modernist liberals purged from them. The modernist movement of the early twentieth century, commonly called liberalism, is one of the most dangerous heresies in the history of the church. Because this heresy was purged from them, the Chinese Christians don't argue about the veracity of the Bible. They just believe what they read and express it in the way they live.

Persecution has tended to cure the underground Chinese church from another dangerous heteropraxy of Western Protestantism, which is proclaiming orthodoxy and living anything but. (I'm using the word *heteropraxy* to mean "The practice of persons who consistently fail to follow the teachings of their avowed belief system.") The Hebrew worldview of the Bible does not allow for us to state one thing with words and live something else. This is exactly the behavior that Jesus chastised the Pharisees about in Matthew 15:8–9: "These people honor me with their lips, but their hearts are far from me. They worship me in vain; their teachings are but rules taught by men."

We have become so used to viewing orthodoxy through the lens of Greek philosophical paradigms that we are quick to proclaim someone orthodox just because he can spout correct propositional truth. We have forgotten that it is not merely by correct propositional truth that we identify each other. Christians should be known by their fruits, not just by what they say. The Chinese church does not struggle with this foolishness, particularly during severe persecution.

Chinese Christians don't like going to jail. They do not like being beaten or tortured. They don't enjoy public humiliation. They do not like having their families torn apart and turned against each other for the sake of the gospel. They certainly don't relish martyrdom. But they have learned that this can be a severe mercy from the Lord. They have learned that through the fellowship of Christ's suffering they can grow spiritually and numerically and enjoy a sustained viral movement of the Spirit.

## Supernaturalism in the Chinese Church

There is one other aspect of the explosion of the gospel in China that should not be overlooked. God is manifesting Himself among the Chinese with signs, wonders, miracles, healings, and the casting out of demons. This is not rare in the Chinese context; it is normal. The following are a brief sampling of stories of God's supernatural power in China.

### Healings

> Zhen Qingfei aged forty-two, had not been able to walk for several years, and medical treatment had brought no improvement.

He decided that he would sell his son to pay for more medical treatments. Then, less than a month after he committed his life to the Lord, he could walk again. It was a miracle. Now he can work again. The Lord has mercy on the poor and saved this whole family.[8]

The son of Wei Yauxi, Wei Jinjian, aged nineteen, had a mental problem for two years. Medical treatments brought no progress. After he put his faith in Christ, however, he was totally healed and is now a strong and healthy young man.[9]

One day, two of Heng Xin's oxen ate grass poisoned with pesticide. The oxen, white foam coming from their mouths, fell to the ground. There was not even time to call for the veterinarian. Heng Xin called a Christian to kneel down and pray, and immediately the Lord healed his animals.[10]

In personal correspondence with my friend Lyle, who traveled to China on vacation and had interaction with Chinese Christians, I was told the following:

I spoke to one man in China who suggested, "You are rich in the West and have doctors. But we are poor and have miraculous healings. I suppose God knows what each of us needs and supplies it." Afterwards I reflected that really in China they know the Spirit's power, but in the West, we don't.[11]

## Victory over demons

Chen Jianguo had been possessed by an evil spirit beginning when he was nineteen. During the following twenty-five years, he would jump around and cause lots of disturbances, sometimes keeping the whole village awake at night. After Chen accepted Christ, however, the evil spirit left him. Every Sunday, Chen goes to church for worship. People in the village are glad now because they can enjoy peace at night.[12]

Yang Zhengju was possessed by evil spirits and was mentally disturbed between the ages of sixteen and twenty-five. During these years, she had been admitted into the mental hospital many times. She had also called upon many deities for help. Yet after she believed in the Lord for forty days, she totally recovered.[13]

## Visions and dreams

I don't have time to write out all sixty testimonies of the new Christian families that joined the church in 1996. Further, the reader would not have the patience. Of those who converted, some had heard the gospel for twenty-eight years, others for three years, but most had just heard it. Anyhow, they decided to accept the incarnated God into their lives. Our coworkers have been busy preaching the gospel in the field. The Holy Spirit often leads us through visions and dreams. As we walk with God, his miracles validate his truth. May all the glory and praise be to the holy name of God.[14]

# Conclusion

In short, the Chinese church lacks wealth, sociopolitical status, social influence, trained workers, access to information, and educated laity.

Yet this church has humbled many missiologists and ecclesiologists. It has grown between ten and twenty times during the past few decades—an accomplishment that challenges most contemporary mission and church growth theories. It seems that the Chinese church can manage without many current mission requirements—funding, trained experts, paid staff, social services, outreach stations, sophisticated programs and strategies, favorable social and political conditions, political influence, international support, concentrated media exposure, coordinated activities and public evangelistic rallies. It seems to come down on the most fundamental question in missiology—mission of God or mission of man, power of God or strength of man—firmly on the side of the former.[15]

In 1949, the year of the military victory of the Chinese Communists, the Catholic church was far larger than the Protestant church. As the government started to clamp down on the church, forcing both Catholics and Protestants to join officially controlled denominations or go underground, an interesting thing began to happen. The underground movement gained spiritual vitality and began to grow explosively. At the same time the underground Protestants, originally the smallest segment of the church, became by far the largest. By 1994 Tony Lambert, an experienced expert on the condition of the Chinese church, could write:

> The phenomenal growth of the church in China since the Cultural Revolution is one of the miracles of the twentieth-century church history. The evidence is now massive. The Party is so concerned about the phenomenon that it has coined the phrase "Christianity fever" (*jidujiao re*) to describe it.[16]

In fact, instead of the officially controlled Protestant Three Self Patriotic Movement clamping down and eventually dominating the underground Protestant house church movement, as was the desire of the Chinese government, the opposite happened. The official Three Self Church started to become exposed and positively impacted by the underground church. The Three Self Church has never shown the ability to grow with the vigor or have the same spiritual fervor and depth as the underground house-church movement, but in the last decades contact with that movement has spiritually and numerically reinvigorated it.

The smallest sector of the church in 1949, the underground house-church movement, became the dominant player on the Christian scene in China. It grew far more rapidly than the official Catholic and Protestant denominations or even the underground Catholic church, which remained faithful to the pope. It went from a tiny religious fringe group to something that greatly disturbed and fascinated the government. It has a spiritual vigor that infects those around them. It has incredible spiritual power. Supernatural manifestation of God's power through miraculous signs and wonders are common. And all of this is happening without trained clergy or outside resources in the face of extreme persecution.

Observers from the West tend to attribute this incredible growth and spiritual power to the effects of persecution. In reality there are a number of interrelated issues involved. The persecution, especially in the early years, led to a shedding of the historical incrustations of Christendom. In effect, the Chinese church reverted to a twentieth-century Chinese expression of the early church. They shed official clergy, yet retained deep respect for godly leaders who demonstrated their faith through life, not mere book learning and positions. They shed the hierarchical structure of Christendom and reverted to the organic structure of a body under the headship of Christ, as described in 1 Corinthians 12. They were forced from congregational and denominational structures to lose relational structures based on personal friendship and reputation. They met in small interrelated gatherings that were connected through relationships with other groups. These networks of small house churches had a significant overlap of participants. In other words, they became much like a huge extended family instead of an organization. This loose relational structure allowed for the viral spread of the gospel.

If this movement were ever to be stopped, it would not be because of heresy or lack of organizational structure. It would be because the Chinese Christians end up making the same mistakes that the early church made in the first few centuries.

> At an international Christian conference in South East Asia recently, several members of the underground church in China appeared on the platform to report on the situation for the church in their country. They asked their audience to pray for them because the communist government has imposed restrictions on them that made being an effective church difficult. In particular they reported on three impositions that they wanted lifted: (1) no unauthorized assembly of more than fifteen people is allowed; (2) no unauthorized church buildings or sanctuaries can be erected; (3) no unauthorized formal training of leaders is permitted.
>
> As they spoke, it occurred to those gathered that these restrictions were the very things that forced the Chinese underground church to be the dynamic and powerful force that it has become. The first imposition forces churches to embrace a cellular-division model of church growth. As a congregation reaches twenty or so members, it must divide into two and launch a new congregation. The second imposition compels the church to meet in homes, restaurants, karaoke bars, and other private spaces. The third restriction drives congregations to equip their own indigenous leadership without the help of formal schools or seminaries. The bitter irony was not lost on many there that day: the communist government is actually forcing the Christian church to rediscover its original genius as a missional movement.[17]

However, if you were to talk to the Chinese Christians about their explosive growth, they would attribute it all to Jesus. They know Jesus. They don't merely preach a set of doctrines called the gospel; rather they introduce people to Jesus Himself. When they do, Jesus manifests His power and gives credence to His presence through healings, signs, and wonders. By shedding the massive lifeless weight of Christendom, the underground Chinese house church found Jesus. And Jesus led them to a viral movement demonstrated through His supernatural power.

The viral movement of the gospel in China continues to this day. The Chinese church continues to grow. It continues to experience powerful supernatural manifestations as part of its spiritual birthright and normal practice for church planting and evangelism. The Chinese believers have gone through cycles of persecution and used them to virally spread the gospel and grow spiritually. They have had relative times of peace, as is the case at the writing of this book. They have learned how to grow numerically and spiritually in times of persecution and times of relative peace. But they have also learned something else, something they can teach us. The sheddable shell of Christendom is not the advantage we think it is. In reality it hinders us from having a viral movement of the gospel. It also tends to hinder true body life and deep spiritual growth. For pointing this out to us, we Western Christians should be deeply grateful to our brethren in China.

## CHAPTER 8

# Viral Discipleship

$\mathcal{M}$Y FIRST EXPERIENCE with discipleship was with a well-known campus ministry. As a new Christian, I was given a series of topical books to look over that would introduce me to the basic doctrines of Christianity. These books were short-answer books in which a question would be posed, a few verses would be suggested, and I would fill in the answer. I learned many more things from this study than was intended.

I learned, for example, that Christianity is a lot like going to school. In this case, it was like learning at about sixth- or seventh-grade educational level. I wasn't expected to meditate deeply; I was expected to read the material and give the obvious answer. Who did John the Baptist say that Jesus was in John 1:29? Answer: The Lamb of God.

I learned that Christianity is about information. It was obvious from the way that Christianity was presented that, to be a good Christian, I needed to know a lot of information called doctrine. It didn't take long to find out that being a good Christian was about knowing doctrine. However, there were lots of arguments about what good doctrine was and what bad doctrine was. In fact, these arguments could be quite heated.

I learned that Christianity was boring. Actually what I learned was that this aspect of Christianity was boring. I was pretty excited about

Jesus saving me from my sin. I needed saving. There was a lot to for-give. I was pretty excited about not only my salvation itself but also that I could start over and that I finally felt clean. I found that I didn't desire to do the things I used to do. Particularly God had taken away my desire for alcohol, carousing, and swearing. What amazes me now is that no one actually explained to me that this was evidence of the Holy Spirit working in my life. No one explained to me how to access and walk in supernatural power to overcome new areas of brokenness in my life. I was told about confessing sin and asking the Spirit to control my life, which was good. But nobody explained to me what the control of the Spirit really was. No one trained me to hear God's voice, to discern God's voice, to trust God's voice and to obey. Instead, I was told to read the Bible. I was trained that the Bible was trustworthy and if I knew my Bible and its doctrines I would be a good Christian. I actually had more of a relationship with the Bible than I did with Jesus.

## Christianity Reduced to Information

In effect, I was being tacitly trained that a major aspect of Christianity was about mastering information. Just as it is in a course in electrical engineering or physics, the issue was the information itself. He who had the most information and could repeat it at will was he who demon-strated mastery of the course, mastery of this thing called Christianity. My faith had become an extracurricular activity, much like taking a course in learning to fly an airplane.

My relationship with Jesus had been reduced to propositional facts. No one was asking questions such as, What is Jesus doing in your life? Where do you sense the Holy Spirit at work? Do you sense God giving you desires to participate in specific kinds of ministries? What do you sense God is saying to you about this issue? What areas of sin are you grappling with right now and how can I help you find Jesus in this? How do you know if this is God's leading or something coming from another source?

# Christianity Reduced to Talents, Techniques, and Tasks

There was another broad area in which I was trained. I was trained to do specific tasks and taught that these tasks were good. I was trained, for example, in how to share my faith with people I met in the cafeteria. I was trained in how to give my salvation testimony. I was trained in how to start and lead a small group. There was particular emphasis placed on small-group dynamics. If I led someone to the Lord, I was to get him to start studying the same booklets I was studying. In effect, I was trained to train him that Christianity was about mastering information. Of course, I could give the friends I led to the Lord only what was given to me.

Christianity for me was reduced to information and tasks, so I could give them only information and tasks. Strangely, no one explained how to experience Jesus in community. No one explained how to learn from each other and hear God's voice through each other. No one explained how to experience God though multiple spiritual gifts being manifest through us by the Holy Spirit, for the benefit of all. Instead we studied information together, mostly by answering questions posed in booklets with Bible references.

I was told to pray. When I asked how to pray, the method was reduced to the acronym ACTS: adoration, confession, thanksgiving, and supplication. I was expected to find things in the Bible, facts about God for which I could adore Him. I was told to try to remember specific bad things I had done and confess them to God, asking for forgiveness. I was told to thank God for good things in my life. And I was trained how to write up a list of things that I wanted God to do for me and ask Him for them. All these things are aspects of prayer. They all have their place. But prayer had been reduced to something I do "at" God. Prayer was like a hose I was spraying God with. It was one directional. My only interaction with God in this schema was to notice if He answered my requests.

I was told that I should have a daily "quite time." This, in effect, was a regular time to study the Bible. I wasn't told much about studying the Bible except what I had learned from reading the aforementioned booklets. So by inference I assumed that we studied the Bible to glean information from it, to learn more and more facts about God and the Christian life.

I was told to memorize scriptures. Actually I was briefly trained to do so. I was trained to state the verse reference, then quote the verse, then state the verse reference again. I was also given little cards that had the reference on one side and the verse on the other. I wasn't particularly good at Bible verse memorization. I found it boring. And other than the verses that were obviously helpful in sharing my faith, I wasn't sure why I was memorizing these verses, except perhaps so that I knew where the Bible stated certain doctrines.

I was trained to go to church. Church was an event that happened on Sunday morning. We went there and listened to a lecture given by a nice guy, a man we were tacitly taught to admire and respect. We also sang some songs and said prayers together. The information from the lecture was the same information we were getting in our booklets and small groups. We also went to adult or college/career Sunday school. There we heard the same information that we were learning at our extracurricular training for our college ministry. So going to church was quite similar to what I was doing at college, only not as fun. However, we were firmly told that we needed to join a church, that we really weren't good Christians until we had done so. We were told that "fellowshiping" at a local church was indispensable. There was something that going to church did for us that we couldn't get by doing what we were already doing during the week. We just couldn't figure out what that was. Frankly the fellowship was much more fun on campus. At least we got to talk to one another.

## Positive Lessons

I was trained to be a leader. More specifically I was given a title as a specific type of campus leader in the organization. This title gave me the right to go to weekly training sessions given by a couple of cool campus ministers. These were probably the best couple of hours of the week. We ate a meal together and actually discussed things, as opposed to being talked at. Looking back, I probably learned more about my faith in those brief weekly meetings than through any other Christian activity I did during the week. Leadership skills weren't taught as much as caught.

Many of those lessons were quite good. I learned how to lead a discussion by seeing a discussion led. This is where I learned that the Holy Spirit tended to manifest Himself differently through different people and that this was a good thing. That wasn't specifically taught, but I absorbed it in my bones from watching it. In other words I was experiencing true discipleship. The message was matched by the behavior of those who were influencing my life. This was not the mere dissemination of information; it was participatory, it was life, and I was involved in it. What I learned I could immediately put into practice. In fact, I was often practicing before I realized what I was learning.

## Untangling the Good From the Bad

Much of what I learned in this stage of my life was good. Bible knowledge is a good thing. So is memorizing scriptures, studying the Bible, and all that I learned about prayer. I'm deeply grateful to the campus ministers who poured their hearts and souls into me. Looking back now, I know they truly loved me. The problem wasn't with the campus ministers. Nor was it with much of what they taught or modeled.

The problem was the underlying system and worldview that was being taught with all the good stuff. It was what was unintentionally taught along with all that was good and right. Further, it was what could and should have been taught and modeled but wasn't. I was taught the rudimentary issues of following Jesus (prayer, Bible study, and memorization) but it didn't go very deep. I was taught that Christianity was basically informational. Worse yet, I was tacitly being taught a form of Christendom. What I didn't learn was how to listen to Jesus's voice in the myriad of ways He can speak to us. I was not taught to compare what I was hearing to the Bible or how to tap into the power of the Holy Spirit to obey God's communication with me. I wasn't taught to discern God's voice from my own or the world's or the evil one's. I wasn't taught the life of faith as I learned to trust the power and direction of the Holy Spirit. In effect, I was tacitly taught to be a follower of the evangelical branch of Christendom's system, as it is currently expressed in the West. What I wasn't taught was how to have a deep, abiding relationship with God.

# What Discipleship Can Be

Today much of Christian activity seems to originate with human plans, and it is then carried out in human strength, with human results. It has nothing to do with the kingdom of God. The world does not need any more religion! It needs Jesus Christ. Religion is people's attempts to do God's work in their own strength. Jesus wants us to live and walk in God's strength. God is only interested in His work, not our work. He oversees and empowers those things that originate in His heart. On judgment day, only that which was birthed and sustained by the Holy Spirit will survive.[1]

The Merriam-Webster online dictionary defines *humanism* as "a doctrine, attitude, or way of life centered on human interests or values; *especially*: a philosophy that usually rejects supernaturalism and stresses an individual's dignity and worth and capacity for self-realization through reason."[2] Most Western Bible-believing Christians are behaving as humanists. Yet most, if they are aware of humanism as a philosophy, would be offended by the idea that they are humanists. However, if we disdain the words yet still behave like humanists, we are humanists.

The basic issue of humanism is that humans make the decisions and cause things to happen by their own will and ability, using their own rational intellects. We may do this for the best of intentions, but since we started from the wrong place and are functioning with the wrong operating system, we end up in a very desperate situation. We are lost in the woods thinking we know where we are going. All the time we are moving farther and farther away from home, away from God.

We have brought this same humanism into discipleship. Hence we focus on such things as witnessing techniques, small-group dynamics, and biblical doctrine. None of these things are wrong, in and of themselves. The problem is the source of our accomplishment. We aren't asking some prior questions. Rather than asking what is a good technique of sharing the gospel, perhaps we should ask: Did God set up this witnessing situation? How is He leading us to share the gospel? Instead of asking how we can utilize good small-group dynamics to lead this group, perhaps we should ask how God is leading in the small group. Through whom does He want to minister? Instead of asking what doctrine this

Bible passage is teaching, perhaps we should ask how God is ministering
to us through the Bible. How is the Holy Spirit activating the truth of the
Bible into our lives though His power?

Real Christian spirituality is not merely about knowing doctrine,
becoming adept at techniques, and practicing disciplines such as Bible
study and scripture memorization. One can master everything the best
seminary has to offer and still live his life as a tacit humanist and still not
be connected to the lordship of Jesus. In fact, it's quite common.

Real Christian spirituality is about God's relationship with us and His
power working in us and through us. It will involve reading and studying
the Bible. It will involve prayer, and it will involve disciplines. But God
controls and leads the process. God will use more mature believers to
guide us in the process. He will use all our Christian community in the
process. But it will be done under His lordship and with His control. It
will be done in a new covenant way, as He ministers to us in the deepest
levels of our hearts and minds through His Holy Spirit. It will not merely
be a matter of our using our rational intellects and wills to affect change
in our lives.

Jesus had great knowledge of the Scriptures. Jesus knew His doctrine.
Jesus had Scriptures memorized; He quoted them. Yet He did only what
He saw the Father doing (John 5:19). He didn't participate in any ministry
unless He saw the Father already at work. He didn't act on His own voli-
tion. And Jesus was God in the flesh. If Jesus could do only what He saw
the Father doing, how can we think we can be any different?

What humanism stripped away from us was the tendency to look to
God instead of ourselves. It is not that God has lost contact with us, but
rather that humanistic Christendom teaches us to rely on our own abilities. He may be in contact with us, but we aren't paying attention. We
are not seeking Him as the source of the solutions to our problems. We
keep trying to handle them ourselves. And this humanistic Christendom
affects everything we do as Christians—the way we think, the way we
meet together, the way we structure "leadership," the way we do ministry, the way we behave. And it affects the way we do discipleship. We
have become enslaved to the *stoicheia*, the foundational principles
of this world. But we are so used to it, that we can't see what is actually happening before our very eyes. We see with our eyes, but we don't

understand with our hearts (Matt. 13:15). It is so comfortable and normal that we don't even think to question this worldview and the behaviors of Christendom that it generates.

So what does discipleship look like when God is leading the process? What roles do other people play in this? What kinds of behaviors, practices, and disciplines do we need to learn in order to live with Jesus as our Lord? How can we learn to cooperate with God's leadership in community so that we can stir each other to love and good works?

This kind of discipleship is not only possible; it is also powerful and satisfying. It connects us with Jesus and teaches us how to live in His supernatural power and with a deep, abiding, fulfilling relationship with Him. This kind of discipleship leads us to become individuals and communities committed to seeing God's will done on earth and with the power to see it through to completion. In other words, it is the kind of discipleship we need if we are to see a viral movement of the Spirit once again in the West. And it will look much like what our Chinese brothers are doing in China. But if we are to experience this, we have to completely rethink what we have come to know as discipleship. We will need to learn to live in a different way than our Western humanistic Christendom has taught us to think, live, and behave.

## Discipleship With a Different Operating System

The worldview, the operating system of biblical Christianity, is different. It is the new covenant. In the new covenant we do what God Himself puts in our hearts and minds. It is centered on God's interests and values. It stresses the dignity, worth, capacity and reason of God without denying human dignity, worth, capacity, and reason as part of God's image in men. It stresses the capacity of God to bring things to pass, not human realization. It stresses God's knowledge, wisdom and intelligence, not man's. His ways are not our ways. Yet He is willing to use us.

Therefore discipleship with Jesus as Lord doesn't stress how to do good things using our human ability; it stresses how to access God's power through the new covenant operating system. It will stress how to learn to listen to God. Bible study stops being merely reading the Bible to know facts about the Bible, although the reader may indeed learn facts. It becomes reading the Bible to also hear the voice of God and obey.

Discipling someone in prayer becomes a more mature Christian teaching a less mature Christian that prayer is a vital part of a multifaceted two-way communication with God. One prays to relationally connect with God. One prays to pour out their hearts' desire to God. One prays to worship and give thanks, to confess sin and express repentance. But one also prays as part of their abiding alignment with God, to hear His voice in the heart and mind so that they can obey God's will for that life. This is done both individually and in community.

Discipling someone in any aspect of Christianity, from sharing the faith, to giving, to training in the growth of spiritual gifts, becomes teaching them to follow God's activity in the heart and mind of the believer, while still remaining deeply connected to a community; all under Christ who is the Head of the church. All of this is both possible and practical because the Holy Spirit of God lives in us. That reality is part of our new covenant heritage. The new covenant then goes far beyond being a correct propositional doctrine. It is a way of life in which believers need to learn how to live effectively. That is a major part of the discipleship process.

## Discipleship With a Different Focus

The discipleship I grew up with was strongly focused on Bible facts and doctrinal facts. I'm not against either one of these things. They are good; they just can't change lives. In a sense they are penultimate goals. We need these things, but we can't stop there. And I believe we can't truly understand the fullness of either the Bible or correct doctrine without the Holy Spirit's help.

We are focused on these propositional issues because we have been trapped by the Platonic philosophical underpinnings of our Western worldview. By that I mean that Plato and Platonic philosophy, which is one of the foundations of our worldview, taught that the most important thing was the "ideal." To put it simply, what counts is the idea, the concept. Human reason can be used by humans to find out all that counts in life. And what is important can be expressed conceptually. Once that is done the game is over.

What are Christian ideas? They are biblical doctrines and facts. They are the propositional truths of the Bible. Again, these aren't bad things. But because we are stuck looking at the Bible and Christian life through the wrong lens, the Western worldview, we get stuck on these things because our worldview tells us that they are what really count. In essence we are stuck in James 2:19: "You believe that there is one God. Good! Even the demons believe that—and shudder." While the truth that God is one is important and good, it isn't enough. We need changed lives, and that is accomplished by the power of the Holy Spirit controlling our lives.

Discipleship with Jesus as Lord will not aim for mere correct doctrine. Rather correct doctrine is an underpinning, not a focus, of this type of discipleship. The assumption of our Western humanistic discipleship has been if our doctrine is correct, we will have a correct relationship with God. This is patently false. I know more than a few people who hold orthodox doctrine and live ungodly lives. You probably know a few too. Instead, we need to learn to access the Holy Spirit's power and leading in our lives, learn to discern what He puts in our hearts and minds, and obey in His power. When we do this, we will live changed lives.

Part of the discerning process is reflecting on our lives individually and in community, through the lens of the Bible and correct doctrine. And any behavior that comes out of the Holy Spirit's leading will reflect the Bible and correct doctrine. But the power for a changed life and the direction for that change come from the Holy Spirit Himself. Therefore, the focus of discipleship with Jesus as Lord is a changed life and action directed and empowered by Holy Spirit.

## Discipleship With a Different Process

If Jesus is truly Lord, He ought to lead the discipleship process. In fact, we are not the disciples of other people, according to the Bible, we are Jesus's disciples. Often, in church as we know it, we tend to get this wrong. I know a number of people who are so firmly entrenched in the theology of John Calvin or John Wesley that everything they believe is formulated through that lens. Personally, I think that is very unhealthy. I know of many believers who are more followers of Joel Osteen, John MacArthur, or Kenneth Copeland than they are of Jesus Christ. And it is not uncommon for one-on-one discipleship to be focused on what the discipler wants the protégée to learn. In other words, the discipler is leading the process. This results in people who are not the disciples of Jesus but the disciples of another person.

Jesus is perfectly capable of speaking with us. It is part of our new covenant birthright. Jesus the Lord is perfectly capable of leading the discipleship process. He may choose to do part of this through other believers, but He doesn't need us to control or determine the process.

The Roman Catholics have developed healthy practices in allowing Jesus to disciple other believers. (The Roman Catholic Church is a huge and diverse institution. It is the most exaggerated expression of Christendom. Yet it has many faithful believers in love with Jesus and loved by Jesus. Their understanding of spiritual direction, as a way of Jesus-centered discipleship, is an area where Protestants of every stripe can and are learning healthy practices from them.) They have become adept at humans learning to help other believers, while still letting Jesus control the process. Over the centuries a discipleship discipline called spiritual direction has been developed which allows for just that. (The term "spiritual direction" sounds like the director is dominating. This is not the case. Think of it as directing them to notice the voice of the Spirit.)

> As we have come to understand it, spiritual direction differs from moral guidance, psychological counseling, and the practice of confessional, preaching or healing ministries (though having affinities with them) in that it directly assists individuals in developing and cultivating their personal relationship with God.[3]

This is far different from what we have come to know as discipleship, in which the main emphasis is on information download. In fact, Barry and Connolly go on to state: "The focus of this type of spiritual direction is on experience, not ideas, and specifically on religious experience, i.e., any experience of the mysterious Other whom we call God."[4]

What would this look like? For many who have been spiritually formed in a Western Christianity that focuses on information, this may be a bit hard to picture. Here is how the authors describe the process.

The ministering person helps the other to address God directly and to listen to what God has to communicate. The focus of this kind of spiritual direction is the relationship itself between God and the person. The person is helped not so much to understand that relationship better, but to engage in it, to enter into dialogue with God. Spiritual direction of this kind focuses on what happens when a person listens to and responds to a self-communicating God.[5]

God is actually leading this process. The spiritual director is only assisting another person in learning to listen to what God is communicating. Further, he is helping the disciple to engage in this divine relationship and respond to it. This is a form of discipleship that is God-focused, not information-focused. People are involved, but God is really controlling the process. He is determining what is being communicated and how.

Further, this is a kind of discipleship that focuses on response to God's communication. If done well, it leads to the disciple's learning not only to hear God but also to engage in a supernatural relationship with Him and respond in obedience to Him. That is a form of discipleship that recognizes Jesus as Lord and fully engages with a God who speaks to our hearts and minds. It allows us to truly become Jesus's disciples, not men's. Jesus said, "If you love me, you will obey what I command. And I will ask the Father, and he will give you another Counselor to be with you forever—the Spirit of truth" (John 14:15–17). When Jesus said those who love Him keep His commandments He wasn't talking merely about keeping the written propositional truths of the Bible. He was talking about what He speaks into our hearts and minds. This passage was given in the context of prayer, and part of the promise that Jesus gives us is that He will give us the Holy Spirit to guide us. This is communication with the triune God that leads to obedience. In the same discourse Jesus said:

> If anyone loves me, he will obey my teaching. My Father will love him, and we will come to him and make our home with him. He who does not love me will not obey my teaching. These words you hear are not my own; they belong to the Father who sent me.
> —JOHN 14:23–24

I don't think we need to copy spiritual direction as some sort of technique as if the power is in the technique itself. Rather, our Catholic brothers have learned how to help fellow Christians engage with Jesus the Lord and obey Him. We shouldn't focus on the technique any more than spiritual directors focus on mere understanding of the relationship itself. The focus is on actually engaging with God and responding, not on the process. Having said this, I do think the Catholics have much to teach us in this kind of discipleship. I believe we would be well served to study with them. They are very open to training non-Catholics in spiritual direction. It would also be helpful for those interested in learning how to disciple like this to be directed themselves.

If Jesus is leading the discipleship process we should also learn to pay attention to what is going on in the disciple's life. Often we tend to be more concerned with cleaning up the new disciple's life, with making them more fit for our subculture. This is a mistake. I'd much rather try to help someone who is rough around the edges engage with God than train someone how to fit into a squeaky-clean subculture. God is interested in holiness, but He works at His own pace. He chooses the issues He wants to deal with. When we take over, we end up discipling people in how to clean up the outside of the cup and not really deal with the filth inside. We are training them to become hypocrites. Only the Holy Spirit can really change a life. We need to learn to let the Counselor do what the Counselor is good at.

## Discipleship With a Different End Point

The end point then in this type of discipleship is changed lives that lead to obedience. The Holy Spirit does the changing. The Holy Spirit leads the process. Someone who engages with God will start to become like God in character. As the Holy Spirit takes control of his life, he will start to express the character of the One who is in control of his spirit: love, joy, peace, patience, kindness, goodness, faithfulness, gentleness, and self-control. This movement from what we are to what God wants us to become can be quite turbulent. I don't think we should be shocked by the turbulence. I doubt God is.

When the Holy Spirit gains control of a life, the life changes to reflect the character of the Spirit. In that sense, true godly Christians are all similar. We all become "little Christs," which is what the term *Christian* means. We become Christlike. However, at the same time God also begins to direct an individual to conform to His special will for that person. This will probably reflect the person's spiritual giftedness. It might reflect other aspects of their human development, such as education, training, personality, experience, and the like. The issue here is that God has designed this person to follow Him into His kingdom purposes. That design will be unique. Jesus taught His disciples to pray "your kingdom come, your will be done on earth as it is in heaven" (Matt. 6:10). Each of us is designed to be part of the coming of God's kingdom, of being part of His will being done on earth. That is part of the joy and privilege of being a Christian, to participate with God, under His direction, in changing His world for the better. So the more each individual matures in God-directed discipleship, the more he reflects the character of Jesus. At the same time the more he participates in this process the more he becomes a unique individual, with unique kingdom purposes and a unique divine calling.

Much of church, as we have come to know it, has focused on the church experience itself and what it supposedly does for those who participate. We are saying with our behavior that this is all about us. We want to experience worship. We want to have fellowship. We want our needs met. We want to be fed. That's nonsense. If God is leading the process, it will be about Him—and it should be. He is the Creator and King of the universe. When He leads the discipleship process, it will lead to holiness and His kingdom purposes. It will not be man-focused; it will be God- and kingdom-focused. If it is not, it is spiritually unhealthy. The end point of discipleship with Jesus as Lord is Jesus manifesting Himself in the lives of believers and Jesus the King leading them to participate with Him in His purposes. That truly is "your kingdom come, your will be done on earth as it is in heaven."

## Discipleship With a Different Structure

To this point our discussion of discipleship has been primarily focused on individual discipleship. However, in reality, discipleship is also a community affair. When we read about the body of Christ in 1 Corinthians 12 we are seeing Christ, the head of the body, leading His body. We are seeing each individual member of that body expressing his giftedness, in the power of the Holy Spirit, for the mutual benefit of the entire body. In other words, we are seeing Christ direct His body to minister to one another in His power. This is community discipleship. Christ is ministering to the gathered individuals through the other individuals. He is guiding. He is directing. He is controlling.

So, just as individual discipleship leads people to engage with God and allow the Holy Spirit to lead them to growth and kingdom purposes, the body gathered will result in the same things for the entire community. And the entire community will be involved in the process. This will lead to the body's engaging in kingdom purposes as a community. We should be highly dubious of groups that meet and feel that they are blessed but never move outside themselves to see others come to Christ, to see God's love of justice and His compassion expressed to the least of these.

As was described in the previous chapter, this does not require human-planned lessons and agenda. It requires learning to let Jesus lead. It also requires that each individual member of the body have an individual relationship with God based on loving obedience. When this is the case, each person is engaging with God individually and has something to offer the body gathered. However, just as the individual seeks to engage in relationship with God and obey what He commands, so does the body gathered.

## Discipleship With a Different Leadership

As should be obvious from what has been said above, discipleship with Jesus as Lord has Jesus as the leader. He is the power source; the new covenant that was sealed with His blood is the operating system. He is the focus, He controls the process, and His holiness and kingdom purposes are the end point. He will use more mature believers who are further along in this process to help direct younger believers to Him, but He is the only real leader.

Actually this has to do with the priesthood of all believers. There are really two basic functions of priests in the Old Testament Law. Priests performed religious duties in the temple. Through those duties, they connected the people with God. In addition, on Yom Kippur, the Day of Atonement, the high priest made the atoning sacrifice that symbolized God's forgiveness for another year. First Peter 2:9 says, "But you are a chosen people, a royal priesthood, a holy nation, a people belonging to God, that you may declare the praises of him who called you out of darkness into his wonderful light." Peter was saying that we all can participate in spiritual duties; we all can minister. We don't need special people, now commonly called clergy, to connect us with God.

We all minister to one another under the power and direction of our head. In that sense we are all leaders when Jesus leads others through us. But it all comes from our Lord. He is our only true leader. There is a special recognition of the maturity some Christians demonstrate. More mature believers, called elders, watch over the less mature and help guide them to Jesus. This is not positional leadership with specific power. It is just recognition of proven spirituality and maturity. It is honored, but such a person always guides people to Jesus Himself.

## Discipleship With No Techniques or Methods

Our Western Christendom, captured as it is by the foundational principles of this world, puts great stock in techniques and methods. This is yet again our Platonic fascination with ideas, methods, and anything else humans can control. It is one more example of not really living with Jesus as Lord. Jesus doesn't need techniques and methods. He knows what is right in every single case, based on the people, cultures, and situations involved.

Having said this, I realize God may give specific individuals or groups certain techniques or methods to use. He may guide them to use them under His direction. And He may guide other believers to use these methods as well. A good example of this is LTGs, or life-transformation groups. God has given Neil Cole and many in the networks he and his friends have started a way to simply teach new believers how to read the Bible, pray for the lost, and be accountable to one another, confessing their sins to one another. All of these things are good ideas. I believe that God directed Neil and his friends to this. I also believe that God uses this beyond the confines of those directly involved with Church Multiplication Associates, the group that developed this methodology. God is using this. But the power isn't in the technique itself; it comes from God's directing people to do this. A group of two or three people can go through the motions of doing an LTG with no particular benefit if it isn't God directed. And there are many other ways God could direct people to spiritually healthy relationships. The power comes from God Himself. Spiritual growth happens when we obey God.

## An Example of This Type of Discipleship

Two of my friends, Ed and Jason, are gifted evangelists. However, Ed is older and more experienced. Ed and Jason have developed a discipleship relationship in their mutual area of giftedness. Their communication takes place both through face-to-face interaction and by e-mail. Here is an excerpt from an e-mail Jason wrote to me describing how this discipling friendship has taken place.

> I remember distinctly my first interaction with Ed about a year and a half ago. My friend Mike introduced me to him as someone gifted in the evangelism area as well. One of the first questions he asked me was this: "What is the gift of evangelism for?" I paused. My instinctive response was, "For the lost." Then Ed gently pointed me back to the Scriptures in Ephesians 4: "to equip the saints."
>
> Right there, my whole paradigm on how the APEST gifts work was refocused and refined. *[APEST refers to the five gifts mentioned in Ephesians 4:11: apostle, prophet, evangelist, shepherd (or pastor), and teacher.]* It wasn't just that God had equipped me to be a proclaimer of the gospel to those who do not yet know Jesus. That was definitely important, but a larger part of the reason that God gifts certain parts of the body with gifts is for multiplication. My gifting as an evangelist is to build into the church to equip more evangelists. That doesn't mean I stop doing what I do personally, but it does mean that, like 2 Timothy 2:2, I am to equip others who will build further into others.
>
> A few months later, when I stepped into a church-planting phase of my life, I created some goals. One of the goals was to

grow in the evangelistic gifting. With that goal, I fashioned some action steps, one of which was to have an ongoing conversation with someone who was a little further along in the E gifting than I. Even in creating that action step, I had Ed in mind as someone who challenged me and someone who was further along than me both in life's seasons and in wisdom in this area. So I e-mailed him to see if he'd be up for it, and he graciously accepted.

I started with a series of questions that were rolling around in my head about evangelism in general. Much of my view on evangelism focused on reshaping some of the preconceptions I had regarding it being programmatic or formulaic. How do I prevent evangelism from becoming a "project"? How do I communicate relevantly without watering down the gospel? How do I say the right thing?

Three principles through this entire process have really shaped how I think, and the way that he stated them in his e-mails— gentle, yet direct, and always founded on the Scriptures—was immensely helpful to me. Along those lines, he was always ready to challenge even my assumptions or preconceptions in my questions, and not worried about pushing me at all. It never felt forced, but always full of grace.

The three principles that are still in my head and heart:

1. We are compelled by the love of Christ (2 Cor. 5:14).

2. Evangelism is about obedience, not techniques.

3. We serve Jesus, not the world.

This is discipleship with a different operating system. Ed has utter confidence in the Holy Spirit's ability to speak to Jason and to him. He believes the new covenant is in effect, not merely as a propositional truth but as something on which we can base our behavior. With this in mind, Ed shares what God has given him as life lessons. He undoubtedly listens to what God would have him give Jason specifically and he has confidence in Jason to ask good questions. This is confidence that the Holy Spirit can speak into the hearts and minds of believers.

This is discipleship with a different focus. Ed and Jason discuss the Bible and biblical principles, but the focus is on Jesus and what Jesus is doing. The Bible is an important resource the Holy Spirit can and will use, but the focus is on Jesus the living Word, not merely the written Word.

This is discipleship with a different process. Jason is not Ed's disciple. He is Jesus's disciple. However, Jesus is using Ed to disciple Jason. Jesus is in control of the process. Ed has the confidence in Jesus that he can wait for Jason to ask questions, for the Holy Spirit to develop divine curiosity in Jason's heart. Ed does not need to control, nor does he need to dominate. He just needs to obey Jesus and encourage Jason to do the same.

Jason's life is being changed by this process. That is because it is discipleship with a different end point. Jesus isn't using Ed merely to download new information or principles. Jesus wants Jason to be a new man, one who is continuing to be conformed to the character of Jesus.

Note that Jason met Ed through his friend Mike. Mike, who also has a mutual discipleship relationship with Jason, had the wisdom to know that Ed would be a great resource for Jason to grow in his spiritual gift of evangelism. Mike wasn't trying to control the process. In fact, Mike understood that real discipleship is a community affair. In this case, the best thing he could do was introduce Jason to Ed, who could help him develop in his spiritual gift. This openness allows for discipleship with a different structure, not one based on hierarchical organization but one based on the organic configuration of the body of Christ.

Jesus is the leader in this type of discipleship. He is the head of the church, and He is Jason's Lord. Jason does need more mature people in his life who can lead him closer to Jesus. In fact, one could say that Ed is acting as a spiritual father to Jason. This reflects what John said about fathers in 1 John 2:12–14. It also reflects Paul's relationship with Timothy in 2 Timothy 2:2. Paul, a spiritual father, teaches Timothy, a young man, in such a way that Timothy could give what he is learning to others, who in turn could pass it on. While Ed is a spiritual father to Jason, he is acting as such under the ultimate leadership of Jesus Himself.

Ed made sure Jason understood that evangelism is about obedience, not techniques. In doing so he not only taught him about good evangelism; he also tacitly taught him about good discipleship. Discipleship, like evangelism and all other aspects of our faith, is not about techniques or methods; it is about following Jesus.

Finally note that Ed is training Jason in a mutual area of giftedness. In doing so Ed is not only equipping the body for the work of service (Eph. 4:12) but also demonstrating the organic nature of the church. Everything can reproduce according to its kind. Ed, an evangelist, is reproducing another evangelist. Elders can reproduce elders. Churches can reproduce churches. Christians can reproduce Christians. Everything is reproduced according to its kind.

## Viral Discipleship

This kind of discipleship can spread from person to person like a virus. In fact, what is actually being spread is Jesus Himself. Anyone who has been discipled like this can also disciple others in the same way. This is the discipleship we see modeled in China. Wherever and whenever Christians meet, they minister to one another. It is both one-on-one discipleship and discipleship in small communities. It doesn't necessarily need to be planned or programmed, although it can be scheduled, if that is best. It doesn't need to be formalized; it just needs to be led by Jesus and lead others to Jesus. Whatever a Christian has—experience, stories, Bible knowledge, songs, encouragement, prophecy, prayer, teaching—can be given to others. All these things can direct another disciple of Jesus toward Jesus. This is as simple and uncomplicated as sneezing, yet it is as profound as Jesus Himself.

## Conclusion

We are disciples of Christ. Jesus is Lord. We belong to Him. We should be in a deep, abiding relationship with Him. That kind of relationship is characterized by loving obedience. It is possible because of the new-covenant relationship we have with the triune God and because Jesus sent His Spirit, who can speak into our hearts and minds, to be our Counselor.

However, the way to live consistently in a deep, obedient, abiding relationship with Christ our Lord has to be learned. For that we need each other in community. We also need the guidance of more mature believers. These believers don't decide for us what we are to learn; they help guide us to the lordship and direction of Jesus Himself. They push us toward Jesus; they don't step between Jesus and us. To do so would be to play the role of priest. We are all priests in that we have a direct connection with God. Yet we have only one High Priest, and His name is Jesus. Viral discipleship will lead us into an ever-maturing and obedient relationship with Jesus Himself. That will end up having a profound impact on our lives and the world around us.

## CHAPTER 9

# Viral Church Planting

OR MUCH OF my Christian life, I viewed the life and ministry of Jesus as something out of the ordinary. Frankly, the things He did seemed out of my grasp. They were certainly not like anything I saw my contemporaries do. It wasn't anything like what I was being taught to do. It never occurred to me that Jesus was modeling exactly what He wanted me to do. It also never occurred to me to look at what He taught His disciples, to see how they responded to His teaching and compare this with what I was doing. If I thought about it at all, I would have probably said, "That was then; this is now." I probably also would have noted that Jesus happened to be God and I wasn't. Therefore, how could my ministry look anything like His? Frankly I think many of us are like Philip.

> Don't you know me, Philip, even after I have been among you such a long time? Anyone who has seen me has seen the Father. How can you say, "Show us the Father"? Don't you believe that I am in the Father, and that the Father is in me? The words I say to you are not just my own. Rather, it is the Father, living in me, who is doing his work. Believe me when I say that I am in the Father and the Father is in me; or at least believe on the evidence of the

miracles themselves. I tell you the truth, anyone who has faith in me will do what I have been doing. He will do even greater things than these, because I am going to the Father. And I will do whatever you ask in my name, so that the Son may bring glory to the Father. You may ask me for anything in my name, and I will do it.

—John 14:9–14

Because Jesus abided in the Father and it played out in the things He did, Philip was expected to believe that anyone who had faith in Jesus would do what Jesus did. In fact they will do even greater things. Is this a pile of religious rhetoric? Was Jesus blowing smoke? Or are we missing something? It sounds to me as if Jesus is saying live like I live, do what I do, and you'll get the same results I get, maybe even better.

The truth is that the early disciples did pretty much the same thing Jesus did, and they got the same results. The same patterns play themselves out in the ministries of Paul, Barnabas, Silas, and Timothy. Of course we can try to take the easy way out and say that this was a time of supernatural power that no longer exists. However, after extensive historical, philosophical, and hermeneutical review of this doctrine, I can no longer buy that argument. (After the aforementioned review I've come to believe that "cessationism," as this doctrine is called, is nothing more than forcing the humanistic Enlightenment worldview onto our own current lifestyle, while turning the Bible into something akin to how some ancient Greeks viewed their own religious myths; both literally true but currently unlivable. For a synopsis of my thoughts on cessationism, see Appendix A.) I am forced to come to the conclusion that Jesus modeled a very specific style of ministry to His disciples. He trained them in how to do it. He called them apostles (sent ones), then sent them out to do the very things He had modeled for them. After Pentecost we see the same pattern playing out over and over again in the pages of the New Testament.

And once one becomes sensitized to the new covenant and the Christian pledge of allegiance (Jesus is Lord) one realizes that the pattern Jesus taught is new covenant and the pledge of allegiance played out in apostolic ministry. This is the same pattern that His original disciples practiced and taught and the same pattern that we see playing itself out in the ministry of the apostle Paul and his associates. It is ministry that takes for granted that God can speak to our hearts and minds. It is ministry practice that reflects that Jesus and Jesus alone is Lord. Is there any reason why we shouldn't be doing these same things today?

You never get an answer to a question you don't ask. So let me ask some questions. Is there a general pattern to ministry that is reflected in Jesus's ministry? Can we see Jesus intentionally teaching His disciples this same pattern? Do we see these patterns playing themselves out in subsequent generations of apostolic ministry? I believe the answer to all these questions is yes. Is this a common pattern in ministry today? The answer to that question is yes and no. Yes, it is common in places where we see viral movements of the gospel such as in China. No, it is not the least bit common in the West, where we don't see a viral movement of the gospel. I don't think that is a coincidence. But I do think it is an indictment of just how disobedient we have become in the West without realizing it.

# The General Pattern As Seen in Luke 10

The general pattern I'm talking about is most clearly laid out in the teaching of Jesus as He sends out the seventy-two in Luke 10:1–23. However, this passage doesn't record the first time Jesus taught His followers this pattern. We have three explicit examples of it as He taught His original twelve how to do ministry in Matthew 10:1–16; Mark 6:7–12; and Luke 9:1–9. (I suspect that the seventy-two were the results of the original twelve's apostolic ministry. We see a progression from Jesus's modeling this pattern to His teaching the twelve to participate in the same pattern in Luke 9. Finally, we see Jesus sending out the seventy-two after the twelve's ministry in Luke 9. This sending of the seventy-two is the first thing mentioned in Luke 10:1.) We also see Jesus modeling this behavior before He taught His disciples to practice it themselves. Obviously this style of ministry is very important to Jesus. For clarity we are going to use the Luke 10 passage as our guide to ministry, Jesus style.

### The prerequisite

It needs to be noted that even the ability to participate in this pattern requires an abiding relationship with Jesus that reflects His abiding relationship with His Father. Jesus Himself did only what He saw the

Father doing. Jesus gave them this answer: "I tell you the truth, the Son can do nothing by himself; he can do only what he sees his Father doing, because whatever the Father does the Son also does. For the Father loves the Son and shows him all he does" (John 5:19–20).

If we are to participate in the general ministry pattern that Jesus taught the twelve and the seventy-two, our first realization must be that we have to do it just as Jesus did. The power is not in the pattern itself. The power comes from Jesus. The power comes from obediently following what we see Jesus, the Lord of the harvest, doing just as He Himself did only what He saw the Father doing. Just as Jesus was totally dependent on His Father, we are totally dependent on Him. We cannot mechanically follow the Luke 10 pattern as if it is a cookie cutter to ministry effectiveness. We need to participate in what Jesus is already doing. Otherwise we may be following the right pattern in the wrong power; the power of the flesh. Jesus is Lord. This is Christian pledge of allegiance ministry. Jesus is Lord; we are not. And in order to do what Jesus is already doing, we must have an abiding relationship with Him. We must hear Him as He speaks His ministry direction in our hearts and minds. This, therefore, is also new covenant ministry.

I am deeply concerned by what I am seeing, as this pattern is beginning to get on the radar screen of those of us in the West. Some have embraced this as if the power were in the pattern itself, as if it were some sort of Jesus technique.

Others are embracing not only the pattern but also the particular application of the pattern God has given to one of His present-day servants, as if the real power is not in Jesus but in the technical application of the pattern that God gave to these individuals. If we follow these "twelve steps" along with these "five principles," as taught by so and so, we will have ministry success.

Who is the Lord of the harvest? Is it Jesus or His servants? I believe that Jesus gives ministry success to a person or team because they are obedient, not because they have great techniques. Jesus may use insights from the techniques He gives them to lead us. There is nothing wrong with that. But the insight is coming from Jesus and the power will come from Jesus, not the technique. We can do everything technically right; but if we aren't obeying the Lord of the harvest, we shouldn't expect much fruit. And some are getting disappointed because "it isn't working." The "it" they are talking about is some technique or set of techniques.

## The Lord of the harvest sends (Luke 10:1)

"After this the Lord appointed seventy-two others and sent them two by two ahead of him to every town and place where He was about to go" (Luke 10:1). Jesus is doing the appointing. This is ministry in which only those who are appointed by Jesus can participate. Volunteers need not apply. We do not get to decide to do this on our own. People who participate in this type of ministry are appointed to it. In fact they are sent. A sent one is an apostle. This is apostolic ministry.

I like to use the metaphor of apostles as sodbusters. The sodbusters were the pioneers who plowed the soil of a homestead for the first time. In the same way, apostles open new territory, virgin territory. They establish churches where the church hasn't been before, or among a group of people who have yet to hear the gospel. They also plant churches where Christendom has become both endemic and ineffective, as in the West. In places such as the West, if we are to again see a movement of the gospel, we can't expect to keep doing the same old ineffective behaviors, get the same anemic results, and expect a movement of the Spirit. So God sends in new apostles to plant a harvest in a long-neglected and abused garden.

Some of those committed to Christendom feel this is an invasion of their territory. They would ask, "Can't these people work within already established churches?" The answer is, not if we want to see a viral movement of the gospel among the lost. There is more than enough kingdom work for all of us. Apostles need to do the work they are designed for. Apostolic work focuses on building the foundation of the kingdom among those who don't already know Christ.

## Apostles tend to work in teams (Luke 10:1)

New Testament apostles tended to work in teams. When Jesus sent out the twelve in Matthew 10 he didn't send out twelve individuals. He didn't call Peter, Andrew, James, John, Philip, Bartholomew.... He called Simon *and* Andrew, James *and* John, Philip *and* Bartholomew, Thomas *and* Matthew.... Just as He later sent out the seventy-two in Luke 10, Jesus sent out the twelve in groups of two.

One of the first things Jesus did in His own ministry was gather a team around Him. Certainly this was so that His work would carry on after the end of His earthly ministry. But I think it also reflects that even Jesus didn't minister as a lone wolf. He worked in a team and He sent out teams. Jesus modeled everything He taught.

The smallest apostolic team is a team of two: Paul and Barnabas, Paul and Silas, or Peter and Andrew. It is not unusual for more experienced apostles to take less experienced apostles with them to teach them the ropes in the real and unpredictable context of ministry. This is evidenced in the ministry of Paul and Barnabas. Barnabas was originally the more experienced apostle. Later we see Paul take a more up-front role. But we don't see Paul and Barnabas fighting over position. They both did what needed to be done without focusing on personal prestige. They both displayed humility about prestige and apparent human leadership in their general relationship together. I believe they both knew that Jesus was the real Lord and the issue was obedience, not human admiration.

When more experienced apostles take less experienced apostles for on-the-job training, all of them should display humility, following Jesus, who is the only true leader of the church. Yet practical experience should be recognized and respected, as John points out regarding the fathers, young men, and children in 1 John 2. (This is not gender specific; I'm just using biblical vocabulary. Women can be apostles, as was Junia, part of an apostolic team of Andronicus and Junia in Romans 16:7. Some have wrongly rendered her name in the masculine "Junias" to avoid dealing with the idea of female apostles. There is not a good textual reason to do so, nor was this gender change in the text done until the Middle Ages. I know a number of female apostles today. The issue is who Jesus sends, not what gender they happen to be.) Experienced apostles teach younger people how to follow Jesus into the harvest.

The issue here is that apostles reproduce themselves. They do so by taking less experienced people into ministry with them. This reflects how Jesus trained others for ministry in the Gospels. We can see this apostolic passing of the baton in Paul (trained and influenced by Barnabas), who trained Silas, both of whom worked with Timothy, who later worked in the team of Silas and Timothy. In 2 Timothy 2:2, Timothy, who was trained by Paul, is exhorted to train faithful men who can train others.

All of these are wonderful examples of apostles reproducing apostles who reflect the organic nature of the church. In the organic world, everything reproduces after its kind. It is part of God's design.

## The harvest is plentiful (Luke 10:2)

I had the privilege of being part of a small but explosive movement of the gospel in Spain in 2005. About 1 in 500 people in Spain would consider themselves evangelical Christians. Spain is very rocky ground for the gospel. It makes most places in the West, including much of Western Europe, look like the Bible Belt. It is one of the most unreached places in the world, outside the Muslim region. Yet when God called us to apostolic ministry there, and we obeyed, there was a plentiful harvest even in rocky Spain.

The problem is not the harvest. It is plentiful. The problem is human obedience. We want to live with our idols. We want to plant simple churches, as long as we can put our denominations' name on them; otherwise we won't fund the project. We want to plant simple churches, as long as we can be financially supported by them or don't have to raise support, or only if we are guaranteed a certain standard of living or a compensation and retirement package. We will plant simple churches as long as we can maintain the business-based structure of our mission. (For those who are unfamiliar with this term of *church planting*, it means to initiate or establish churches, preferably among previous non-Christians. It is a good organic metaphor, but it is not a biblical term.)

The other option to all of this is we can proclaim Jesus is Lord and do what He says in utter obedience. If He wants to plant churches through a traditional missions structure, that's His business. He is Lord. If He calls people out of that structure, that's His business too. What we don't want to do is blame the field for the lack of harvest.

## Being lambs among wolves (Luke 10:3)

Jesus's statement in Luke 10 that He sends us out as lambs among wolves strikes many as odd. Why would He say that? What is His point? However, once we view church planting as new covenant ministry, which reflects our pledge of allegiance to Jesus our Lord, it makes perfect sense. Vulnerable lambs, living among wolves, had better know where their Shepherd is. They must know His voice. They need to know when it is their Shepherd speaking into their hearts and minds and not some other voice—the voice of the world, the flesh, or the devil.

A sheep in wolf country had better not decide that he is lord. That is a great way to be a lamb cutlet dinner for a hungry wolf. Sheep are great followers, but they are terrible leaders. Yet our twenty-first-century Western ministry practice more commonly reflects sheep as leaders and the Shepherd as a follower. I think we have things terribly backward. We make sheep decisions, based on sheep parameters and sheep paradigms, and wonder why we don't get the same results as Jesus and His immediate followers. They understood that they were sheep in wolf territory and lived like it.

## Working without a purse or bag or sandals (Luke 10:4)

> The first question anyone should face who believes himself truly called of God is the financial question. If he cannot look to the Lord alone for the meeting of his daily wants, then he is not qualified to be engaged in His work, for if he is not financially independent of men, the work cannot be independent of men either. If he cannot trust God for the supply of needed funds, can he trust Him in all the problems and difficulties of the work? If we are utterly dependent on God for our supplies, then we are responsible to Him alone for our work, and in that case it need not come under human direction. May I advise all who are not prepared for the walk of faith, to continue with their secular duties and not engage in spiritual service. Every worker for God must be able to trust Him.[1]

Watchman Nee addresses a very important but very touchy issue, the issue of finances. Jesus explicitly addressed the same issue. Both Jesus and Nee make the same point, supply of money (the purse) and daily needs (the bag and sandals) are supplied by God, not by men.

Nee also points out why this is such an important issue, because it is really an issue of control. Who is in control of the ministry, God or men? In new covenant ministry that functions within the pledge of allegiance to Jesus the Lord, we should be able to trust God to supply and therefore be free to live only under His control. As Nee points out in another place,

"Further, he who holds the purse holds authority. If we are supported by men, our work will be controlled by men."[2]

This is an issue of dependence. We need to be utterly dependent on the Lord, living a supernatural life of faith where Jesus supplies. Can it be nerve-racking? Absolutely. But it is also supernatural, so we get to see God supply in supernatural ways.

It is not mine to judge how God will do this. Does He call some as tent makers, who hold some sort of job so they can be financially free to minister? Yes, He does this, and I know a number of apostles who live just this way. It is God's calling on their lives. Will He lead others to live by utter faith, expecting God to supply supernaturally? Yes, I know others who have this call. Will He have some who live by faith and yet have a spouse with a secular job? A number of other apostles I know live like this. The issue is that Jesus the Lord determines what this looks like.

However, I have strong reservations, as does Nee, about those who are focused on humanly provided and controlled financial security. Jesus told us to go without a purse or bag or sandals. If we are not willing to do so, perhaps we have either misread our call or are not willing to completely follow it in utter obedience. If we can't go without the security of a 401(k) plan or a retirement package, we are probably not ready for apostolic work.

Jesus's instructions do not stop here though. Just before His arrest He talked to His disciples.

> Then Jesus asked them, "When I sent you without purse, bag or sandals, did you lack anything?"
>
> "Nothing," they answered.
>
> He said to them, "But now if you have a purse, take it, and also a bag; and if you don't have a sword, sell your cloak and buy one. It is written: 'And he was numbered with the transgressors'; and I tell you that this must be fulfilled in me. Yes, what is written about me is reaching its fulfillment."
>
> —Luke 22:35–37

Is Jesus talking out of both sides of His mouth? I don't think so. I believe what He is really saying is that provision is provided by God. We need to trust Him to give us what we need. His way of doing this can change over time. However, the real dangers of finance are control and a sense of financial security provided by men. If finances come with strings attached, so that humans make decisions rather than God, we are on very dangerous ground. It is much better to do without than to depend on seeming financial security that requires our putting Jesus in second place. We need to be willing to be obedient, radically so.

### Do not greet anyone on the road (Luke 10:4)

Here is another strange statement from Jesus in the Luke 10 passage: "Do not greet anyone on the road." Is Jesus asking us to be unfriendly? No, I think He is telling us something similar to His statement in Matthew 7:6: "Do not give dogs what is sacred; do not throw your pearls to pigs. If you do, they may trample them under their feet, and then turn and tear you to pieces."

The mandate not to greet anyone along the road needs to be understood in its immediate context, including the last section of Luke chapter 9. In verses 57–62, Jesus encounters three people along the road. To each He offers the challenge to follow Him. Jesus's interaction with each one highlights why people end up not following Him. The first apparently isn't ready to live a lifestyle of a disciple, in which there is not even a place to lay one's head, let alone security. The second wants to wait until his familial responsibility to "bury his father" is out of the way. The third will likewise follow under the condition that he can say good-bye to his family. All these people explicitly or tacitly want to set conditions on their obedience to Jesus. Those along the road, in this context, become those who want to follow as long as discipleship is easy and secure. Jesus doesn't bother with such people. He tells His disciples not to bother either.

We have somehow come to the conclusion that preaching the gospel is a matter of getting the message out about salvation to anyone who will listen. Some even try to force people to listen who aren't the least bit interested. I think randomly preaching the gospel to those to whom we haven't been directed is also Luke's greeting people along the road: "Hi, do you know who the Lord is? Let me tell you all about Him." The question needs to be asked, did Jesus the Lord direct you to this person? Did He ask you to preach publicly? If Jesus truly asked you to preach publicly, then obey. However, don't do so as some church-planting technique without prompting from the Holy Spirit. Do it out of obedience.

## The house of peace (Luke 10:5)

When we read Luke 10:5, which mentions a house, we tend to think the word *house* refers to the building. In the original text the word is *oikos*, which does mean the building we call a house. But it much more commonly refers to the household, the people who live in the house. In fact, it can even mean the sphere of influence of that household; in other words, the folk who would hang out in that house. The people were in focus, not the building.

The point is this: the house mentioned here is referring to the people, not the building. So if an apostle encounters a household of people, he blesses them by saying, "Peace to this household." If the key person called the man of peace, which we will discuss next, is there, the blessing will rest on them. In other words, they will accept the presence of apostolic people among them as a blessing, not a curse. (The "man of peace" is the phrase used in the text. However the concept itself is not gender specific, for example the woman at the well in John 4 was a woman of peace. A common term now for the concept is a "person of peace.")

As in the principles of not speaking to those along the road or casting pearls before pigs, if a household is not interested in the Lord you represent, don't bother going any further. So we don't speak to random individuals who aren't interested. In the same way, we don't speak to households who aren't interested. However, if they do show interest, we stay. We stay in the home. We spend time with them. We eat with them—anything they set before us. We don't make special demands.

This is how Jesus's ministry pattern works. If God directs us to a group of people who show interest in knowing Jesus, we spend time with them. This time is not just some formalized discipleship hour. It is social and very human. This is their chance to see Jesus, as He lives His life through us. It is our chance to be salt and light, a beacon on a hill. Our words should match our message, and our interaction with them should be lasting enough, whole enough, and deep enough, that they can read our message in our lives as well as understand our words.

## The man of peace (Luke 10:6)

If in this household we find a person of peace, we are to stay. We know that he is the person of peace because we have blessed him and he has received that blessing. I suspect that these instructions carry an ancient Middle Eastern flavor. I think this "man of peace" was often the household's patriarch. In that day, if one were invited to a home, let's say by one of the teenage sons, but the family patriarch didn't find the apostle's message appealing, it is doubtful the other family members would feel peaceful about accepting that message.

Our Western society is structured quite a bit differently. Most of the people of peace stories I know here in the West start with finding a person of peace who then leads the apostle back to the household or sphere of influence. I started chapter 1 with the story of my friend Vincent and a woman of peace named Connie. First Vincent met Connie, who led him to her sphere of influence. I suspect this is just a cultural difference. In our Western society we are much more autonomous. We are free to make religious decisions without the direct permission of the male head of the household. In fact, it is not uncommon for individuals to not even consider consulting their parents or spouses.

The best way to think of persons of peace is to think of them as people of influence, either good or bad. If it is good influence, people will be open to hearing this good news based on the quality of their relational standing. On the other hand, if they are people with bad reputations, their changed lives will be their testimonies. Cornelius was a person of good influence. The Gerasene demoniac was a person of bad influence, yet he impacted the entire Decapolis (Mark 5:20). The woman at the well was not a person of good reputation, yet the whole village came out to meet Jesus based on what she said. People of peace can be popular politicians or drug addicts. We don't pick them; Jesus does. I know of a movement of the Spirit in Spain that started because one drug addict came to the Lord and demonstrated his changed life to other drug addicts and their families.

Even though we in the West are more autonomous, the people of peace and the households of peace are not moot points in our society. Even though our culture has different practices than those of the ancient Middle East, there are still some important common features. We humans, by our very nature, are involved in interconnected relational groups. These are the "households," the spheres of influence. In our Western society these "households" are not always necessarily connected to a house or home. Nevertheless, they are a social unit. One woman may have not only a nuclear and extended family but also a bowling league, a network of friends at work, and old school friends with whom she has coffee every week. Each one of these affinity groups can be considered an *oikos*, a sphere of influence. This same woman, who for our purposes is the person of peace, may be able to easily take the gospel to her bowling group. However, it may take more time for the gospel to penetrate her work and her coffee group, and longer still to penetrate her extended family.

There are two important points here. First, if we see an individual merely as an autonomous person, devoid of spheres of influence, we will retard or stop the flow of the gospel through our society. Second, individuals have more than one sphere of influence.

Our common Western ministry practice is to preach the gospel to individuals without taking the least notice of their spheres of influence. If we are fortunate enough to win someone to the Lord, we immediately take them out of their social groups and take them to a congregational church. Soon they have replaced their old contacts with their new Christian ones. We actually encourage this behavior. It is exactly counter to what Jesus taught His disciples to do.

Each of the overlapping spheres of influence may be more or less open to the gospel. Yet the same person often opens more than one sphere of influence to Jesus. In the case above there is not only the family but also work, the coffee group, and the bowling league. It is not uncommon for some people to have many spheres of influence. And in turn, the individuals in her spheres of influence each have their own overlapping sets of spheres of influence.

It was Jesus's particular genius to understand the reality of these overlapping relationships as the highway for the gospel. It is this insight that allows for a viral movement of the gospel. He didn't aim just for the autonomous individual. He was looking for the households, the overlapping spheres of influence. This is how a viral Jesus movement works. The gospel enters into a group, or multiple groups, through an individual.

Once there, it becomes explosive. Each set of friends or relatives the gospel enters introduces it not only to a number of new individuals but also to whole sets of additional relational groups. This is exponential growth, once the Holy Spirit sets it loose. This growth can be explosive or more leisurely; that depends quite a bit on the culture in which the kingdom is being announced.

### Stay in that house; eat what is set before you (Luke 10:7)

Apostolic ministry requires tact. We are outsiders who have been invited into a new sphere of influence. We need to earn trust. In the ancient Near East this was accomplished by participating in offered hospitality through actually staying in the home. In our Western culture we might phrase it "hang out with them." If you are going to hang out with people you should learn to enjoy what they enjoy, even food and drink. If they eat pizza, so should you.

There is nothing more annoying than the new person who has all sorts of prerequisites for hanging out with a group. "Oh, I'm sorry, I have to get my beauty sleep; I'm always in bed by 9." "I'm a vegan, so I can only eat food that is not associated with animals." If you are going to do apostolic ministry you need to eat what is set before you; that is, eat what the sphere of influence eats. Certainly if one is a diabetic one shouldn't gorge oneself on donuts and sodas. But God will give a tactful way to deal with dietary restrictions. However, I would suggest that such nonparticipation is ruled by true health issues, not personal preference or nonbiblical ideology.

Bill Hoffman, one of my close apostolic friends, was raised in the meat and potato culture of Southern Idaho. However, God has allowed him to plant churches among a number of ethnic groups, including Mexicans and Singaporeans. When he is among them he eats what is set before him with a joyous heart, even though it is often not something he would ever eat on his own outside of apostolic ministry.

### Do not move around from house to house (Luke 10:7)

One way to encourage a viral Jesus movement of the gospel is to make sure apostles are not taking the gospel to each household. Apostles are sodbusters, they are not settlers. They get the gospel going; they make sure it has a good foundation and then they encourage the new Christians to take the gospel to new spheres of influence. Good apostles avoid becoming another form of clergy who do all the important work. They "prepare God's people for works of service, so that the body of Christ may be built up" (Eph. 4:12). They don't do it all themselves.

Let's go back to our example of the woman of peace, in the bowling league, mentioned above. Let's call her Angela. Angela meets an apostolic person named Lena. Lena leads her to the Lord. Angela is excited about this and introduces Lena to her bowling league friends. Soon a church is meeting at Sunset Lanes. In the mean time, Lena is training and encouraging Angela to tell her friends about Jesus. She is doing the same with her new friends at Sunset Lanes. Angela can take the gospel to her family, her work, and her coffee friends. At the same time Angela's friends at Sunset Lanes are beginning to preach the gospel to their respective spheres of influence. What we don't want to see is Lena the apostle and her experienced apostolic team doing all the work.

In the introduction, I told the story of my friend Vincent and the person of peace, Connie. In that story you were also introduced to Andrea, Connie's friend from work. What I didn't tell in that story was that within about a year Andrea had planted six churches among her spheres of influence. Vincent didn't plant them; Andrea and her sister, to whom Andrea had preached the gospel, did the work. Vincent coached Andrea, but she was the one preaching the gospel and following Jesus as He built His church.

The point is this, apostles open up new territory. They do this through planting churches in new spheres of influence. From that point on, they want the evangelism and church planting to radiate out from that point of contact, most of the work being done by the new Christians themselves. Apostles don't try to move from house to house planting all the churches themselves. They allow the viral nature of organic Christianity to spread the virus through new Christians spreading Jesus along through their network of relationships.

## Healing the sick (Luke 10:9)

Jesus expected apostolic ministry to be validated through supernatural power. In the Luke 10 passage He mentions healing the sick. If we review all the passages in which Jesus teaches about apostolic ministry, the list grows to include other signs and wonders. These signs and wonders are intricately linked to preaching the gospel of the kingdom.

Jesus seemed to take the supernatural power of His disciples for granted. He didn't tell them to pray for miracles; He told them to perform them: "When you enter a town and are welcomed, eat what is set before you. Heal the sick who are there and tell them, 'The kingdom of God is near you'" (vv. 8–9). When Jesus trained the original twelve apostles and later the seventy-two, He told them to heal the sick, raise the dead, heal lepers, cast out demons, and proclaim the gospel of the kingdom. These activities seem to pretty much summarize the initial behavior of apostolic ministry. When the seventy-two returned, they were shocked and amazed. They had seen demons submit to the name of Jesus.

## Blessing and cursing (Luke 10:10–16)

In the same way that we don't preach to people along the way (those individuals who aren't interested) and those households who don't receive our blessing, we don't preach to towns who reject our apostolic presence. Once the gospel is set loose in a true viral movement of the gospel, it might not take long for it to become the talk of the town. I'm sure this was true in small, first-century Middle Eastern villages. In huge Western metropolises, or in culturally resistant areas, it might take considerably more time. However, God doesn't deal just with individuals; He deals with interconnecting spheres of influence and with cities, towns, and regions. In the same way that individuals and spheres of influence can accept or reject our blessing, so can cities, regions, and counties.

Either the town welcomes an apostolic presence and offers help, or they reject it. If they are receptive, we are to bless them. If they reject us, we are to curse. Jesus actually gives us a significant example of a curse—His curse on Korazin and Bethsaida. Cursing and blessing in the Bible are not small things. We rational Westerners view these acts as just a bunch of words. In the biblical worldview the blessings and curses of Christians have real authority and spiritual power. We should not take them lightly.

When do we bless or curse? I think the answer might seem trite, yet I believe it is accurate. Jesus will tell you what and when. He will tell you exactly what to say and He will tell you when to say it. As of the writing of this book, my friends and I are working in the San Francisco Bay Area. We do not sense our time has come to an end. We still all feel God is calling us to continue making disciples and planting churches in Northern California. We have seen significant movement. We have had significant setbacks, and we have been guided to practices, places, and new understanding of the Scriptures we weren't expecting. It has been a tremendous learning experience. I don't think our learning curve is over. But we have not been told to pull out yet. I am praying that when we do, it will be because Jesus has unleashed a viral movement of the gospel here and our work will be done. We will bless the place and move on.

The other option is much more difficult, but just as important. I hope I never have to curse a city or region. But if Jesus asks me to do so I will. However, I can do this only under the direction of the Lord. If I wake up one morning frustrated that things aren't going as fast as I hoped, it does not give me the right to curse. Such a drastic step should be done only under the clear direction of the Lord.

## Debriefing and praise (Luke 10:17–22)

After the disciples returned excited about what they had seen, Jesus took the opportunity to deepen their learning. In our modern parlance, He debriefed them. They were particularly excited by the fact that demons had submitted to them. Jesus used their excitement to take them into deeper teaching on supernatural ministry and overcoming the power of the enemy.

Next Jesus used what had already happened to praise His Father. This was natural because Jesus had taught the apostles to do only what they saw the Father doing. This was actually His work done in His power, so, as Jesus demonstrates, He deserves the praise. Yet this praise is also an encouragement to the apostles. By being obedient, they had had things revealed to them by the Father. And their work caused Jesus to break out into spontaneous praise.

## Being blessed to see (Luke 10:23)

Jesus ends His apostolic training with a blessing of those who had participated: "Blessed are the eyes that see what you see." I believe this pattern of debriefing, encouragement, praise, and mutual blessing should be a normal part of apostolic ministry. In the network of friends with whom I work, there are a number of groups around the Bay Area of California that meet regularly to tell stories, learn from one another, encourage one another, and praise God for what He is doing. In doing so, we realize we are truly blessed to see things most Western Christians don't see.

# The Luke 10 Pattern in the New Testament

Jesus taught the seventy-two how to minister in Luke 10. It was the same pattern He had taught to His disciples earlier. It was the same pattern He had already demonstrated to them in His own ministry, and it is the same pattern they later lived out as apostolic workers themselves. Sometimes we see the whole pattern played out; sometimes we see parts of the pattern. I suspect that this pattern was so much a part of the *modus operandi* of the church that it didn't need to be spelled out each time.

I strongly suspect that the early church would have recognized Zaccheus as a person of peace in the story of Jesus's entry into Jericho (Luke 19:1–10). I'm sure they would have viewed the house of Mary, Martha, and Lazarus as a natural sphere of influence, and Martha as the woman of peace (Luke 10:38–42). They would have taken it as the most natural thing that Jesus would hang out with this household, teach there, and then expand His ministerial reach through raising Lazarus from the dead while people were gathered for his funeral. Among many other things, Lazarus's resurrection was the gospel moving into new spheres of influence. (See John 11:1–46.)

Our problem is that we have lost contact with Jesus's pattern of ministry through 1,700 years of Christendom. We have been doing everything but this for so long that even when we do see it plainly laid out for us in the pages of Scripture, we don't notice. These stories of Jesus and His disciples living out Jesus's teaching on apostolic ministry become just another Bible story because we have lost eyes to see the pattern of how Jesus taught us to minister.

## Examples of Luke 10 pattern in the ministry of Jesus

Jesus met a woman at a well in Samaria. She was a person of peace. Jesus demonstrated His spiritual credentials by giving her a supernatural word of knowledge about her broken past. She was so amazed that she ran to the village, which was her sphere of influence, and the entire village turned out to hear the truth from Jesus. The response was so fruitful that Jesus and the disciples (an apostolic team) needed to stay for extra days as they equipped the Samarian village through teaching (John 4:7–45). After one is sensitized to the pattern, it is pretty obvious.

The story of Vincent and Connie could be seen as a modern-day woman-at-the-well story. Connie wasn't necessarily a woman of great reputation; yet God used her to be the flash point for many people's coming to Christ and a number of churches being planted.

Jesus met a tax collector named Matthew at his tax tables. He was a man of peace. He had a pretty bad reputation and a pretty bad sphere of influence. Yet that didn't bother Jesus, who went to his house filled with other tax collectors and assorted scoundrels so that He could bring the gospel to Matthew's *oikos*. Jesus's willingness to eat what was set before Him in the sphere of influence of a rather disreputable man of peace was deeply offensive to the religious establishment. However, Jesus was just living what He taught. (See Matthew 9:9–13.)

I once led a businessman to the Lord and a church got started in his house the very next day. He wasn't the most reputable of businessmen. In fact, he was quite similar to Matthew the tax collector. You may remember that story from chapter 3.

## Examples of Luke 10 pattern in the ministry of the disciples

A man of peace named Cornelius was visited by an angel who told him to go look for a man named Peter in Joppa. Cornelius immediately sent some people from his household to go find Peter. The next day Peter was praying on a rooftop in Joppa. He had a prophetic vision that prepared him to preach the gospel to Gentiles. One thing led to another and Peter the Apostle, along with his team, ended up at the house of Cornelius, the man of peace. Peter entered the house and found a large group of people gathered there. This was Cornelius's *oikos*, his household, his sphere of influence. While Peter was still preaching, the Holy Spirit came on the entire bunch, and they supernaturally manifested God's presence. Later Peter caught flack for eating what was set before him in the *oikos* of a Gentile. But in reality, Peter was just doing what Jesus had modeled for him and taught him. (See Acts 10.)

Peter and John were walking in the temple precinct near the Beautiful Gate. A man of peace, who happened to be a cripple, asked them for money. Instead they demonstrated the power of God through a notable miracle. The crippled man jumped up and began to loudly praise God. This got the attention of his sphere of influence, since he was a person known to many who came to the temple. Peter and John, an apostolic team, used this occasion and the supernatural healing to proclaim the gospel of the kingdom. (See Acts 3:1–10.)

The story of Mariluz healing the woman through prayer in the hospital in Spain and this leading to a whole sphere of influence coming to Christ and a church being planted among them is a modern-day example of Jesus using miracles to confirm His apostolic ministry. I told that story in chapter 2.

### Examples of Luke 10 pattern in the ministry of Paul

On a Sabbath day Paul and his team met a woman named Lydia by the riverside in Philippi. She was the woman of peace. This meeting of a woman of peace ended up with a church planted in her home (Acts 16:13–15).

But the church they planted in Lydia's house was not the only church to be planted in Philippi. Due to persecution, Paul and Silas were severely beaten and thrown into jail. Instead of complaining, they sang hymns. There was a violent earthquake. All the prison doors were thrown open and Paul's and Silas's chains miraculously fell off. The jailer, realizing that he would be executed for allowing prisoners to escape, prepared to commit suicide. Paul shouted, "Don't harm yourself! We are all here!" When the jailer realized that as an act of kindness to him, Paul and Silas had not escaped, he fell at their feet asking what he needed to do to be saved. This jailer was a man of peace. When Paul and Silas met this Philippian man of peace, they assumed that he would be saved along with his *oikos*. And that is exactly what happened. The jailer took Paul and Silas to his home to clean their wounds and meet his family. As a result his family was all saved. Then to cap it off, Paul and Silas ate what was set before them, just as Jesus had taught. (See Acts 16:25–34.)

# Luke 10 Pattern in the Ministry in the US Bowling Alley "Church"

My good friend Isaiah Hwang shared an experience that shows how the Luke 10 pattern can be effective in ministry today. Isaiah grew up with a number of friends, but when he became a young adult he felt as if some of them had fallen off the face of the earth. One day he happened to encounter one of these old friends named Jeff. Jeff loved to go bowling, so Isaiah and Jeff started to bowl together. Bowling became a regular activity for them.

Soon some of Jeff's other friends began meeting with Jeff and Isaiah to hang out together and bowl. At first it was just a time to bowl, eat some hot dogs, and have a beer or two. But soon the group that seemed to be connected by Jeff started bonding not only around Jeff but also around their regular bowling time.

Smokers are not allowed to smoke in the bowling alley, so most, if not all, of the group would go outside between games and form a "smoking circle." Isaiah doesn't smoke, but he did want to connect with his new friends and have a spiritual impact in their lives, so he would accompany them. While they smoked and swapped stories, Isaiah would quietly pray for them. He found that God particularly put Jeff on his heart, so he prayed earnestly for him.

Through the prompting of the Holy Spirit, Isaiah interjected spiritual comments into the conversation. Because of the growing depth of the relationship, his input was acceptable to the group, and the group became an *oikos* with whom Isaiah was gently sharing Jesus. The *oikos* had been gathered by Jeff, the person of peace. The bowling alley and the "smoking circle" outside became their "church building." Ministry was accomplished by merely following Jesus into the harvest, not by trying to make things happen.

## Luke 10 Pattern as Normal Operating Procedure

The pattern Jesus taught was normal operating procedure for biblical apostolic ministry. We see it played out time and time again. Sometimes we see the whole pattern and sometimes, like shorthand, we see bits and pieces. I believe it was such a commonly known pattern, it was assumed the reader could fill in the blanks.

I also believe that this was not some special pattern for a distant time in the past. It is how Jesus expects His church to do apostolic ministry. I've done this many times myself and have watched my friends do the same. This is the way virgin territory is opened up. This is how the apostles bust the sod. But in general the church has become distanced from it by 1,700 years of Christendom's disobedience. We need to reconnect with Jesus's way of doing things if we are going to see a viral movement of the gospel in the West.

My eyes have been blessed to see these things. I've met many people of peace. I've seen Jesus form churches among their spheres of influence. I've seen people healed and seen it lead to church planting. God has used my friends and me to cast out demons in apostolic ministry. And frankly, I would agree with Jesus; it has been a blessing.

It has also created a hunger and thirst in me to see much more. I never get tired of watching God set up seemingly spontaneous meetings with people of peace. His infinite creativity to do so amazes me. I never get tired of leading people to Christ. I love to equip new believers in the basics so they can do the work of service. I love to see a person God has trained through me win people to Christ and plant churches. Truly my eyes have been blessed. I hope yours have been too, or soon will be.

## Conclusion

In the following chapter we are going to look at a subject commonly discussed in evangelical circles but not often carried out in actual behavior: evangelism. This practice is deeply connected with viral church planting but distinct from it. Church planting is often carried out by apostles, who participate in evangelism. Yet apostles are distinct from evangelists. What is the difference? How do both equip the body for the work of service? How are these practices interrelated? How can each and every Christian participate in real Jesus-led evangelism? Can evangelism be something that is actually exciting and fun for every believer? What would evangelism look like if Jesus were leading the process? What are the principles of this kind of evangelism? How do we participate in Jesus-led evangelism without becoming technique driven? How does this fit into a viral Jesus movement?

## CHAPTER 10

# Viral Evangelism

*I*N THE INTRODUCTION, I told the story about the Lord's arranging for my friend Vincent to witness to a woman of peace named Connie and how that led to a church being planted. In the last chapter I mentioned that this was not the end of the story. In fact, a woman named Andrea came to Christ in that first meeting. She preached the gospel to her sister, both of whom were subsequently involved in church planting and evangelism. What we are seeing here is how apostolic ministry leads to further evangelism by new Christians, resulting in further viral church planting and evangelism.

I have mentioned that it is not a good idea for apostles to plant all the churches in a viral Jesus movement. Rather it is much better to equip new believers to share their new story with their ever-expanding sets of relationships. If we are to see the good news become a viral epidemic, we need to see it spread from person to person. Think of it this way. If twelve people are infected with a cold and they spread it to 20 percent of the people they speak with, many people will get a cold. However, if the only people infected are those who have direct contact with those original twelve people, the cold will never reach epidemic proportions. For that to happen, we also need to see those infected infect others, and those to infect others. This is the difference between addition and multiplication. Actually, this is the difference between addition and exponential growth.

Equipping new believers to share their story is one of the most important ways evangelists "prepare God's people for works of service, so that the body of Christ may be built up" (Eph. 4:12). If we want to see salvation once again become a viral epidemic in the West, we must move beyond a bunch of apostolically gifted people witnessing. We need every Christian sharing his faith. And for that to happen we need evangelists. One of the most important phrases in Ephesians 4:11–12 is *"to prepare God's people for works of service"* (emphasis added). What is the function of the five gifts mentioned in Ephesians 4:11? It is preparing God's people for works of service. So, what is the function of an evangelist? It is to prepare all the saints to share their faith. This is one of the ways we have gotten so off track in Christendom. We have gifted evangelists do the work for us, instead of preparing us to do the work.

We will never see a viral movement of the gospel if a few specially gifted people do most of the work. An apostle's greatest joy should come not in controlling the work but in watching Jesus cause it to spread faster than we could ever imagine. Apostles are sodbusters. They open up virgin territory. But that gives us a crop for only one year. After that we need settlers. Settlers plant crops year after year. To extend our analogy just a bit further, suppose, as in US history, the settlers came from the rainy East Coast to the semiarid plans of the Midwest. Someone needed to teach the settlers how to have healthy crops, year after year, in a new environment. That is the role of the evangelist in Ephesians 4:11. Evangelists don't do all the farming. They train settlers in how to farm effectively year after year. They train them to have good crops the first year and to keep the soil healthy so they can have good crops, even better crops, ten and twenty years later.

Let me extend our analogy just a bit further. A good evangelist is not just a good farmer; he is the county extension agent. Here is one of the definitions of a county extension agent: extension personnel have the task of bringing scientific knowledge to farm families in the farms and homes. The object of the task is to improve the efficiency of agriculture.[1] In the same way, a good evangelist teaches us all how to be effective in sharing the faith. We want to see salvation spread like a virus. That means that it is traveling down the networks of relationship from person to person, from household to household. To spread the gospel quickly, we need evangelists who don't do all the work themselves but teach us how to roll up our sleeves.

One of the most encouraging verses in the Book of Acts is Acts 8:4, which describes what the believers in Jerusalem did after the persecution that arose with the martyrdom of Stephen: "Those who had been scattered preached the word wherever they went." Phillip is used as one example, perhaps one of the more spectacular ones, of what that looked like. Philip is never called an apostle, but he is called an evangelist in Acts 21:8.

Most likely much of what these scattered believers did was much less spectacular than what Philip did in his ministry. That doesn't mean it was devoid of supernatural power, just that much of it was probably sharing with friends, neighbors, and work associates. I am not suggesting that there is no further work for apostles to do once the faith is spreading rapidly. They also need to equip. They also need to train. They need to keep their fingers on the pulse of the movement so that they can deal with any problems that arise. That seems to be what Peter and John did with the explosive outbreak of salvation in Philip's ministry in Samaria. But they didn't try to control it either. They did not impose limits, structures, or traditions that stopped the flow of the gospel. They didn't take over for Philip. They came, they helped, they made sure things were going well, they dealt with problems, and they left.

Every believer should feel that each one of us can and should share his faith with his spheres of influence. We should have resources available to us that will help us do so. That will most likely come through evangelists. These evangelists are usually spiritually gifted people from our own network of Christian friends. New believers may need some help as churches begin to form in their households and spheres of influence. Abundant sowing and church planting should be part of the ethos of a viral Jesus movement. In fact, it won't become viral without it. Church planting, network health, and development are roles for apostles. Continued abundant sowing of the good news by every believer is the role of evangelists.

It should also be noted that viral evangelism, like every other aspect of viral Christianity, is all about Jesus and His leading. Our foundational principle and practice is that Jesus is Lord. Our operating system is based on the new covenant reality that the Spirit of Jesus not only lives in us but also communicates to our hearts and minds.

# What Does Viral Evangelism Look Like?

So what does viral evangelism look like? For that I'd like to refer to the teaching of a gifted friend and evangelist, Ed Waken. Here are a few of the key principles that he teaches to help normal, everyday Christians share the Good News with their friends and family, as they live normal, everyday lives.

Most of us are more than a bit intimidated by the thought of sharing our faith. Part of this may be that just about the only evangelism we've seen has been in one of the following two scenarios: evangelism by extraordinary evangelists and evangelism by insensitive evangelists. In the first case, we feel we can't do that because we are not gifted like they are; so we are intimidated. In the second case we are justifiably offended. We would not want someone confronting us in insensitive ways, and we don't want to talk to our friends and family in insensitive ways. We instinctively know that it most likely will do more harm than good, and we are correct in our assumption.

Ed likes to say we can be 100 percent effective in evangelism 100 percent of the time. To do this we need to do exactly what Jesus leads us to do—no more, no less. For me this is a very encouraging statement. In fact, it is a relief. We don't need to hit a home run every time we speak to a non-Christian friend. All we have to do is trust Jesus to know what to do. Jesus doesn't want to insult, intimidate, or harm our friends and family any more than we do. Jesus can read their hearts, even if we can't. So, can we truly trust Jesus to do the right thing—no more, no less? If Jesus leads us to let a non-Christian friend know we are Christians, do that and no more. If He prompts us to offer to pray for an illness, do that—no more, no less. If He stimulates us to ask leading questions, then drop the subject; do that. If He leads us to share the entire story of salvation, do that. This is following the Lord of the harvest into the harvest. It is allowing Jesus to be Lord and not taking over for Him. It is paying attention to Jesus's voice as He speaks to our hearts and minds. In other words, it is new-covenant evangelism.

## Phil's story

Let me tell you a story of new-covenant evangelism that happened to my friend Phil and me. Phil and I met every Sunday morning in a restaurant in San Rafael, California. Sometimes we met with students from our English-as-a-second-language ministry who wanted to know about Jesus. Sometimes no students came. When that happened, we didn't worry about it. In that case Phil and I met up for breakfast and talked about how Jesus was working in our lives. For a few months we had been noticing that a regular customer of the restaurant, who speaks Spanish, had been positioning himself to listen in on our little group, as we discussed Jesus and the Bible in Spanish. He laughed when we cracked a joke. He frowned when someone told a sad story.

One day just Phil and I met. One of the topics of our discussion was learning to respond immediately to the gentle prompting of the Holy Spirit, even if it didn't make sense to us. As I was talking to one of the restaurant staff, Phil felt the Spirit's gentle prompting. He sensed that the Holy Spirit was asking him to acknowledge the regular customer and comment that he was often at the restaurant on Sunday mornings just like us. The regular customer smiled and pointed to Phil's Bible, then asked what we did every week.

Before long Phil and I were sitting at his booth having a friendly conversation. As we talked, we were also trying to tune into Jesus's frequency, asking Him what to do next. The customer told us that he had a bunch of questions about the Bible. We told him that was a good thing, that one of the things we did was explore the Bible together. I suggested that he ask Jesus to tell him the most important question he could bring to explore together the next Sunday. He thought that was a wonderful idea. Then I sensed the Holy Spirit tell me that was enough. I had done all that he wanted done right then. So I smiled, made an appointment to see the guy the following Sunday, shook his hand, and we left on friendly terms.

Now, let's apply Ed's "100 percent effective 100 percent of the time" principle to the above example. Phil and I love to share our faith. But we don't like humiliating people. We don't like buttonholing people. And we don't like making nuisances of ourselves. We had noticed this customer happily listening in on our meetings. Did the customer want us to invite him to the group? Was this guy ready to hear the good news? How could we know? Yet when the time was right, Jesus gave Phil a gentle nudge. Will the Holy Spirit always lead us to start up a conversation? No, but we should always follow Jesus's lead. Every case is different, but we can trust Jesus to lead us effectively 100 percent of the time. That does not mean that we will respond the right way 100 percent of the time. But it's OK to make mistakes; they are part of the learning process.

Note that we had a friendly conversation with the customer. Is that always the case? No, but I think it is often the case. There may be instances in which Jesus asks us to confront people, perhaps in what seems to be uncomfortable ways. But in general we will probably end up having normal, friendly conversations with people. Jesus is probably leading us to many more opportunities to share than we respond to. Part of growing in 100 percent effective evangelism is learning to respond to the prompting of the Holy Spirit and trust Him that He will show us exactly what to do—no more, no less.

Will our encounter with the customer in the restaurant result in our leading him to Jesus? We have no idea. It could. It could actually lead to salvation flowing through multiple generations of people. That is certainly what we desire. But perhaps our job is only to plant seeds. Perhaps seeds have already been planted by someone else and our job is to water. Perhaps he's already a Christian and we need to train him to take his faith to his friends. Perhaps in the long run he will be the rocky ground that Jesus talks about in the parable of the soils. At the point of contact Phil and I don't know. But we can trust Jesus to know what to do. Our job is to follow His lead; only in doing that can we be 100 percent effective.

## Why Are We Afraid to Share the Gospel?

Most of us are intimidated to share our faith. I don't think we need to beat ourselves up about that, nor do I think we should allow that to stop us from graciously sharing the good news. Here are a few reasons why we tend to get stuck not sharing our faith when Jesus gives us opportunities.

## "I don't know enough."

You're right, you probably don't. Neither do I. Neither does Phil or Ed. But we all know someone who does—Jesus. If we are going to be 100 percent effective 100 percent of the time, we don't need to be experts who know everything; we need to trust Jesus—no more, no less. The apostle John writes, "As for you, the anointing which you received from Him abides in you, and you have no need for anyone to teach you; but as His anointing teaches you about all things, and is true and is not a lie, and just as it has taught you, you abide in Him" (1 John 2:27, NAS). Let me paraphrase that: "Don't worry. Jesus will give you what you need, when you need it, and it will be true. Just abide and trust Him."

In effect we can do only what we see Jesus already doing. In the same way, Jesus did only what He saw His Father doing. The issue here isn't really information; it is relationship. If you are abiding in Jesus, He will give you the right information when you need it. We need to maintain our abiding relationship with Him. That is an important key. Just make sure it is Him leading and not your human will, skill, or even guilt.

## "I'm afraid of rejection."

Aren't we all afraid of rejection? Nobody wants to be rejected. However, we need to be careful that the rejection we fear is realistic. First of all, most of the rejection we face in evangelism has to do with evangelism done poorly. By that I mean evangelism that involves forcing others to listen to a message they really don't want to hear or one that Jesus hasn't initiated. When we force people to listen to something they really don't want to hear, they probably will reject the messenger. However, if we are truly following Jesus, can't we trust Him to lead us to say the right thing to the right person?

Second, we should make sure we know where our fear of rejection is coming from. Of all the beings in the universe, who is most likely to want to keep us from sharing salvation through Jesus? I think the answer is obvious. I believe Satan is behind much of our fear of sharing our faith. One of his key ways of doing this is by stirring up our natural fear of rejection and reminding us of the negative emotions generated by evangelism done poorly.

Finally, if Jesus really is asking us to share our faith, it does not mean

179

that everything will go smoothly every time. It does mean that if we are obedient He will accomplish what He wants to accomplish, and He will reward us for it. Even if we are rejected, we will be rewarded. "Blessed are those who are persecuted because of righteousness, for theirs is the kingdom of heaven. Blessed are you when people insult you, persecute you and falsely say all kinds of evil against you because of me. Rejoice and be glad, because great is your reward in heaven, for in the same way they persecuted the prophets who were before you" (Matt. 5:10–12).

Honestly most evangelism done by following Jesus's initiative doesn't lead to persecution or rejection. It is much more common to have a situation like the one Phil and I had. It ends up being a friendly conversation. Our fear of rejection and persecution is way out of proportion to the actual instances of rejection. Of course, the only way we can find this out is by allowing Jesus to lead us into evangelistic opportunities and then obeying. And an important part of that is to pray that Jesus would begin to lead us into such opportunities. By the way, Satan won't like you praying about that, so expect him to attempt to distract you away from such prayer.

### "I might make a mistake."

Paul talked about people preaching the gospel out of wrong motives. Here was his response to that situation: "But what does it matter? The important thing is that in every way, whether from false motives or true, Christ is preached. And because of this I rejoice" (Phil. 1:18). I think we can apply the same logic to making evangelistic mistakes. Still, Christ is preached. And Jesus knows how to use mistakes for His glory. Romans 8:28 applies in all situations, including this one: "And we know that in all things God works for the good of those who love him, who have been called according to his purpose."

### "Whose job is it, anyway?"

In Luke 18 the rich ruler rejected Jesus's offer of eternal life. Jesus may have been 100 percent effective, but not everyone He spoke the good news to came into the kingdom. In this case the rich ruler didn't want eternal life if it meant giving up his worldly wealth. In response, Jesus said it was very difficult for wealthy people to gain eternal life. "Who then can be saved?" His disciples asked. Jesus replied, "What is impossible with men is possible with God." Actually this is a general principle of evangelism. We can't lead people to Christ, but the Holy Spirit can lead people to Christ through us. We don't have the power to change the human heart, but He does. Salvation is God's job, but He wants to use us in the process. And He wants us to be willing to be used. He also wants us to pray toward that end.

## Overcoming the Objections

With these common objections in mind, notice how my friend Isaiah overcame them through prayer and by having a normal friendship.

When Isaiah was in college, his church was emphasizing "friendship evangelism." So Isaiah began praying for a couple friends in particular whose names were Ricky and Annie. Rather than bombard them with gospel presentations, he decided to "live Jesus in front of them." He also began to share snippets of his spiritual life with them to see how they would react. If, out of curiosity, they asked for more, he would give them more. If they didn't show interest, he would drop the subject. Slowly but surely, they became more open to talking about spiritual things. After a while, Isaiah began not only praying for them in his private time with God but also asking them if he could pray for specific concerns in their lives. Soon they were requesting prayer from him.

Isaiah's friendship with Ricky and Annie has turned into a long-term relationship. Isaiah makes the effort to keep the relationship fresh. Ricky once commented that Isaiah was different from Christians he knew. He knew others who tried to force their opinions on him. "If you were like that, we wouldn't be friends."

Isaiah inquired, "How am I different?"

"You don't shove it down my throat."

Over time both Ricky and Annie began asking questions such as, "Hey, Isaiah, what does the Bible say about...?" And Isaiah would answer their questions. Sometimes this led to deeper spiritual conversations, sometimes not.

It has gotten to the point now that if Isaiah doesn't say grace before he eats, they remind him to do so. Out of this relationship, Isaiah has taken both Ricky and Annie step by step closer to Jesus by just doing what Jesus prompts him to do—no more, no less.

# Five Principles of Effective Evangelism

Ed Waken has graciously shared five principles of effective evangelism with me. I'd like to share them with you.

## PRINCIPLE #1:
### Jesus wants more communicators, not more listeners

The Great Commission is for every Christian. We are all to make more disciples of Jesus. The problem is never lack of listeners; after all, the fields are still white unto harvest. The reason the Great Commission hasn't been completed yet is that we Christians tend to be stingy in sharing our faith. We treat it as if it is our own little secret.

Another issue we have is that we have become so accustomed to the clergy mentality that we are waiting for the experts to do the job. We send missionaries overseas and to different ethnic groups in our own country. We expect the clergy to share the gospel in our own spheres of influence. We're much more likely to try to bring our friends to the preacher rather than preach to our friends.

Here is Jesus's perspective on that issue: "My prayer is not that you take them out of the world but that you protect them from the evil one. They are not of the world, even as I am not of it. Sanctify them by the truth; your word is truth. As you sent me into the world, I have sent them into the world" (John 17:15–18). All of us as Christians are on a Jesus mission, to be in the world, to be salt and light for that world. Just like His Father sent Him so He sends us—all of us. It is His job to protect us from the evil one.

Instead of acting on our commission of being sent into the world, we have a tendency to hide from the world, often fearing that it will contaminate us. Light chases out darkness. Salt purifies decay. We have God's truth to sanctify us. He protects us from the evil one. Even when we do suffer, He uses it for our growth. Can we trust Jesus to do His job? Can we trust Him to send us into His broken world and give us what we need in His power?

Another factor in our inability to respond to Jesus's sending us into

His world is that we expect evangelists to do the job instead of training us to do it. We are treating evangelists like another category of clergy, instead of what they really are—resources to equip us. We are supposed to do the job. They are supposed to help us in that task.

A final factor in our failure to complete Jesus's task of evangelizing the world He loves is that evangelism has become technique-driven and human-empowered instead of Jesus-driven and Holy Spirit–empowered. We seem to have more faith in a one-size-fits-every-situation technique than in Jesus's ability to lead us and the Holy Spirit's ability to let us know what to do and say. In effect we trust human ability rather than God. We might as well call this what it really is: a lack of faith.

How can you begin to follow Jesus into His harvest, no matter how you are spiritually gifted? What would He ask you to do? Can you ask Him? Will you obey, even if it is embarrassing? Are you willing to learn from your mistakes and try again?

## PRINCIPLE #2:
### We can all live like missionaries

We can live like missionaries and in the process live an exciting life full of God-stories, stories of how God has used normal people like us to tell others of His good news. This is what the Thessalonians were famous for. Here is what Paul said about their lifestyle.

> …because our gospel came to you not simply with words, but also with power, with the Holy Spirit and with deep conviction. You know how we lived among you for your sake. You became imitators of us and of the Lord; in spite of severe suffering, you welcomed the message with the joy given by the Holy Spirit. And so you became a model to all the believers in Macedonia and Achaia. The Lord's message rang out from you not only in Macedonia and Achaia—your faith in God has become known everywhere. Therefore we do not need to say anything about it, for they themselves report what kind of reception you gave us. They tell how you turned to God from idols to serve the living and true God, and to wait for his Son from heaven, whom he raised from the dead—Jesus, who rescues us from the coming wrath.
>
> —1 Thessalonians 1:5–10

The Thessalonians first became imitators of Paul, which in reality means they were imitators of the Lord. They recognized the good news for what it was—a message direct from the Holy Spirit. As a result they not only received it; they also began to spread it. Paul said the message rang out from them not only in their own region but also to the south in Achaia. Note also that as they trusted the Holy Spirit to work through them in spreading the message, their lives were sanctified, as shown by their rejection of their former idols.

This is exactly as it is supposed to be. All the believers experienced changed lives and told their stories to others. The results were wonderful for them and for those who needed to hear their message, a message testified to not only through words but also through the lives themselves.

We will not experience a viral movement of the gospel in the West until every Christian is equipped and willing to participate in the Great Commission as missionaries. This can be an exciting process. Wouldn't it be wonderful if every time we gathered together as a body one or two of us had stories of how God had used him in the last few days to share God's good news and change people's lives for the better? It really can be like that. Evangelists are God's resource so that we can learn to live like that. The end result will be that God's divine will can be done on earth as it is in heaven.

How can you learn to live like a missionary? Do you know gifted evangelists who can train you to start to reach the people around you? To whom is Jesus calling you? What are you going to do about it?

## PRINCIPLE #3:
### The Bible gives every believer a guarantee

The apostle Paul was no different than we are. He struggled with evangelism too. But he did believe that God gives us a guarantee to provide us the resources we need. Paul's response to his struggle was to rely on that guarantee. So he prayed and asked others to pray for him so that he would live as God designs every believer to live. "Pray also for me, that whenever I open my mouth, words may be given me so that I will fearlessly make known the mystery of the gospel, for which I am an ambassador in chains. Pray that I may declare it fearlessly, as I should" (Eph. 6:19–20).

Paul didn't want to rely on some canned technique. Instead he had confidence that the Holy Spirit would be faithful to put words in his mouth at just the right time. The result was fearless preaching. Paul had confidence in God to lead the process, not in his or any other human's ability or in a canned technique. Paul's resources were the power of the Holy Spirit as he lived in abiding relationship with Jesus, his prayer, and the prayer of others. Paul thought it only right that he participate in this confident (fearless) preaching of the faith.

This is the same fearless sharing of the good news that Jesus was talking about in Matthew 10:18–20: "On my account you will be brought before governors and kings as witnesses to them and to the Gentiles. But when they arrest you, do not worry about what to say or how to say it. At that time you will be given what to say, for it will not be you speaking, but the Spirit of your Father speaking through you."

This is the guarantee that Paul was relying on. The Holy Spirit Himself will give us the words to say. In fact, it won't actually be us speaking but the Spirit of our Father speaking through us. Now that's some guarantee. We don't have to worry; we can be fearless, bold, and confident. We can be like this not because of who we are but because of who He is. This is living in exciting supernatural power.

We can live like this. We can live in the same guarantee; it is given to us too. It will require faith and practice, but the results will be an exciting life as we see God use us to complete His desires for His world. Are you willing to trust Jesus to be faithful to His guarantee? Are we willing to make mistakes along the way and consider them gifts from Jesus?

## PRINCIPLE #4:
### The spontaneity principle

We are used to planning, but we need to learn to trust God to lead us in spontaneous situations in which He is already at work. Just like Jesus, we are to note where the Father is at work and cooperate with Him. Here are just a few examples of this spontaneity principle from the New Testament as believers lived their normal lives and God worked through them spontaneously and unexpectedly.

In Acts 4:8–20 Peter and John were arrested. Instead of complaining to God about how unjust this was, they viewed it as an opportunity to witness about Jesus to the rulers and elders of the Jewish people. Peter and John did not wake up in the morning and work out a detailed plan on how to get arrested so they could share their faith. I'm sure this day did not go according to their plans at all, yet it was a spontaneous opportunity.

In Acts 6:8–10 Stephen didn't see the opposition of the Synagogue of the Freedmen as a hindrance but as an opportunity to boldly preach the good news. This spontaneous preaching was a step in the apostle Paul's journey to faith. In Acts 8:25–40 we see the evangelist Philip responding to a spontaneous situation that resulted in an Ethiopian eunuch coming to faith. In Acts 14:3 we see Barnabas and Paul spontaneously doing signs and wonders that led to the bold preaching of the gospel.

We see this spontaneity principle at work over and over again in the New Testament. This same principle was at work in Phil's and my interaction with the regular restaurant customer. However, we need to accustom our eyes to notice. My friends and I are learning this very same thing as we live our normal lives in the Bay Area of California. We are finding that Northern California in the twenty-first century is no different from Jerusalem in the first. If we trust God and pray, He will spontaneously lead us into situations in which He is already at work. Then we can rely on the guarantee He gave us to show us what to do and what words to say.

Think back over the last few months. Has God given you spontaneous situations that afforded you an opportunity to share Jesus? How did you respond? What would happen if you began to pray for these situations to occur more frequently? What could happen if you asked God to open your eyes to notice these situations and open your ears to His voice so you would know what to say?

## PRINCIPLE #5:
### Every believer is empowered for success

Perhaps our ideas of success in evangelism should be revised. We tend to think effective evangelism is leading someone to Christ. Here is how Ed Waken defines success: "Success is not measured in results when it comes to evangelism. Obedience to Jesus is to cast the seed of truth into the lives of people. However, we do know that if we cast an abundant amount of seed, we will see a great harvest—100 percent success 100 percent of the time!"[2]

Are you willing to consider it a great success if you just get to plant seeds or water? Are you willing to sow seed abundantly and allow Jesus to do what He wants with it? Are you willing to allow Jesus to take you on a journey in which you come closer and closer to becoming 100 percent effective in evangelism 100 percent of the time?

# Conclusion

The principles shared in this chapter should give us confidence in Jesus. He wants all of us to be successful in evangelism. We just need to learn that Jesus wants us as His communicators. He already has prepared the listeners. There are more than enough listeners to go around. We need to trust God's guarantee to give us the words and the power at just the right time. And we need to have eyes to see God's leading us into seemingly spontaneous situations, ones in which He has already been at work.

The results of this are confident, Holy Spirit–led, Holy Spirit–empowered sharing of the faith in which we can be 100 percent effective 100 percent of the time. When we do this, we will begin to see a viral movement of salvation again in the West. And in the process we will joyously participate in God's harvest.

### David's story

I'd like to share what some friends and I have done, not as a technique but as acts of confidence in Jesus's ability to lead us into the harvest. The following story is from my friend David Nyquist. David was asked to train a young adult group in Redwood City, California, in a way of following Jesus into the harvest called "treasure hunting." Here is David's story.

> After sharing some testimonies from past treasure hunts, it was time for us to embark upon on our own. We asked Jesus what He wanted us to look out for, these things were our treasure map. The small group that I had joined was in search of the owners of a small black dog. Less than 50 feet away, we spotted James, his wife, and Maria, their little black dog! I shared with them that we were on a treasure hunt and showed them our list of clues. The young adults I had recently trained jumped right in with encouraging

affirming words for this couple. It wasn't very long into our conversation that I discovered I was holding a clue for the healing of James's hamstrings, which had been terribly strained from his job lifting and raising enormous tents and canopies.

With such a promising list of clues, we asked if we could pray for James. He agreed, and we began to minister to several areas of need in his life: some that he shared and some that were received as words of knowledge right on the spot. When we finished praying, it was evident his countenance had changed and he was feeling better. His legs were not completely healed, but we believed that they may continue to loosen as time went on.

Later that evening I got a report from some members of our group that James had come running up to them (an action he couldn't have done an hour earlier) testifying to the healing in his legs. He also shared that when we laid hands on him, a warmth began to envelop him and remained on him even after we left. James also wanted us to know how encouraged he was by some of the words spoken over him. He had not shared some of the personal difficulties he was having parenting his teenage son, and yet, the words we spoke to him about him having "great strength, despite having a very tender and kind heart" gave him hope for the challenge of loving and fathering his son, despite his son's rebellion.[3]

We really have nothing to fear in evangelism. What we need is Jesus the Lord, and we need to function in His new-covenant operating system. When we do that, we can be 100 percent effective 100 percent of the time.

# ☙ CONCLUSION ❧

OUR SPIRITUAL FOREFATHERS, often with the best of intentions, stepped away from our new-covenant heritage. They foolishly followed the foundational principles of the world. This process took centuries, but what it gave us, in place of new-covenant Christianity, was Christendom: a form of godliness that denies the real power behind it, Jesus the Lord. Slowly but surely we succumbed to worldly principles of Greek philosophy, as well as pagan and Old Testament Jewish structures. We replaced the lordship of Jesus with the control and will of man. In doing so, we created a Christian religion that is now being rejected by Western society. The rejection of society, as serious as that is, is not nearly as serious as the damage this does to our relationship with Jesus Himself.

Sadly, we have become like the people whom James exhorted, the ones who could state the central truth of the Jewish faith, God is One, but didn't live it in the practical outworking of their lives. In the same way, we state Jesus is Lord as a mere propositional fact, but the way we structure leadership, the way we gather, the way we do ministry—in fact, the way we live life and think—has more to do with Greek philosophy than it does with the lordship of Christ.

We don't do this out of malice for our Lord; we do it because our Western society has given us a Greek-based worldview. And our Christian forefathers, in succumbing to this worldview, have given us Christendom rather than Christianity. We have become used to this Christendom, justifying it with the very Scriptures that it negates. We do this because it is all we know. We don't realize we have become like the church of Ephesus in Revelation chapter 2. We have forsaken our first love, Jesus Himself. We must recognize the height from which we have fallen. We need to repent and do the things we did at first.

In essence we have become Christian humanists. We proclaim that Jesus is Lord but live as if what really counts is our own values, effort, structures, techniques, and will. We have forsaken the power that comes from being individuals and communities in abiding relationship with Jesus and behave as enlightened rationalists, who are impressed with our own human ability. In the process, we have stepped away from a deep connection with Jesus the vine, both individually and in community—not because we wanted to, but because the way we think, the systems we use, the human structures we have imposed on God's church, separate us from Jesus Himself. We cannot repent and return to the things we did at first until we recognize the behaviors and values that dampen Jesus's power. Like the character in the Pogo comic strip, we have met the enemy and he is us.[1]

In this book I have tried to both develop and document a new way for the church of the West. It is both new and very old. I say this because what we need is what the church had in the beginning, Jesus her Lord and an operating system, the new covenant, which allowed her to live under His lordship. With this, we have all that we need.

I have developed and documented this in three ways. First, I described and developed the realities of viral Jesus movements. In chapter 1, I described and developed the elements and characteristics of a viral Jesus movement. In chapter 2, I discussed stability and control in a viral Jesus movement. I showed how the right kind of fragility is good and described the type of structure that provides for divine stability and control. In chapter 3, I described how supernaturalism is inherent in viral Jesus movements and how we too can live in this supernatural power.

Second, I described the history of viral Jesus movements. In chapter 4, I developed the history of the first viral Jesus movement, the early church, and how its structure and worldview allowed it to explode on the Roman world. Next, in chapter 5, I showed how through succumbing to the foundational principles of the world our forefathers stepped out of a viral Jesus movement and gave us Christendom in its place. In chapter 6, I gave a quick tour of partial viral Jesus movements through the history of Christianity. I showed how each was a God-given opportunity to once again experience the power of a viral Jesus movement, an opportunity we sadly missed, time after time, because we were trapped in Christendom. In chapter 7, I documented the first real viral Jesus movement in the modern world, the explosion of the house-church movement in China. I showed that our Chinese brothers have much to teach us, lessons they learned because their Christendom was stripped away from them. Yet what was left in its place, only Jesus their Lord and a new-covenant connection with Him, was enough to spark the fastest, most powerful movement of the gospel in the history of Christianity.

Finally, I discussed the practicalities of a viral Jesus movement. In chapter 8, I developed viral discipleship, a discipleship based on Jesus the Lord and intimate connection with Him. In chapter 9, I developed what viral church planting looks like when we follow the Lord of the harvest into the harvest and allow His natural, organic, kingdom structure to work for us. In chapter 10, I discussed viral evangelism, showing how we can learn to let Jesus set up our evangelistic contacts and by doing only what he directs be 100 percent effective in evangelism 100 percent of the time.

My friends and I long to see an organic, viral, contagious pandemic of the gospel sweep through the West. We long to be a part of it. We hope to see Jesus sneezed from one person to another like the spread of the Jesus virus. We desire to see Jesus's supernatural power become normal again here in the West. We dream of a time when viral discipleship, church planting, and evangelistic practices become normal. Will you join us? Will you not only dream with us; will you also ask Jesus to make it happen? Will you trust Him and obey Him when He asks you to participate with Him in the impossible? I believe that this is one more instance in which Jesus would say, "With man this is impossible, but with God all things are possible."

# Cessationism

COMMON DOCTRINE AMONG non-Pentecostal evangelicals is the doctrine of cessationism. This doctrine posits that everything the Bible says is true and that it really happened in history. But, and here is the caveat, somehow, sometime after the writing of the New Testament, the miraculous stopped. The timing of this cessation of the miraculous gifts is debated among cessationists. Some say the miraculous ended with the death of the last apostle. By this they mean the original twelve apostles. So the miraculous probably ended near the death of John, who lived into his late nineties or even a bit beyond; so roughly at the close of the first century. The second group places the cessation of the miraculous at the completion of the canon of Scripture. This would place the cessation of the miraculous around the time of the Synod of Hippo (A.D. 393) and the first and second Councils of Carthage (A.D. 397 and A.D. 419 respectively). So even among cessationists, there is disagreement about when the miraculous ceased, with a difference of around two hundred fifty to three hundred years in their estimations. Some cessationists further posit that there is a geographic element to the supernatural. God does miracles on the mission field or in the Third World, but He doesn't do them where people are more enlightened and don't really need miracles.

Why can't cessationists agree about when the miraculous ceased? Why can't they come into agreement about where the miraculous happens? Does it happen in some places and not others? Why the confusion?

Of course the worst problem for cessationists is that the doctrine is not mentioned anywhere in Scripture. The New Testament closes with the premise that every believer is to expect supernaturalism as part of their birthright. However, there is one Scripture that some cessationists argue indicates that supernaturalism will cease.

This classic argument of cessationism revolves around 1 Corinthians 13:8–10:

> Love never fails. But where there are prophecies, they will cease; where there are tongues, they will be stilled; where there is knowledge, it will pass away. For we know in part and we prophesy in part, but when perfection comes, the imperfect disappears.

This is an important verse for many cessationists, principally because it is the only reference in the entire Bible that could be construed to mean that supernaturalism will cease. There are really only two understandings of this verse. The cessationists, argument is that the "perfect" of verse 10 is a reference to Scripture. Those who are not cessationists argue that the "perfect" is a reference to Christ at His Second Coming.

The cessationist argument says when the canon of Scripture was completed, there was no longer a need for such things as prophecies, tongues, and words of knowledge. In this point of view, we have full revelation in written form, so revelatory gifts are superfluous. Further, those who view this verse in this way note that the "perfect" in the New Testament Greek, *teleion,* is in the neuter, which could be and often is translated, "the perfect thing." The argument goes that this is a reference to a thing (the Scriptures) not a person (Jesus), or it would not have been written in the neuter.

On the surface, this seems to make good sense. It is true that this construction is usually, but not exclusively, used for things rather than persons. While it can be used for persons and translated "the perfect one," this would be the less common translation. This is the strongest point of the cessationist view of 1 Corinthians 13:10. From that point on, the view becomes significantly weaker. First of all, there is a time marker in the immediate context that clearly weakens the idea that this is referring to the completion of canon. Verse 12 of 1 Corinthians 13 states: "Now we see but a poor reflection as in a mirror; then we shall see face to face. Now I know in part; then I shall know fully, even as I am fully known."

It should be noted that the ideas that verse 12 is stating make more sense when viewed in the time context of the Second Coming of Christ rather than the completion of canon. At this point in time, when the perfect One (Jesus) comes, we will see face to face and we will be fully known. It is difficult to make the argument by the Scriptures that we currently, having the complete canon, know fully and are fully known. There are still many scriptural mysteries. There are still many unanswered questions. We do not fully know, but we certainly will after the Second Coming of Christ.

Furthermore, this also makes more sense when viewed as interaction with a person. We don't have "face to face" interaction with the Bible; we read the Bible. The Bible doesn't know us, although the God of the Bible does. We are knowing, and we are being fully known. Again, this is language reserved for personal relationship rather than interaction with an inanimate object.

Finally, it needs to be noted that while on the surface the cessationist view of 1 Corinthians chapter 13 seems to make sense, it is actually a clumsy theological construct rather than a straightforward biblical interpretation. For the cessationist argument to work, one has to surmise that "the perfect" is a thing and that this thing is the completed canon of Scriptures. There are no verbal cues in the text that would lead one to believe that the passage is talking about the completed canon of the Bible, or the Scriptures in any way. One needs to impose this concept upon the text from silence.

Further, the Scriptures do not refer to the concept of the completion of canon in any other place. These concepts of the canon and the completion of the canon come from later theology but not from the Bible. To decide that this vague reference to "the perfect" is a clear reference to the completion of canon when this is a concept that is not discussed scripturally is quite a stretch. This is a violation of the logical principle of Occam's Razor, which states "one should not increase, beyond what is necessary, the number of entities required to explain anything."[1] However, if "the perfect" is referring to the second coming of Christ, we are on solid ground. This is a major theme of both the Old and the New Testaments and fits the language of the immediate context.

Consequently, when one hermeneutically investigates this passage in depth and in context, it becomes highly unlikely that it actually bolsters the cessationist view. This is why most branches of the Christian faith, including the Roman Catholics, would view 1 Corinthians 13 as a proof against cessationism. This is also why some cessationists do not use this passage of Scripture for textual support. (This, however, leaves them in the dubious position of trying to prove a "biblical doctrine" without any biblical reference. At that point they can only string together a series of theological and/or historical arguments. This is an unconvincing line of reasoning.) Even to some cessationists it is more objective to view 1 Corinthians 13:8–10 as referring to the second coming of Christ. Richard B. Gaffin Jr., in arguing for cessationism in *Are Miraculous Gifts for Today? Four Views*, states:

> To argue, as some cessationists do, that "the perfect" has in view the completion of the New Testament canon or some other state of affairs prior to the Parousia is just not credible exegetically.[2]

# Postmodernism

ESTERN SOCIETY IS currently undergoing a worldview shift called "postmodernism." The title itself is hotly debated since it defines postmodernism by what came before "modernism," or the Enlightenment. While in its early stages postmodernism did indeed define itself as an angry rejection of the values of the Enlightenment, this is no longer necessarily the case. Therefore some are suggesting that postmodernism should refer only to the early stages. Other titles such as post-postmodernism, referring to the worldview without the reference to modernism itself, should refer to what seems to be more common now: the values of postmodernism without the rejection or reference to modernism. To date, no better widely accepted title has been found for the very real and significant shift the Western world is currently undergoing.

*Viral Jesus* mentions postmodernism a number of times. This appendix will help the reader who is unfamiliar with postmodernism briefly understand its tenets as well as briefly compare it to modernism or the Enlightenment. The following are slightly adapted from my own articles on postmodernism "The Gospel and Postmodernism"[1] and "Practical Considerations for Postmodern Sensitive Churches."[2] When I wrote these articles in response to the strategic impact of postmodernism on the ministry context of Spain, where I was living at the time, I was not adequately aware of the current phenomena called alternately "simple," "organic," or "house" churches. I currently believe this is the most relevant ecclesiological expression to answer the strategic challenges of postmodernism. I also believe simple/organic/house churches are the most relevant ecclesiological response to the other issues brought up in this book.

## A Postmodern Encounter With a Traditional Church

Let's imagine for a moment that a non-Christian, Western postmodern,[3] the kind of person we meet every day on the street, came for the first time to a traditional church. What would the experience be like for her? Let's take a look as she experiences what we call a "worship service."

*Wow, interesting music, I don't think I've ever heard that song before. Not bad, but isn't there an ordinance against loud music? Oh, it's coming out of the church. First Baptist: are they in competition with each other? Is being a first Baptist better than being a third Baptist? Does being a second Congregational trump being a first Presbyterian? Do Christians have trump suits? Wow, this is creepy. This is supposed to be religion, yet they advertise like they're a business in a strip mall. Is religion supposed to be like going to the dry cleaners? I thought religion was about connecting with something higher. Why do they need to advertise? Why do they need a name? This is so institutional—buildings, signs, names. How can this be spiritual and so institutional at the same time? Does God need an institution? Is He chairman of the board? Still, the music is kinda cool. It's creative and I like creativity. Maybe the music will outweigh the creepy institutional feel. I'll go inside and check this out.*

*This is so weird! Look at that! They sit in rows...rows! This is like the Stepford Wives. What, are they a bunch of automatons? Boy, you can sure see who has power in this place. One hundred people lined up in rows facing one way, one dude raised on a platform and behind the podium of power facing the other. He tells them to stand up, and they stand up. He tells them to sing, and they sing. He tells them to pray, and they all pray in unison. Where are the strings for these puppets? I'm beginning to feel my skin crawl. Can't these people think for themselves? Why do they need this guy up there to tell them what to do? Finally, the big boss is going to speak. Now I'll find out what makes these people tick....*

*...OK, I've been listening to this for the last fifteen minutes and I don't have any idea what he is talking about. Redemption, speaking in tongues, and why do they need to always talk about being justified? Are they that insecure? Isn't religion supposed to make people better for society? These guys are just talking about justifying themselves. Is their God that angry that they need some sort of excuse? Enough with the excuses; show me a better life. You guys are no different than I am, except you let Chatty Cathy up there control you like the chief puppet master. I'm outta here.*

Would this really happen? It probably wouldn't, mainly because most nonchurched postmoderns would never actually enter the door. However, if they did, our behavior would not speak to them of spirituality. It would speak to them of institutional behavior. It wouldn't inspire them to connect with God. For postmoderns, the traditional church experience is like going to the dry cleaners except when they get inside. Once inside, it's more like the Twilight Zone. Actually the closest non-Christian experience I can think of that resembles a conventional church is a lodge meeting. All we lack are the moose antlers and the handshakes.

Am I being too harsh? Let me ask you this. When was the last time an unchurched, non-Christian came to your church uninvited, without any relational connections, and became a Christian? That is a rare story indeed. In my nearly forty years in the faith, I've seen that happen only once. And honestly, when we bring our non-Christian friends to a church service (if we can get them to go), how many come back on their own until they come to faith? It's not all that common, is it?

How do we reach a lost world when almost everything we do alienates us from the people we are supposed to be trying to reach? How would a prostitute feel in your church? How would a New Age practitioner feel in your church? How would a beer-swilling investment banker feel in your church? Would they see Jesus? Would they be amazed at the power of God being demonstrated? Would the most positive comment they could make be about music? Or would it just be creepy?

The issue I'm bringing up here is the concept of sentient boundaries or barriers of feeling. Most people have a number of ways they make decisions. Some of these ways are not necessarily about reason and logic. They are about feelings. When people have an encounter with something they find emotionally uncomfortable, there has to be some sort of reward to spur them on or they will retreat from that experience.

In my story above, there was only one positive thing, the music. But there were tons of barriers of feeling: from the sign out front, to our synchronized bobbing and sitting, to the strange way we line up. Most of all, our services speak of the personal power of the person up front. Sometimes they even dress differently, in a robe or suit. This is weird to anyone who hasn't been raised in our small subculture or acculturated into it.

Names for churches, synchronized behavior, pulpits, buildings, pews, lined-up chairs—none of this comes from the Bible, not one thing. It all comes from Christendom, and it is keeping people out of the kingdom of God. However, just changing the add-ons from Christendom to some other form will not be enough. Changing from sitting in rows to sitting in a circle or making our groups smaller, in and of themselves, are not adequate changes. We have to change the essence of who we are and how we connect with God and the society around us.

# Tendencies of Postmodernism Compared to Modernism

## Postmodernism

The following tendencies were taken from an article by Dr. Mary Klages, which is no longer available on the Internet:[4]

| TENDENCIES OF POSTMODERNISM |
|---|
| Subjectivity |
| Rejection of rigid distinctions |
| Local, personal, and specific truth |
| Rejection of absolute truths |
| Rejection of "grand narratives" that explain reality such as capitalism or communism. These grand narratives are seen as old and simplistic and don't adequately explain the world's complexity. |
| Practicality |
| Inclusiveness or tolerance |
| Diversity of morals and lifestyle |
| Tendency to perceive information that does not fit their worldview as "noise" |
| Tendency to see conservative religion or politics as the enemy |
| Language is fluid and subjective (the listener brings as much to the conversation as the speaker). |

Other tendencies not specifically mentioned by Klages:

- Desire for spirituality
- Desire for community
- Rejection of negativity

## Modernism/The Enlightenment

| TENDENCIES OF MODERNISM/ THE ENLIGHTENMENT |
| --- |
| Rationality |
| Autonomy |
| Objectivity |
| Science as the objective arbiter of truth |
| Knowledge produced by science is "truth" and is eternal |
| Value of progress and perfection |
| Order |
| Language is rational and transparent (it means exactly what it says) |
| Rejection of that which does not represent order |
| Rejection of that which is considered "other," i.e., lack of tolerance |

# The Postmodern Person

How does the postmodern person act? How is he different from modern people? The following is a profile of postmodern people from their own perspective.

- I'm looking for a truth that works for me.
- I can only try to see life from my own perspective; reality is too complex to understand it all.
- I'm interested in the values of my group and my community.
- I believe in being tolerant.
- I believe in letting others live like they want to.
- I don't like it when people argue about how their group or beliefs are better.
- I want practical answers to life. I'm not drawn to idealistic schemes.

- I am suspicious of schemes that try to explain everything or give simplistic answers to complex questions.
- When people talk to me about these schemes I think of it as "noise" to be ignored.
- I like to have a group of close friends with whom I share common values.
- I don't like institutional religion.
- I do have a vague desire for noninstitutional spirituality, but I don't know how to find it.

These are a few of the more common values of postmodernism. Not every person in a postmodern society holds each one of these values. However, there is a strong tendency in the society for these values, and most people hold many, if not all these values.

One needs to distinguish between philosophical postmoderns and "street" postmoderns. Philosophical postmoderns, like philosophers and their philosophy students in universities, tend to state that there really is no such thing as truth. The average person on the street is not nearly as philosophical. In fact, few ponder the deep questions of life, but they have still absorbed the basic postmodern worldview. If forced to express in words how they view life, the average street postmoderns would more likely state that truth exists; it is just impossible to fully understand. Because of its complexity they tend to look for a "truth" that works for them. Most of the people we meet are not philosophical postmoderns but street postmoderns. The good news is that street postmoderns tend to be quite open to considering the gospel if it is expressed in postmodern-sensitive ways.

As stated above, postmodernism is a shift of worldview on a world-wide scale. Worldview is the most profound level of cultural expression. It expresses the most deeply and widely held values. These are the values that form the framework of how we view and understand our world. Worldview values are often held by many cultures in many parts of the world.

As a worldview shift, postmodernism is a change in the way people view and understand their world. It is the deepest kind of cultural shift.

Worldview changes are extremely infrequent. The last complete world-view change in Western culture was the Renaissance, which occurred about five hundred years ago. Modernism or the Enlightenment was not a complete worldview shift. Instead, it was an intensification and amplification of the Renaissance values that were already prevalent. Both found their inspiration from ancient Greek philosophy, particularly the writings of Plato and Aristotle. It would not be reasonable to expect post-modernism to go away soon. It will probably be here in some form or another for a number of generations.

Since postmodernism is a worldview shift, it will have regional and national expressions. France is postmodern and so is the United States, but they are culturally different from each other because they have different cultural values and histories. However, these cultural values will still express themselves within the worldview framework of postmodernism.

Roman Catholicism and the various expressions of Eastern Orthodoxy are cultural expressions of Christianity based on their historical roots of the Ancient worldview, the worldview before the Renaissance. The Protestant Reformation was the Christian response to the new values of Renaissance, as are the denominations, which sprang from this period—for example, the Lutheranism and the various Presbyterian/Covenant denominations. Evangelicalism and fundamentalism are the Christian responses to the Enlightenment. As such, evangelicalism and fundamentalism as Christian cultural expressions of Enlightenment values will find themselves increasingly isolated from the culture surrounding them. They will find themselves increasingly unable to adequately engage with meaningful dialog that will lead to others coming to Christ. Indeed, this is already the case.

# ⌒ NOTES ⌒

## PREFACE

1. New Advent, *Fathers of the Church: The Epistle of Ignatius to the Romans*, translated by Alexander Roberts and James Donaldson, http://www .newadvent.org/fathers/0107.htm (accessed January 23, 2011).
2. Ibid.

## INTRODUCTION
### Following Jesus Into a Viral Jesus Movement

1. Michael Frost and Alan Hirsch, *The Shaping of Things to Come* (Peabody, MA: Hendrickson Publishers, 2003), 116.
2. Ibid., 120.
3. Ibid., 126.

## CHAPTER 1: What a Viral Jesus Movement Looks Like

1. Alan Hirsch, *The Forgotten Ways: Reactivating the Missional Church* (Grand Rapids: Brazos Press, 2006), 86.
2. For a historical development of this process see Frank Viola and George Barna, *Pagan Christianity* (Carol Stream, IL: Barna, 2008).

## CHAPTER 2: Stability and Control in a Viral Jesus Movement

1. Merriam-Webster.com, s.v. "apostle," http://www.merriam-webster.com /dictionary/apostle (accessed July 14, 2011).
2. Ibid.
3. Merriam-Webster.com, s.v. "mission," http://www.merriam-webster.com /dictionary/mission (accessed July 14, 2011).

## CHAPTER 3: Supernaturalism in a Viral Jesus Movement

1. Merriam-Webster.com, s.v. "mysticism," http://www.merriam-webster.com /dictionary/mysticism (accessed July 14, 2011).
2. Ibid.
3. Ibid., s.v. "prophecy," http://www.merriam-webster.com/dictionary /prophecy?show=0&t=1318423433 (accessed October 12, 2011).
4. Wolfgang Simson, *The Starfish Manifesto*, (Starfish Publishing, 2008), 13, public domain. *The Starfish Manifesto* is a free e-book. One pays for it by

paying it forward, i.e., by sending it to at least ten other people who they feel would benefit from reading the book. You can download *The Starfish Manifesto* for free at http://www.box.net/shared/yns46ncgsc (accessed July 14, 2011).

## CHAPTER 4
### The Early Church—the First Viral Jesus Movement

1. Early Christian Writings, "Pliny the Younger and Trajan on the Christians," http://www.earlychristianwritings.com/text/pliny.html (accessed July 14, 2011).

2. Alexander Roberts and James Donaldson, trans., Alexander Roberts, James Donaldson, and A. Cleveland Coxe, eds., *From Ante-Nicene Fathers*, vol. 1. (Buffalo, NY: Christian Literature Publishing Co., 1885.); as quoted in Kevin Knight, ed., "The Manners of the Christians," *The Epistle of Mathetes to Diognetus*, NewAdvent.org, http://www.newadvent.org/fathers/0101.htm (accessed July 14, 2011).

3. USGS.gov, "VHP Photo Glossary: Plinian eruption," http://volcanoes.usgs .gov/images/pglossary/PlinianEruption.php (accessed July 14, 2011).

## CHAPTER 5
### The Crumbling of a Viral Jesus Movement

1. Suscopts.org, "St. Ignatius' Letter to the Romans," http://www.suscopts.org /stgeorgetampa/Letter_to_Romans.html (accessed July 18, 2011).

2. ChristianAnswers.net, "Magnesians," http://www.christiananswers.net /q-eden/magnesians.html (accessed July 18, 2011).

3. Crossroadsinitiative.com, "Letter of Ignatius of Antioch to the Ephesians," http://www.crossroadsinitiative.com/library_article/124/Ignatius__of _Antioch_s_Letter_to_the_Ephesians.html (accessed July 14, 2011).

4. Frank Viola and George Barna, *Pagan Christianity* (Carol Stream, IL: Barna, 2008), 112.

5. Ibid., 111.

6. *Ante-Nicene Fathers Vol.1*, chap. 44, translated by Philip Schaff et al., Christian Classics Ethereal Library, http://www.ccel.org/ccel/schaff/anf01.ii.ii .xliv.html (accessed Otober 13, 2011).

7. Viola and Barna, 113.

8. Ibid.

9. Ibid.

10. Wikisource.org, "Ante-Nicene Fathers Vol. IV, Tertullian: Part Fourth, On Monogamy by Tertullian," http://en.wikisource.org/wiki/Ante-Nicene_ Fathers/Volume_IV/Tertullian:_Part_Fourth/On_Monogamy/Elucidations (accessed August 8, 2009).

11. Wikipedia.org, "Pontifex Maximus," http://en.wikipedia.org/wiki/Pontifex _Maximus (accessed July 17, 2008).

12. Ibid.

13. Frost and Hirsch, 225.

## CHAPTER 6
### A History of Partial Viral Jesus Movements

1. HistoryMatters.gmu.edu, "A Religious Flame That Spread All Over Kentucky," http://historymatters.gmu.edu/d/6370/ (accessed February 18, 2010).

2. Peter Marshall and David Manuel, *From Sea to Shining Sea* (Grand Rapids, MI: Fleming H. Revell, 1986), 67-68.

3. "A Religious Flame That Spread All Over Kentucky" (accessed February 18, 2010).

4. WisdomQuotes.com, "George Santayana," http://www.wisdomquotes.com /quote/george-santayana-5.html (accessed October 13, 2011).

5. Euan Cameron, *Waldenses: Rejections of Holy Church in Medieval Europe*, (Carol Stream, IL: Barna, 2008), 21.

6. National Humanities Institute, "Jonathan Edwards: On the Great Awakening," *Who We Are, The Story of America's Constitution,* http://www.nhinet.org /ccs/docs/awaken.htm (accessed August 8, 2009).

7. Marshall and Manuel, 67-68.

## CHAPTER 7
### China: A Current Viral Jesus Movement

1. Roderick MacFarquhar and Michael Schoenhals, *Mao's Last Revolution* (Cambridge, MA: Harvard University Press, 2006), 102.

2. Kenneth W. Harl, "Early Medieval and Byzantine Civilization: Constantine to Crusades," http://www.tulane.edu/~august/H303/handouts/Population.htm (accessed March 19, 2009).

3. Robert A. Guisepi, ed., "A History of Christianity," http://history-world.org /origins_of_christianity.htm (accessed March 19, 2009).

4. Jonathan Chao, *Wise as Serpents Harmless as Doves: Christians in China Tell Their Story* (Pasadena, CA: William Carrey Library, 1988), 27. Permission requested.

5. Ibid., 35-36.

6. Ibid., 39.

7. Ibid., 20-21.

8. Tetsunao Yamamori and Kim-Kwong Chan, *Witnesses to Power: Stories of God's Quiet Work in a Changing China.* (Milton Keynes, UK: Paternoster Press, 2000), 46. Permission requested.

9. Ibid.

10. Ibid.

11. Personal correspondence with Lyle Wilkinson, Richmond, CA, August 20, 2009.

12. Yamamori and Chan, 47.

13. Ibid.

14. Ibid., 48.

15. Ibid., 82.

16. Tony Lambert, *The Resurrection of the Chinese Church* (Wheaton: OMF Books, 1994), 139.

17. Michael Frost, *Exiles: Living Missionally in a Post-Christian Culture* (Peabody, MA: Hendrickson Publishers, 2006), 138.

## CHAPTER 8
### Viral Discipleship

1. Brother Yun, *Living Water* (Grand Rapids, MI: Zondervan, 2008), 54.

2. Merriam-Webster Online, s.v. "humanism," http://www.merriam-webster .com/dictionary/humanism (accessed July 20, 2009).

3. William A. Barry and William J. Connolly, *The Practice of Spiritual Direction* (San Francisco: Harper & Row, 1986).

4. Ibid., 8.

5. Ibid., 6–7.

## CHAPTER 9
### Viral Church Planting

1. Watchman Nee, *The Normal Christian Church Life* (Anaheim, CA: Living Stream Ministry, 1994), 142.

2. Ibid, 141.

## CHAPTER 10
### Viral Evangelism

1. Wikipedia.org, "Agricultural Extension," http://en.wikipedia.org/wiki /Agricultural_extension (accessed September 26, 2009).

2. Ed Waken, unpublished notes.

3. David Nyquist, unpublished e-mail correspondence with the author, September 29, 2009.

## CONCLUSION

1. Wikipedia.org, "Pogo (comic strip)," http://en.wikipedia.org/wiki/Pogo _(comics)#.22We_have_met_the_enemy.....22 (accessed 23 July 2009).

## APPENDIX A: Cessationism

1. Francis Heylighen, *Principia Cybernetica Web: Occam's Razor,* 1997 http://pespmc1.vub.ac.be/OCCAMRAZ.html (accessed March 24, 2009).

2. Richard B.Gaffin et al., *Are Miraculous Gifts for Today?: 4 Views* (Grand Rapids, MI: Zondervan, 1996), 55.

## APPENDIX B: Postmodernism

1. Ross Rohde, "The Gospel and Postmodernism," http://thejesusvirus.org/ wp-content/uploads/2011/07/The-Gospel-and-Postmodernism-Final-Ed.pdf (accessed November 23, 2011).

2. Ross Rohde, "Practical Considerations for Postmodern Sensitive Churches," http://thejesusvirus.org/wp-content/uploads/2011/07/Practical-Considerations-for-Postmodern-Sensitive-Churches.pdf (accessed November 23, 2011).

3. For a discussion of postmodernism and how it interacts with current modern Christianity please see my articles "The Gospel and Postmodernism," http://thejesusvirus.org/wp-content/uploads/2011/07/The-Gospel-and-Postmodernism-Final-Ed.pdf, and "Practical Considerations for Postmodern Sensitive Churches," http://thejesusvirus.org/wp-content/uploads/2011/07/ Practical-Considerations-for-Postmodern-Sensitive-Churches.pdf (accessed November 23, 2011).

4. Mary Klages, "Postmodernism."

# ❧ INDEX ❧

Ross & Margi Rohde

Ross is available for:

- Conference Speaking
- Organic church planting training
- Organic church planter coaching, mentoring and consulting
- Organic discipleship coaching, mentoring and consulting
- Ross is fluent in both English and Spanish

If you would like to contact
Ross to discuss ministry opportunities
please contact him through:

Email: rossrohde@gmail.com
Facebook: rossrohde

Ross' wife Margi is available for:

- Spiritual direction via various media
- Workshops in contemplative practices and creative expression
- Consultation in greater spiritual and artistic freedom
- Training in the process of spiritual discernment (co-led with Ross)
- Workshops in hearing the voice of God (co-led with Ross)
- Margi is fluent in both English and Spanish

If you would like to contact
Margi to discuss ministry opportunities
please contact her through:

Email: margirohde@yahoo.com